About the Author

Gene Steinberg first used a Mac in 1984 and never looked back. He is a fact and science fiction writer and computer software and systems consultant. His more than fifteen computer-related books include Que's *AOL 4.0 Quick Reference* and *Sams Teach Yourself AOL in 10 Minutes*. Gene's commentaries and product reviews appear in *MacHome* magazine and his "Mac Reality Check Column" for the *Arizona Republic*'s Arizona Central Computing page. He's also a regularly featured guest on Craig Crossman's "Computer America" radio show. In his spare time, Gene and his son, Grayson, are developing a new science fiction adventure series, *Attack of the Rockoids*.

Dedication

For Wally, who showed me that miracles are indeed possible!

Acknowledgments

There's never enough time to do a book of this size and scope all alone. And so I'm grateful to the many people who contributed information, tips, tricks, and, most of all, advice in the preparation of this book.

I want to give thanks to my friend and agent, Lew Grimes, for his sage advice, and Apple's corporate communications team, including Rhona Hamilton, Matt Hutchison, Keri Walker, and Nathalie Welch. I'd also like to offer special appreciation to a pair of former members of Apple's Customer Quality Feedback crew, Thom Franklin and Min Wang, for letting me see the future.

And extra kudos go to Apple's Jonathan Ive and his industrial design team for giving us the iMac.

In order to deliver complete details about the latest generation of iMac personal computers, I had the cooperation of two dedicated Mac dealers, who let me and my son, Grayson, spend hours poking, prodding and testing their newly delivered products without a word of protest. Special thanks go to Computer Town's Priyantha Kalupahana (whom we all call PK), Brent Krah and Tim Romero, and CompUSA's Jerod Havel.

I must give special praise to the team at Macmillan for putting up with my many eccentricities and for allowing me a great deal of latitude in outlining and writing this book. They include Betsy Brown, Scott Meyers, Kate Givens, and Carol Bowers. I'd also like to express my appreciation to Macmillan's dedicated, fearless technical editor, Jeff Keller, for poring through every written word and every illustration to verify that they were absolutely correct to the last, minute detail.

And last, I wish to offer a heartfelt, loving thank you to my wonderful, beautiful wife Barbara and my extraordinary son Grayson for putting up with the long hours I spent chained to my computer so that my work could be done on schedule.

Tell Us What You Think!

As the reader of this book, *you* are our most important critic and commentator. We value your opinion and want to know what we're doing right, what we could do better, what areas you'd like to see us publish in, and any other words of wisdom you're willing to pass our way.

You can fax, email, or write me directly to let me know what you did or didn't like about this book—as well as what we can do to make our books stronger.

Please note that I cannot help you with technical problems related to the topic of this book, and that due to the high volume of mail I receive, I might not be able to reply to every message.

When you write, please be sure to include this book's title and author as well as your name and phone or fax number. I will carefully review your comments and share them with the author and editors who worked on the book.

Fax: (317) 581-4770
E-mail: internet_sams@mcp.com
Mail: Mark Taber
          Associate Publisher
          Sams Publishing
          201 West 103rd Street
          Indianapolis, IN 46290

Introduction

It's hard to think of a product as a legend in its own time.

But in the 1987 movie *Star Trek IV: The Voyage Home*, it was clear that one computing product had achieved that status. In the movie, the crew of the Enterprise goes back through time to visit San Francisco of the 1980s. In one memorable scene, the ship's salty engineer, Scotty, walks over to a 20th century computer, picks up the mouse, and says, "computer," expecting it to respond to his verbal commands.

The computer was an Apple Macintosh.

Long gone are the days when that low-powered, uniquely designed computer captured anyone's imagination, but rising from the ashes of lost market share and low profits are worthy successors, such as the iMac (and the new iBook). And you can also see it featured prominently in TV shows and movies.

The iMac is designed for folks like you and me, who just want computing "appliances" that will get the work done fast, with as little fuss and bother as possible. Well, at least with as little fuss as you can expect from such a highly complex device as a personal computer.

About a third of the folks buying Apple's consumer computers are new to personal computing. Others have switched from that "other platform" to the Mac. In either case, I'm sure you'll want to get up and running as quickly as possible, and safely navigate around whatever hurdles may stand in your way.

When I bought my first Mac back in the 1980s, Apple included several big instruction books with their new products—but big computer manuals are history.

New Apple computers these days usually just come with a quick setup card and a brief troubleshooting book. If you want to know more, you've got to check the Help menu on the computer itself.

Or, even better, read this book.

If you're an experienced Mac user—or this is your first Mac—you'll find that *Sams Teach Yourself the iMac in 24 Hours* is the best book you can buy. I've written the lessons just for you, and I've tried to avoid "geek" talk as much as possible. And where I have to be a little technical, I'll try my best to explain everything to you as clearly as possible.

This Book Is Not Just for iMac Users

This book covers the subjects any Mac user would want to know. So whether you have an iMac, an iBook, or a regular PowerMac or PowerBook, you'll find lots of information in this book that will help you master your new computer.

For this second edition, I'm adding full coverage on the second generation of iMacs (including the DV models), the ones Apple calls "slot-loading," because of the new automatic loading CD or DVD drive. I've also focused on the version of the Mac operating system that shipped at the time this book was written, Mac OS 9, and I'll also tell you the ways it differs from previous versions of the Mac operating system. So bear that in mind if you are using a different Mac operating system version and find that a few things work, well, a little differently.

But that's no problem. If you bought an iMac with the older operating system (from version 8.1 to 8.6), just contact Apple at 1-800-335-9258 and ask about their Mac OS "Up-To-Date program." Depending on when you bought your new computer or Mac OS upgrade, you may be eligible for a discount when you buy the OS 9 upgrade direct from Apple.

How to Use This Book

This book is divided into 24 segments that each take roughly an hour to complete. You can work through the lessons in the space of a day (if you don't plan to eat or sleep) or you can take your time and work through the hour lessons.

The lessons begin with unpacking your new iMac and setting it up in your work area. From there, you'll learn about the great features of Apple's "Mac OS" operating system, and discover all the terrific software that came with your new computer. In addition, you'll learn lots of tips and tricks that will help you do things it took years for the experts to discover.

At the end of each hour, you'll be able to accomplish a new set of tasks. The lessons contain clear explanations of the program features and how they work. In addition, each hour provides you with the opportunity for hands-on training, simply by following the steps described.

Conventions Used in This Book

Sams Teach Yourself the iMac in 24 Hours uses a number of conventions that are consistent throughout this book:

- Each hour begins with an overview of what you will learn and the highlights of every hour.
- Step-by-step instructions are preceded by a To Do icon.
- Every hour ends with a summary and a series of commonly asked questions and answers; hopefully, you'll find the answers to your questions among them.

In addition, these elements appear throughout the book:

Notes provide you with comments and asides about the topic at hand.

Tips offer shortcuts and hints on getting the task done.

Cautions explain roadblocks you might encounter when you work with your iMac and tell you how to avoid them.

NEW TERM *New terms* are introduced with this special designation.

At the end of each hour, a list of questions and answers covers real-life questions about the material covered in the hour.

The Thrill of Discovery Is Just Beginning...

Your new iMac has the power that was formerly reserved for the largest mainframe computers. And it all fits in a cute little polycarbonate plastic case. Truly amazing.

A book such as this can only be a starting point. After you've spent those 24 hours discovering the great features of your iMac and the Macintosh operating system, you'll be ready to go on and surf the Internet, write that great American novel, or just sit back and have fun with a colorful computer game.

I hope you will be able to share the excitement and thrill of discovery that I felt when I bought my first Mac. And if you have any questions or comments, feel free to email me or just pay a visit to one of my two Web sites when you have a chance.

Gene Steinberg
Scottsdale, AZ
email: gene@starshiplair.com
http://www.starshiplair.com
http://www.rockoids.com

PART I
Opening the Box

Hour

HOUR 1

Setting Up Your iMac

Your new iMac is a marvel of technology. Inside its cute plastic box lies the incredible power of Apple's G3 microprocessor, a supercharged chip that's no larger than a postage stamp. This miniature technological wonder has the ability to process millions upon millions of computer instructions every single second. In addition, your new computer comes with a sharp, bright color screen, a graphics accelerator, a fast CD-ROM (or DVD player on the DV models) and a built-in modem, along with lots and lots of great software.

NEW TERM A *microprocessor* is a little electronic component that crunches numbers and gives your computer its incredible computing power. A *Graphics accelerator* is a chip that makes the images on your computer's screen show up very, very fast. A *modem* is a clever device that turns the ones and zeros generated by your iMac and other computers into analog signals that can be sent back and forth over telephone lines.

In the first hour of this book, I'll take you beyond those first six steps in Apple's "Welcome" card, and show you

- How to set up your new iMac
- How to get it running
- How to use Apple's Mac OS Setup Assistant
- How to use Apple's Internet Setup Assistant
- And if you're new to the Mac operating system, you'll get some advice on how to master your mouse skills and what all those strange symbols on the keyboard mean

 Although many of you have worked on other Macs or the computers from that "other" platform (Windows), I realize that some of you are first-time computer buyers. So I'm going to cover a few basics in this first hour, such as how to figure out what plugs in to where, and how to use the mouse. If you've already worked on a Mac and have installed new computers, you'll be able to advance to Hour 2, "Exploring the iMac Desktop," in much less time.

Unpacking the iMac

Before you unpack your new iMac, find a convenient table or desk for it. It's not too large to fit on a small desk, but many of you will purchase a special table for it. In addition, you might want to buy a mouse pad. You can use the iMac's mouse on a regular smooth surface, but the porous character of the mouse pad will offer more precise mouse movement. And because it only costs a few bucks, it's worth having.

 When you register your new computer with Apple, you can choose from among several free gifts. One of those choices is a genuine Apple mouse pad, but you might prefer to accept one of the complimentary computer magazine subscriptions and buy a mouse pad from your dealer.

As with any new purchase, before you attempt to use your new computer, give it a once over for visible signs of damage. If something looks broken (or the shipping box is badly damaged), contact your dealer for help. It's a good idea not to try to attempt to use a computer that might be damaged until it has been checked or (if need be) repaired.

1

The View from the Front of Your iMac

Let's take a closer look at your new iMac and see what features are available. First the front view (see Figure 1.1):

FIGURE 1.1
The iMac will be ready to roll as soon as you hook it up.

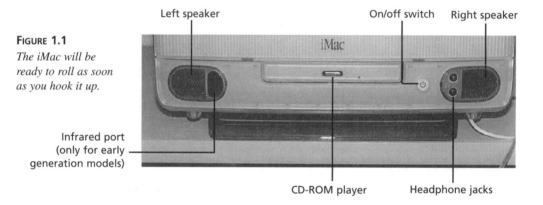

Let's take a look at the iMac's "face":

- At the very top of your iMac, just above the screen (not pictured in Figure 1.1), is a little rectangular hole. It's not a keyhole; there's actually a microphone inside, and it lets you record sounds on your iMac. And yes, after a fashion, you can give it commands (not like they do in those *Star Trek* movies, but good enough for simple functions). You'll learn how when you get to Hour 14, "Using the iMac Speech Recording Features."

- The grills at the lower left and right are your iMac's loudspeakers. And, you can plug in earphones to either of the two jacks at the right.

- The Infrared port (only available on so-called Revision A and Revision B iMacs) is somewhat similar to the one on any electronics product with a remote control (such as your stereo). The feature lets you network with another iMac or PowerBook, or any peripheral device that supports Apple's version of wireless networking.

- Right at the bottom center of the iMac is your CD drive. Just press the little rectangular green button to open the CD tray. To close the drive, press the tray in gently.

> The second-generation iMacs, which Apple calls "slot loading," have a different type of CD or DVD player. The players on these models are similar to the ones you find on some cars. There is no pull out tray. Just push the CD or DVD in until the drive grabs the disc and pulls it the rest of the way.

- To the right of the CD drive is the on/off switch. We'll get to that in a moment (after you've plugged everything in, of course).
- The two holes at the left of the right speaker are the headphone jacks. They let you (and a friend) listen to your iMac in silence.

> The earphone jacks are next to the left speaker on the second-generation "slot loading" iMacs, and the speaker grills are differently shaped, because of a new design licensed by Harman Kardon, the audio manufacturer.

Hooking Up Your iMac

I know you're excited to turn on your iMac. I remember when I bought my first new car and just wanted to go out and cruise the highways and try out the engine and handling.

But you can't just turn on your iMac and browse the Internet. You have to hook up a few things first. So let's go through the steps:

1. Place your iMac on a desk.
2. If you want the screen to be a bit higher, lift it slightly from the front and swing out the little "foot" from beneath it. That will tilt the front of the iMac upward a few inches.
3. Plug in the power cord, and take the other end and plug it into a convenient AC jack. *Don't turn it on yet! You need to do a few more things before it will work properly!*
4. At the right end of your iMac is a little plastic cover, beneath which are the jacks to which you attach the iMac's various components (see Figure 1.2). To open it, just reach into the top of the round hole and pull out. Figure 1.3 shows the view of the second generation iMac's connection panel (there's no cover provided for this model).

FIGURE 1.2

The connection jacks to your iMac are protected by a plastic cover.

External microphone jack

External speaker jack

Ethernet networking jack

Recessed reset switch (use only in emergencies)

Built-in modem jack

Universal Serial Bus jacks for keyboard and mouse (and other peripherals); there are two of these

FIGURE 1.3

The iMac DV, has jacks for FireWire and an easier-to-use emergency reset switch.

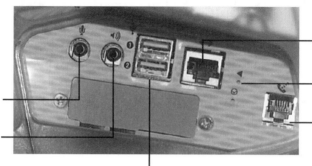

External microphone jack

External speaker jack

FireWire jacks (*only* on iMac DV and iMac DV Special Edition)

Reset switch (use only in emergencies)

Built-in modem jack

Interrupt switch (for programmers only)

Ethernet networking jack

Universal Serial Bus jacks for keyboard and mouse (and other peripherals); there are two of these

5. Take the keyboard's cable and connect to either of the Universal Serial Bus jacks (it really makes no difference). Don't force the plug, it only connects in one direction (the side with the special symbol on it is at the top).

NEW TERM A *Universal Serial Bus*, or USB for short, is a piece of technology that lets you connect up to 127 different accessories to your iMac. In addition to the keyboard and mouse, you can add extra drives, printers, scanners, digital cameras, joysticks, and more.

▼   NEW TERM   *FireWire* is a high speed peripheral standard that lets you connect digital
                  camcorders, fast hard drives, and other products to iMac DV models.

      NEW TERM   A *network* is not as complicated as it sounds. Whenever you hook two
                  computers together, or just attach a printer to your iMac, you are on a
            network. Just as in your office, when you try to make new friends or business
            contacts.

      NEW TERM   An *Ethernet* is a technique for networking—that is, transferring data to
                  and from other computers and printers.

   6. Plug the mouse into either jack on the keyboard. It really doesn't matter if you use
       your mouse left-handed or right-handed. I'm a lefty, myself, but I learned the
       mouse with my right hand. Go figure!

   7. If you want to use your iMac's built-in modem, connect a modular phone plug into
       the modem jack (the one at the extreme right of the connection panel). Put the
       other end in your phone jack, or connect to the second jack (if any) on a telephone.

   8. To connect your iMac to a regular Ethernet network or just to a single printer with
       Ethernet connection, plug in the network cable to the jack on your iMac.

   9. If you have an iMac DV or DV Special Edition, you can hook up a FireWire hard
       drive, digital camcorder or other high performance device to either of the two
       FireWire ports. I'll tell you some more about FireWire in Hour 20, "Adding More
       Goodies to Your iMac."

  10. Direct the cables to the open slide at each side of the cover, and then close the
       cover gently until it snaps shut. Those little slots keep your cables nice and neat.
       No unsightly messes as you find on many of those "other" computers.

  11. Turn the iMac on. Press the white, circular "on" switch on the front of the iMac, or
▲   the one at the upper right of the keyboard (doesn't matter which one).

Your iMac's Startup Routine

As soon as you start up, the iMac will make a little sound. (I'll talk about that a bit more
in the Question & Answer session at the end of this lesson.)

For the next minute or two, you'll see a procession of little colorful, square pictures
(icons) appearing at the bottom of your computer's screen. These icons represent little
programs that are needed to give your computer certain features. I'll tell you more about
those when you get to Hour 15, "What's a System Folder and Why Do I need One?".

After the process is done, you'll see a sort of shimmering green backdrop on your
screen, with little square pictures (icons) spread around it. I'll clue you in on how to
change that desktop backdrop when you get to Hour 16, "Using Control Panels to
Customize Your iMac."

Questions, Questions!

In addition to seeing that desktop backdrop, you'll also have a close encounter with Apple's Setup Assistant (see Figure 1.4).

FIGURE 1.4

Your iMac's "Assistant" needs to ask you a few questions before you get to play around with your new computer.

Point the mouse cursor on the right arrow and click to continue

Actually, you don't have to answer any of the Setup Assistant's questions. You can dismiss the Assistant whenever you want and answer the questions later. The Setup routine is needed to set the correct time zone on your computer's internal clock. It's also needed if you're going to use a printer, share files with another computer, or you want to explore the Internet. If you don't want to make these settings now (and it only takes a minute or two), just choose Quit from the File menu. You'll get a little prompt on the screen asking if you really, truly want to quit. Just click the Quit button and the Assistant will go bye-bye.

If you decide to take the quiz, just read the questions you see on the screen before answering. (You can always change the answers later if you come up with a better one.) Click the right arrow to move ahead; click the left arrow to back up and recheck a question or answer.

That little pointer you see on your screen when you move the mouse around is the mouse *cursor*. Its shape changes for different functions. For example, it will become a blinking vertical bar if you click an area where you enter text, and it will switch to a little hand if you point the cursor at something that can be activated with a single mouse click. And when your computer is "thinking" over an operation you activated, the cursor changes to a little spinning watch.

I'll list most of the important questions the Assistant will ask you. Just read the directions carefully and the answers will come easy (as explained below):

- **Regional Preferences**: Just indicate the country you're in.

- **Name and Organization**: You can keep the second text field blank if you just bought your computer for your own personal use. Or you can give it a name anyway, such as "Spaceship Old Ironsides" or something. It's just used for networking purposes anyway, so as long as it's unique, it doesn't really matter.

- **Time and Date**: More than likely your iMac was built in another time zone, so these settings might be off. So go ahead and change them to the proper setting (see Figure 1.5). Just click the up or down arrows next to the time and date settings. Then indicate whether you're on Daylight Savings Time or not. This is one setting you might want to make, even if you don't do the others, so your built-in clock shows the right time.

FIGURE 1.5

Pick a time, anyway. These settings adjust your iMac's clock so it displays the correct time.

- **Geographic Location**: You can be inventive here if you wish, but some Internet services (and even AOL) want to know what time zone you're in.

- **Finder Preferences**: This option sets "Simple" Finder preferences. Just leave it be for now. I'll explain what is simple about "Simple" when you get to Hour 16.

NEW TERM   The *Finder* is the program that runs all the time on a Mac OS computer. It really manages more than it finds, controlling such things as desktop backdrop, icon display, disk management, and copy functions.

- **Local Network Introduction**: You only need worry about this stuff if you plan on hooking up a printer to your Ethernet jack or you want to share files with another Mac.

- **Computer Name and Password**: Again this setting (see Figure 1.6) is only needed if you plan to hook up to a network consisting of other computers. The password you enter appears as little bullets on the screen, so the person who might be looking over your shoulder doesn't see what you type. If you don't need security, just use your name as the password (so you don't forget it). If you need to keep your password protected, pick a random combination of letters and numbers and write it down on a piece of paper and put that in a safe place (in case you forget it).

FIGURE 1.6

Name your computer and give yourself a password if you plan to network your iMac.

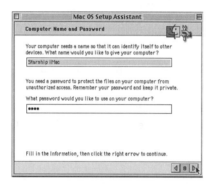

OS 9   If several people will be working on your new computer, you'll be pleased to know you can create a set of custom access privileges for each. I'll tell you how to use Apple's Multiple User feature in Hour 21, "Backup, Backup, Backup...How to Protect Your Files."

- **Shared Folder**: This choice lets you specify a place (folder) on your hard drive to be a drop box, where folks can add or copy files on your computer. The rest of your computer will be private. You really only need to worry about this sort of thing if you're in a large office, or in a situation where your personal files have to be protected from other users.
- **Printer Connection**: Here's a choice that takes a bit of an explanation. The instructions Apple gives you (shown in Figure 1.7) are apt to be confusing. A networked printer is any printer than can be shared by more than one user, or any printer that attaches to your computer's Ethernet jack. For the most part, laser printers are considered networked, ink jet printers (unless they have a special network jack) aren't (although they are technically on a network, too). That's true even if you are using a special adapter plug to hook up an older printer to your iMac. If your printer connects to the USB jack, it's a "direct connection."

FIGURE **1.7**

*Is your printer
networked or not?
Apple clouds the issue
a bit here.*

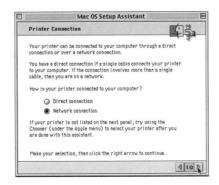

- **Printer Selection**: If you are hooked up to a networked printer, you'll click its name here to select it. If you have more than one printer at hand, not to worry. You can do hookups for additional printers later on (as I'll show you in Hour 16).

- **Conclusion**: Are we really done? Well, not quite. The setups you make are shown on this screen (see Figure 1.8). If everything is OK, just click the Go Ahead button with your mouse and move on.

FIGURE **1.8**

*If you made a mistake,
click the left arrow
multiple times, until
you see the setup
screen you need to
change.*

Internet Setup Questions

We aren't quite done yet (I know you're anxious to try out your new computer). If you plan on joining an Internet service, or bringing over the settings from the one you have, the Go Ahead button will open Apple's Internet Setup Assistant (see Figure 1.9). Click Yes to go on. Click No to end the process (you can always return to it later on). As with the Mac OS Setup Assistant you just used, the right arrow moves to the next screen, the left arrow to the previous one.

FIGURE 1.9
Do you want to explore Internet? Click Yes to go on.

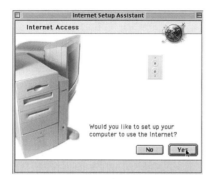

I'll cover the basic questions you'll be asked here. Just follow the actual text on the Assistant screens before you type your answer.

Those Assistants don't disappear when you quit them. They are still on your computer, in a folder labeled Assistants.

- **Internet Access**: If you have an Internet account, click Yes, and the screen will ask you some questions about transferring the settings. If you don't know the answers, check the settings on your other computer and copy them over, or just call your Internet service for help. If you want to sign up to a service, click No, and continue.

Your iMac also includes a copy of America Online's software, but you cannot set it up with the Internet Setup Assistant. AOL's program has its own setup routine. I'll cover the specifics on joining AOL in Hour 3, "Getting on the Net." The America Online 4.0 software that you need is available in a folder labeled Internet.

- **Introduction**: Just to avoid confusion here, clicking No means you want to join a new Internet service, not transfer the settings from the one you have. If you opt to join a new Internet service, the Assistant will ask you a few questions (see Figure 1.10) to help find you the right service and get you set up quickly. Time to click the right arrow.

FIGURE **1.10**

*If you want to join an
Internet service, click
the right arrow to
move on.*

Some iMacs come with a different type of Internet Setup Assistant. Rather
than taking you to Apple's referral center to get an account, the revised version of the Assistant will, instead, give you the option of installing Internet
setup software that's already on your iMac. This setup software will let you
establish an Internet account with EarthLink. You'll learn more about
EarthLink in Hour 3.

- **Modem Settings**: Apple has already made the proper settings here (see
  Figure 1.11). The only changes you might need to make apply if you are
  connecting from an office and need to specify a prefix to dial an outside line.

FIGURE **1.11**

*Leave the settings
alone unless you need
to dial a special access
number at your office.*

- **Disclaimer**: Just something Apple's lawyers put in to tell you they aren't recom-
  mending a specific Internet service nor are they responsible for your dealings with
  that service.

- **Country and Area Code**: Apple needs this information to select an Internet service that's in your own city (or nearby anyway). Click Register to have the Assistant dial up Apple's "referral" service to dig up a list of local Internet service providers for you.

> Apple's referral center is sometimes busy. Don't be surprised if there's a busy signal. If this happens, you'll see a Retry button on the Assistant screen. Just click it to redial. If you don't hear a dial tone from your computer's speaker, check to be sure that your modem cable is connected between your computer and wall jack. Then try again. If you still get those busy signals, you can quit the Internet Setup Assistant and try it at a later time; it should retain the answers you've already entered.

- **Conclusion**: The Assistant will select an access number for you to continue the setup. Just double-check the number, in case you have to dial an outside line prefix (just type it before the number that'll be displayed on your screen). Click the right arrow to connect to a second screen labeled Conclusion (sort of reminds me of those horror movies that have extra endings tacked on when the villain comes back to life). On the second screen, click Go Ahead to continue the setup process.

- **The Real Conclusion**: From here you'll receive several prompts you need to answer to create an account with an Internet service. You'll need to enter your billing information, so keep your credit card handy. At the end of the process, you'll have the option to log on and try out the new service.

> Most Internet services (sometimes called Internet service providers, or ISPs) give you a short trial period, usually from 14 to 30 days. At the end of that time, you might cancel and try another service if you don't like the choice selected. Some services even come with their own installer CDs, so you don't have to use the Internet Setup Assistant if you don't want to.

Turning It All Off

All Macs, including the iMac, have to do a little internal housekeeping whenever you shut them down. So there are two ways to turn off your computer.

- Click the Special menu and choose Shut Down. Within a few seconds, the iMac will comply and turn itself off.

- Press the on/off switch (on the iMac's keyboard or on the front of the computer). You'll see a little screen with four options (see Figure 1.12). Choose the one to Shut Down.

> The Sleep button is used to put your computer into a low-power mode. The screen will darken, but the computer will still be on, and a simple press of any key on the keyboard will restore it to life. And anything you worked on before it went to sleep will still be there, ready to be worked on again.

If you listen carefully after the Shut Down command is engaged, you'll hear the hard drive on your computer churning a little bit. That's normal. The Mac OS is designed to do a few chores with the drive before the computer is ready to turn itself off.

FIGURE 1.12
Turn me off? Just click the last button on this screen.

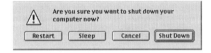

> If you accidentally shut the computer off by pulling the power cord, or there's a power failure, in most cases it will work just fine the next time you start it up. But if you happened to be working with a file at the time, there's always the possibility the file might become damaged, or there might be minor damage to the hard drive's catalog directory. So just be careful. I'll tell you how to fix common problems in Hours 23, "Crashin' Away: What to Do?" and 24, "An iMac Safety Net."

Mouse-er-size

Are you new to the Macintosh world? Or to computers in general? Well, take it from me, the mouse takes a little while to get used to, but after a couple of exercises, you'll be working it like a pro.

Unfortunately, to learn to work with the mouse you have to use it to get to a tutorial. It's sort of like that old joke, "If you don't know how to spell the word, how do you look it up?"

Apple has a built-in mouse tutorial (it takes just 15 minutes to do). To run that tutorial, you do need to do a little work with the mouse. Just click the Help menu on your computer's screen and choose Tutorial. The first option in the tutorial will run you through some basic mouse lessons.

> If you're having a bit of trouble getting to the Help menu, here's a fast tip. Just point the mouse to the item on the menu bar labeled Help and click the mouse button once. The Help menu will sit there until you pick a command (or about 15 seconds if you don't make a selection). Then just move the mouse downward till the pointer (or cursor) reaches Tutorial and click again on the mouse button. From there just follow the screen instructions on what to do. After a few seconds, you'll see a large rectangular button labeled "Mouse Skills." Click that and you're ready to learn.

Keyboard Power

Don't feel that using the your computer will confine you to the mouse. As you'll see throughout this book, there are many ways to use the keyboard to help you get around.

If you haven't used a computer before, you'll find a few odd keys surrounding the normal range of letters and numbers.

Here's what they do (from left to right, top to bottom, and so on and so forth):

- **Esc**: This is similar to the option on a Windows-based computer. For some programs, it lets you stop a function.
- **F1 through F12**: These are function keys. For some programs, you'll find they activate additional features. The manuals or online help for those programs will explain what they do.
- **Help**: Opens the Help menu for most programs.
- **Home**: They say you can't go home again, but the purpose of this is to take you to the top of a document page or directory window.
- **Pg Up**: This keystroke takes you up a page or single screen in a program (but not all software supports the feature).
- **Pg Dn**: The reverse of Pg Up. It takes you down a page or single screen in a program that supports the feature.

- **Numeric keypad**: It's similar to a calculator, and you might find it convenient to enter numbers in a program.

- **Enter**: Used to activate a function. In many programs, the Return key and the Enter keys each trigger the start of a function, but only the Return key is used to end a paragraph when you write text in a program.

- **Control**: This is a modifier key. You press Control along with an alphanumeric character to activate a special function in some programs.

> You can also use the Control key and a mouse click (pressed at the same time) to activate a special feature called Contextual menus. This feature opens a menu of command functions that apply to the item you're working on. If you've used Windows, the result is much the same as a right-click.

- **Option**: Another modifier key. It's often used (along with an alphanumeric key) to get you a special character when you're typing a document (such as a foreign accent or symbol). This key is identical to the Alt key on a Windows keyboard.

- **Command**: It's sometimes called the Apple key because some keyboards show the Apple symbol there instead of the cloverleaf. It's another modifier key, used along with an alphanumeric key, to activate a command.

Summary

In Hour 1, you unpacked your brand new iMac. Then you connected everything together and turned it on for the first time. From here, you ran through Apple's setup assistants to get your computer set up and to connect to the Internet. If you're new to Macs or to personal computers in general, you also received some advice on how to use Apple's own "Mouse Skills" tutorial to get you up to speed. You also got a quick primer on the purpose behind those extra keys on the iMac's keyboard.

In Hour 2, you'll explore your computer's desktop to see how to invoke simple commands to make your computer do things for you.

Q&A

Q What's that startup sound?

A Your iMac (and all new Macs) begins with a startup chime. On most current models, the sound resembles a G chord played on a synthesizer. Don't be alarmed; it's very normal. And don't be concerned if it takes a few moments for the screen to light up. Your computer has to do a little self-diagnostic routine before it's ready to roll.

Q What's the *i* in iMac stand for?

A It's not a play on the old movie line, "Me Tarzan, You Jane." The iMac is meant as a convenient computer to connect to the Internet—hence the i in its name. And it sounds "cute" in all those ads.

Q Okay, tell me the truth: is the first generation iMac blue or green?

A According to Apple, the color is "bondi blue." It's based on the color of the surf at Bondi Beach in Australia. Not having been "down under," I can't confirm this. The lighter color is called "ice."

The later generations of iMacs use fruit-based colors, such as blueberry, strawberry, lime, grape and tangerine; that is, except for the iMac DV Special Edition, which comes in graphite.

Q That cute plastic exterior on these computers doesn't look terribly sturdy. What's the real "skinny" about it?

A The iMac is made of polycarbonate plastic, similar to the material used for Apple's PowerBook line. It's pretty sturdy under normal circumstances, but you've got to treat it with a bit of care. Don't scratch it with a sharp object, or rub on it with an abrasive cloth or other material. Keep liquids elsewhere. If you need to clean your iMac, shut it down, and use a slightly damp, lint free cloth.

And if you drop the iMac, it definitely can break.

Q Can I expand the iMac to make it run better or add things to it?

A Yes to both. You can install additional random access memory (RAM), which lets you add more memory to a program or run more at the same time. I'll tell you more about hardware expansion in Hour 22, "Giving Your iMac New Software, More RAM, and Other Things," but if you're not mechanically inclined, you might want to let your friendly, neighborhood Apple dealer do it for you.

If you have a first generation iMac, you can also add more video memory (they call it VRAM), which lets you run in the highest resolution color mode and get more performance from your iMac's onboard 3D acceleration feature. Only the so-called Revision A iMacs need this upgrade (later models are already fitted with the maximum possible amount of video memory).

You can also add a wide variety of extras to your computer, such as printers, additional drives (such as the SuperDisk, which can read floppies), joysticks (for games), digital cameras, and lots more. The iMac DV series can also be used to edit videos from your digital camcorder. Your favorite computer store no doubt has lots of great products to expand the horizons of your iMac. I'll cover some possibilities for you in Hours 20 and 21.

Q **A friend of mine is an illustrator, and she has two displays hooked up to her Mac. Can I connect a second or a larger display to my iMac?**

A Yes, but only if you have a DV model. The DV model has a standard display jack at the bottom just above the access panel where you add a memory upgrade or an AirPort wireless networking card, to which you can connect a regular display. But it's normally hidden away, covered by a little plastic cover (you'll find a replacement cover with an opening for the jack in your iMac Accessory Kit). Just pry off the original cover, snap on the replacement, and the jack will be accessible. One thing, though, when you hook up a second display to your iMac DV, it will only duplicate or mirror the contents of your regular iMac display. It won't let you see a wider desktop. And don't forget to turn off iMac before you attach that second display.

HOUR 2

Exploring the iMac Desktop

In the very old days of personal computing, the screen was just plain text. To tell your computer to do something, you had to type the instructions on the keyboard. There wasn't even a mouse to click.

When Apple created the Mac, they did it differently (and that's, no doubt, where the idea for the commercial—Think Different—was first spawned, though it came years later).

The Mac was designed to relate to you in a way that was familiar to anyone who works in an office, using a desktop. Common elements on the computer are shown as little pictures (icons) to serve as illustrations of the purpose of a specific item.

It's very true that there are still computers today that are set up to work with a text (command line) interface. There's of course DOS on the PC side of the personal computer arena, and UNIX, an industrial-strength operating system that can work with either a text or a graphical user interface.

For Hour 2, you'll take a tour around your iMac's desktop. You'll learn

- What all those little icons represent and what they're used for.
- What the menu bar is all about.
- How to select menu commands.
- About your iMac's desktop folders and what they contain.

What Do the Icons Stand For?

The items on your iMac are identified by little pictures, or *icons*, that tell you what they do.

Here's a quick look at some of the icons you'll see most often and what they represent:

FIGURE 2.1

Each icon on your iMac's desktop accesses a specific item or feature.

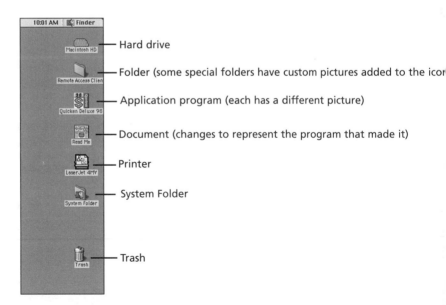

The iMac's Menu Bar

Your TV's remote control has buttons to activate functions to turn the TV on, or change channels. On the iMac, there are several ways to give the computer instructions to do something. The first one I'll talk about is the menu bar, that long, gray (or "platinum," as Apple calls it) strip across the top of your iMac's screen.

If you've used Windows, you'll see one big difference between the way the menu bar works on the "other side" and on the Mac. Under Windows, each program you use has its own menu bar, so you might find several menu bars across your computer's screen. On a Mac, there's one menu bar, at the very top, which changes to reflect the features of a specific program. The advantage is that you only have to point your mouse in one specific place for it to work properly.

Let's Take a Menu Bar Tour

The iMac's menu bar has a set of labels that you click on to open a list of functions (commands). In the next few pages, I'll take you through the Finder's menu bar, where you'll discover what all those commands really accomplish. In later Hours, you'll learn specifically how to use these commands in other applications.

As you explore menu bar commands, you'll see that many of them are common from one program to another. That's a reflection of how consistent the Mac OS interface is. So when you learn what these commands do for the iMac's Finder, you'll also see how they work in other programs, such as the ones I'll describe in Hour 3, Hour 8, Hour 9, and Hour 10. And that knowledge goes a long way toward learning how to use those programs.

Touring the File Menu

Let's start with the File menu (see Figure 2.2). To open this screen, just perform the following steps; these basic steps apply to activating any menu bar function.

1. Move your mouse cursor to the File menu.
2. Click on the File menu and hold down the mouse button. A list of the commands that are available from that menu will pop up on your screen.

FIGURE 2.2

*The File menu
controls basic file
manipulation features
of your computer.*

Actually, the pop-up menu drops down, and if you use Windows, you are probably used to calling them "drop-down menus." But because this is a Mac, I'll use the word "pop-up" to be consistent with Apple's term.

3. To activate a command, move the mouse cursor to that item. You'll see a dark rectangle around it to show it has been chosen (or *selected*).

4. Release the mouse button to activate the command.

If holding down the mouse button isn't comfortable for you, just release it after you click on a menu bar label. The pop-up menu will stay there for 15 seconds, which will give you enough time to point to a specific command. After you've done that, click on that command. The menu will disappear and the command will be activated.

You'll notice that some items are gray (or *grayed out*). Those commands are only available under certain conditions (such as "Print" when you have a document open), or if you select a specific icon to which the command applies. You won't be able to activate grayed-out commands.

The following items appear on the File menu:

- **New Folder**: Creates a container in which to store files (or more folders). You can insert folders within folders to your heart's content (but don't overdo it) just by dragging one over to the folder you want to put it in. Wait for the target folder to highlight before releasing the mouse button.

You don't have to use your mouse for all commands. Some functions have keyboard shortcuts, too. You'll see them listed at the right of the command label on a menu. The clover-leaf symbol stands for the "Apple" or Command key on your iMac's keyboard. If you hold down that key plus the second key listed, it will activate that function.

2

- **Open**: Opens a folder, or launches a program and brings a document to your screen.
- **Print**: Prints the document you have open on your screen.
- **Move to Trash**: Puts a selected item in the little trash can at the lower right of your iMac's screen (the equivalent of the Hefty bags you keep in your garage).
- **Get Info**: Use this command to learn more about a selected icon.

NEW TERM Some commands in a menu have a right arrow next to them. If you see the right arrow, it means clicking on it will open a second menu (a *submenu*) showing additional functions that apply to that command.

- **Label**: You can use this feature to change the color of an icon, which is helpful in sorting things by priority. You can also change the names that apply to a specific label category.
- **Duplicate**: As it says, it will make a copy of the item you've selected.
- **Make Alias**: I'll cover this in more detail in Hour 5, "Files, Folders, Windows, and Other Things." But an Alias in Mac OS parlance is an icon that points to the original (it's like running something on remote control). It has lots of cool uses, as you'll see later.
- **Add to Favorites**: If you want to call up a program or document often, you'll want to make it a Favorite, so you can get to it quickly. You'll be able to access it directly whenever you want from the Apple menu.
- **Put Away**: This command can be used to eject such things as a CD or floppy disk. And if you move an icon from its original location, this command puts it back from whence it came (to get literary about it).

OS 9
- **Encrypt**: Use this command to scramble (encrypt) a selected file, so it cannot be opened by someone unless he has the correct password.

- **Find**: This command opens the great Sherlock search feature. You can use Sherlock (or Sherlock 2 for Mac OS 9) to locate files on your iMac's drive or the text inside files.

> If you see three dots (an ellipsis) next to a menu command, you'll see another screen (a dialog box) when you select that function. You will have to make some choices from the dialog box to activate a function (that's why it's a "dialog"). I'll tell you more about this in Hour 5.

NEW TERM A *dialog box* is a screen or window where you can interact with your computer to make choices about a selected function. For example, if you want to print something you'll see a dialog box where you type how many copies you want of each page and what pages you want to print.

NEW TERM A *window* as described here is not that "other" platform, but a rectangular-shaped object that displays such things as a list of files, the contents of a folder, or the contents of a document (such as your letter to your mom and so on). I'll explain more about how this all works in Hour 5.

OS 9
- **Search Internet**: This command brings up Sherlock 2, which lets you search for information on the Internet.
  - **Show Original**: When you make an Alias (file reference), this command brings up the original item.
  - **Page Setup**: This command is used to set up your printer to handle a particular type of document. I'll cover printing issues in Hour 17, "Now That I Wrote It, How Do I Print It?"
  - **Print Window**: Use this command to print an open directory Window, so you can have a hard copy of your list of files.

Touring the Edit Menu

The next menu is called Edit (see Figure 2.3). It's used to make changes to a selected item.

Here's the list of commands that are used to Edit something. Once again, if something is grayed out, it means that command isn't available to work on the item you've selected.

FIGURE 2.3

Use the iMac's Edit menu to make changes to a selected item.

2

The Edit menu includes the following items:

- **Undo**: They say there's no going back. But on the iMac, this isn't always true. If this command is black, it means that the last action you took to edit something can be rescinded. Except for a very few programs, you can only do this sort of thing once (after which the command changes to Redo, which gives you the choice to make the change you undid all over again).

- **Cut**: This isn't used for removing files. It's designed to remove a text or picture you've selected and store it in a little "invisible" place called the "Clipboard."

 NEW TERM The *Clipboard* is a little cupboard or place in the iMac's memory where the item you copy is held in storage until replaced with another copied item—or until your computer is restarted or shut down.

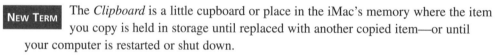

Be careful what you do after you Cut something. If you perform another operation (even typing a single letter), you won't be able to Undo the function.

- **Copy**: This command makes a duplicate of the selected word or picture and stores it in the Clipboard.

- **Paste**: This command inserts an item you've copied with the Copy command or removed with the Cut command.

- **Clear**: This command wipes out the selected item. It's gone, history. You won't be able to retrieve it from the Clipboard (though you can Undo the operation).

- **Select All**: This command does precisely what the name implies. It highlights all of the items in the selected window.

- **Show Clipboard**: This command opens a small document window showing the contents of the Clipboard.

- **Preferences**: This command opens a dialog box where you can make a few settings on Finder functions (see Figure 2.4). I'll cover more about this when you get to Hour 16. Feel free to play with the settings for now. You can always change them back.

FIGURE 2.4

Click on a tab at the top of the Preferences dialog box to change specific settings that cover the Finder display.

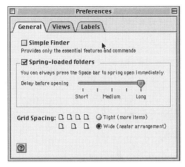

Touring the View Menu

The next stop on our little trip around the iMac's menu bar is the View menu (shown in Figure 2.5). It's used to control how items on your computer's desktop are displayed. The first three choices are either/or propositions. And there's a checkmark to the left of the one you select.

FIGURE 2.5

The View menu shows how items are displayed on the desktop.

Here's a quick look at how the View settings work:

- **View as Icons**: This is the normal setup; everything is displayed as a colorful icon (shown in Figure 2.6).

FIGURE 2.6

The normal display scheme for items on the desktop is the Icon view.

- **View as Buttons**: Converts your icons to large buttons (see Figure 2.7). A single click will activate the function that applies to the button.

FIGURE 2.7

If two clicks are one too many, try the Button view instead.

- **View as List**: Sometimes known as list view. It offers you a simple text listing or directory (see Figure 2.8). If you have lots of items in a directory, this option makes them all take up a lot less screen space.

FIGURE 2.8

This is a simple text view of a directory.

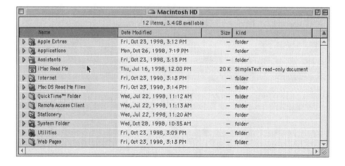

Sorry, you can't change the desktop icons to List view. As someone once said, that's the way it is.

- **View as Window**: Your standard setting for windows displayed onscreen.
- **View as Pop-up Window**: This alternative setting is a desktop space saver. It moves the window to the bottom of the screen and the window title changes to the shape of a file folder label (see Figure 2.9). Click once to reduce it to a file folder icon that will grace the bottom of the iMac's screen, and a second time to bring it back to regular size.

FIGURE 2.9

Click again to reduce the window to a little folder label at the bottom of your screen.

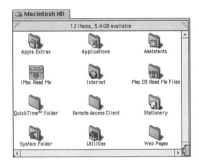

- **Clean Up**: If your icons are spread around, this helps clean them up with a neater arrangement. Now if it would only work that way in my office, I'd be all set.

- **Arrange**: Click on the arrow to open a sorting sequence, such as by Name, Date Modified, and so on.

- **Reset Column Positions**: This restores the directory display to the way it was previously set up.

- **View Options**: This will open a Setting dialog box (see Figure 2.10) that allows you to make further adjustments on how items on the desktop are set up.

FIGURE 2.10

Pick your View setup choices from this dialog box.

Touring the Special Menu

The Special menu has some very serious functions, as you'll see shortly (see Figure 2.11). You'll have to think twice about some of these commands before you activate them.

FIGURE 2.11

You use the Special menu to activate some heavy-duty functions.

Let's take the Special menu items one by one:

- **Empty Trash**: When you put something in the trash can, it's not really gone. To remove the item, you have to use the Empty Trash command.

> Think carefully before you use the Empty Trash command. It is more or less a one-way ticket, and after the item you remove is gone, you probably won't be able to retrieve it later. I say "probably," because there are programs, as I'll explain in Hour 24, which are designed to retrieve files you deleted by mistake. But they are not guaranteed to work all of the time.

- **Eject**: This command is used to eject a CD or other mounted disk. Before you use the Eject command, make sure the item you want to eject isn't being used by a program or running something, or otherwise your computer might crash or freeze. The function is the same as the Put Away command in the File menu.

- **Erase Disk**: Use this command with caution. It is designed to erase the contents of the selected disk (fortunately you cannot erase the disk that you use to start your computer this way).

- **Sleep**: This command puts your iMac into an idle mode or low-power mode. The screen will turn off, but the computer will remain on with anything you're working on still intact. Just press any key to awaken your sleeping computer. And it doesn't even snore.

- **Restart**: After installing a new program (or in case a program crashes or stops running for some reason), you should always use the Restart command. It causes the iMac to go through its normal shutting down routine, but then it starts up normally.

- **Shut Down**: Turns your computer off.

> The above three functions in the Special menu can also be activated by pressing the power button below the iMac's screen or on the keyboard of the iMac. It will open a menu giving these choices (plus one more, the ability to Cancel the operation). Clicking on the appropriate function will activate it.

OS 9 • **Logout**: If you've set up your Multiple Users Control Panel (see the section on security in Hour 21), you'll see this additional presence on the Special menu. Otherwise you won't and you do not need to fret over it.

Touring the Help Menu

When you run into a problem while working on your iMac, or if you just have a question, you'll want to keep this book at hand. But you'll also want to consult Apple's Help menu (see Figure 2.12).

FIGURE 2.12

How do I do that? Let Apple's Help menu guide you.

Each program will have its own set of Help choices, but these are the ones Apple gives you:

* **Help Center**: This is your introduction to Apple's help feature.
* **Show Balloons**: Not everyone's cup of tea. It puts a little comic book-type "balloon" describing the function of an item over which the mouse cursor is pointed. It's fun for a while, but some folks (such as your fearless author) get tired of it after a while and turn the feature off.
* **Tutorial**: I mentioned this briefly in Hour 1, in the section entitled "Mouse-er-size," where I explained how to use Apple's online mouse tutorial. You can also get a fast tutorial into basic functions of your computer here, too. But it's very, very basic.
* **Mac OS Help**: This introduces you to Apple's complete Help menu for the Mac OS (see Figure 2.13).

A quick way to get around Apple's Help menu is to use the Search feature. Just click on the text field to the left of the Search button in Figure 2.13, type the subject of the information you want and, if available, it'll show up in a few seconds.

FIGURE 2.13

Click on an underlined item to learn more about it.

Touring the Apple Menu

Our last menu bar option is actually the first on your screen, the Apple menu, which is, of course, identified simply by the symbol of an Apple (see Figure 2.14).

FIGURE 2.14

The Apple menu offers quick access to more programs and documents.

The Apple menu isn't set in stone, and might look different from the way it's shown here. That's because it can be easily configured to display the items (folders, files, programs) you want. I'll tell you more in Hour 16. For now, here's a very brief look at some of the standard contents of the Apple menu:

- **About This Computer**: This one opens a screen that gives you some basic information about the Mac OS version you have, and the amount of memory installed and in use.

- **Apple System Profiler**: This is useful for troubleshooting. It's a fast way to create a report of what you have installed on your iMac in case you need help to resolve a problem.

- **Automated Tasks**: Click on the arrow to open a submenu of some canned AppleScript functions. They are clearly labeled as to what they do.

> **NEW TERM** *AppleScript* is a set of tools that allow you to automate many repetitious tasks on your iMac. I'll tell you more about it in Hour 19, "AppleScript: Putting Your iMac on Automatic Pilot."

- **Calculator**: A very, very simple calculator.

- **Chooser**: This program is used to choose (select) a printer, or connect you to a network (see also Network Browser below).

- **Control Panels**: This opens a submenu listing programs that let you control certain features on your iMac. It's sort of like the buttons on your stereo because it lets you adjust many things the way you like. I'll tell you more in Hour 16.

- **Favorites**: This is a place where you can put your favorite programs, documents, or Web sites for easy access.

- **FaxStatus**: If you see this item, it means your computer comes with software that lets you use your modem as a fax machine. You'll discover more about this feature in Hour 10, "Faxing, Cooking, and Other Software."

- **Graphing Calculator**: Takes the iMac's calculation abilities to the next level.

> If you're wondering where your Graphing Calculator is, all right, I'll confess. This interesting little program isn't part of Mac OS 9, so if you have a new iMac, don't be overly concerned if it's no longer there.

- **Internet Access**: This choice opens a submenu of Internet connection choices.

- **Jigsaw Puzzle**: As the name implies, it's just for fun.

- **Key Caps**: In Hour 1's discussion on "Keyboard Power," I explained there were optional keys available for certain characters, such as accents or math symbols. Here's where you can open a display of the available characters and how to access them.

- **Network Browser**: This program lets you access another iMac, iBook, or other Mac on a network.

- **Note Pad**: This is a very simple word processing program that lets you keep notes for later review.

- **Remote Access Status**: On online display, used when you've connected to the Internet or another Mac with Remote Access software.

- **Scrapbook**: This program lets you create a little repository of pictures and text for quick retrieval later. It's useful for inserting items into a document you're working on.

- **Sherlock**: Sherlock is Apple's search tool that lets you find things on your computer, inside documents, and on the Internet. For Mac OS 9, it's called Sherlock 2, and sports a brand new interface. I'll tell you more about this in Hour 10.

- **SimpleSound**: Lets you pick and record sounds.

- **Stickies**: If your office is filled with little yellow sticky notes, isn't it nice to know that you can fill your iMac's desktop with the same sort of notes (see Figure 2.15)? Just select this program and see what it does for you.

FIGURE 2.15

Here's a way to fill the desktop with lots and lots of "sticky" notes.

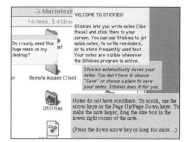

The Rest of the Menu Bar

To the right of all the command labels I've just described is your iMac's clock. And at the right end of the menu bar, you'll see a label identifying the application you're in.

You can switch from one application to another (if you've opened more than one) simply by clicking on the application's name and choosing another program from the list (all open applications will be shown there).

Another way to zip through your open applications is via a keyboard shortcut: Command+Tab.

Here's a neat trick: Just click on the application menu. Hold down the mouse and pull (drag) it away from the menu bar. Guess what? You'll see a floating screen (palette) showing you the applications you've opened on your iMac (see figure 2.16). Just click on the one you want to activate.

FIGURE 2.16

Click on any item shown here to switch to that program.

What Is All That Stuff on My Desktop?

When you set up your new iMac, you'll see a little icon labeled Macintosh HD near the upper-right corner of your screen (below the menu bar). Just double-click on that icon to see the bill of fare (see Figure 2.17).

FIGURE 2.17

Most of the files stored on your new computer are in little containers (folders).

I'll assume here that you've tried out the various settings in the Views menu to see what they do.

Here's a brief idea of the contents of those little folder icons in the Macintosh HD window:

- **Apple Extras**: This folder contains a number of options and instruction sheets that Apple gives you on various features. For example, you'll find information about its automation program, AppleScript, the files for the Mac OS Tutorial, some ReadMe files (last-minute updates to your iMac's features), and so on.

2

> If you've already hooked up a printer to your iMac, you can get a hard copy of any of those ReadMe files you open on your screen. Just choose Print from the File menu and indicate how many copies you want (the default is one). Then click the Print button to make it so. I'll cover more about printing in Hour 17.

NEW TERM A *ReadMe* or *Read Me* is a document file that contains important, late-breaking information about your iMac, the Mac OS, or a specific program or product. It's always a good idea to check these files out as soon as you can.

- **Applications**: This folder includes all of the programs that were bundled with your iMac, plus new programs you might have installed. However, some programs put their own little folders in the top level (root level) of your drive directory instead.

- **Assistants**: Here's where you can find the Mac OS and Internet Setup Assistants, plus any other Assistants Apple might give you at a later time.

- **iMac ReadMe**: Double-click on this icon to learn last-minute news from Apple about your new computer.

- **Internet**: Check out this folder for your Internet-related programs, including your Web browser software and other software.

- **Mac OS ReadMe Files**: This folder includes late-breaking information files about the version of the Mac OS you're using.

- **QuickTime Folder**: QuickTime is Apple's software that lets you see movies and other productions on your iMac. Check the information in this folder to learn more.

- **Remote Access Client**: Apple uses a program called Remote Access to let you connect to the Internet or share files via modem to the Macs at your office.

- **Stationery**: Don't worry too much about this one. Only the original iMac units that Apple shipped included this folder. It covers a program, OpenDoc, which Apple once included with its computers. It's one of those cool technologies that never quite got off the ground.

- **System Folder**: This is the "guts" of your iMac. It contains the Mac OS software needed to make your computer run.

- **Utilities**: Apple gives you some extra stuff to check and update your iMac's hard drive. You'll learn more about these programs, which include Disk First Aid, in Hours 23 and 24.

Summary

In Hour 2, you began to discover how to make your iMac do things for you. You toured the menu bar, and discovered the folders that contain all the great programs that Apple has thoughtfully provided for your computer. In Hour 3, I'll show you how to begin to explore the Internet, using such services as EarthLink or AOL.

You'll even get some information to help you decide which service to join (or whether it makes sense to pick both).

Q&A

Q I tried double-clicking on an icon as you said and it doesn't work. What did I do wrong?

A Mouse skills take a bit of time to master. You might want to use Apple's own "Mouse Skills" tutorial. I explained how to access it in Hour 1, in the section titled "Mouse-er-size." Double-clicking requires getting used to the right rhythm. And you can adjust the setting to fit in with your own taste. I'll tell you how when you get to Hour 16.

Q What happens when I double-click on a file? Am I launching the file or a program?

A Well, both. When you double-click on a document file, such as one of those ReadMe files, first your computer launches the program that made it. Then the document itself is opened. So it's doing double duty. When you click on a program's icon, just the program is opened. I'll cover this subject in more detail in Hour 7, "Opening, Saving, Finding, Moving, Etc."

Q My iMac's desktop doesn't look like the one in this book. What am I doing wrong?

A Probably nothing at all. If you are working on an iMac that has already been set up by someone else, perhaps the Views options are different, or a different desktop backdrop has been selected. It's even possible the folders that contain your computer's software have been organized in a different fashion (or have been placed within other folders). Or that some of the programs my new computer contains aren't available on yours. The beauty of the Mac OS is that, like that fast-food burger, you really can "have it your way."

Q Help—my iMac's keyboard and mouse won't work. What's up?

A Your iMac might have crashed (see Hours 23 and 24 for some help on dealing with such problems). But for now, you should make sure that both your mouse and keyboard are plugged in securely. Don't feel shy about pulling out plugs and putting them in agian. The iMac's USB port is capable of "hot swapping."

2

HOUR 3

Getting On the Net

In Hour 1, "Setting Up Your iMac," I explained that the *i* in the iMac name stands for, at least in part, the "Internet."

And many of you bought one of these great little computers to do just that, explore all the great features on the world wide Internet.

For Hour 3, you'll explore the subject of the Internet. You'll learn

- The differences between an Internet provider and an online service (and which to pick and why).
- How to sign up with EarthLink or a similar service.
- How to join AOL and what it offers.
- Some advice for getting started as an Internet surfer.

The Internet is not a physical place to go (such as your corner bakery). It's, well, a little more complicated than that. Back in Hour 1, I explained that whenever you connect two computers together, you have a network.

The Internet is a network, too, only it doesn't contain just two computers, but millions of them, spread across the world. These computers not only share information but work as relay stations, forwarding the information they receive to other computers. Think of it as a gigantic relay race.

And what's more, these computers aren't restricted to Macs or PCs. They run the gamut of many operating systems. Some are personal computers not much different in capability from your iMac. Others are huge mainframes, filling entire offices. The Internet is, in a sense, a worldwide computer network that doesn't have any boundaries as to computer, operating system, or location.

EarthLink or AOL? What's the Difference?

AOL bills itself (correctly, of course) as the "world's largest Internet online service." And EarthLink is an Internet service, too, right?

Well, there *is* a difference. AOL, like EarthLink, does indeed give you an Internet connection and a Web browser to explore the Internet.

NEW TERM A *Web browser* is a program that calls up the information you want on the Internet and presents it on your computer with full color, animation, and sometimes sound.

Although its custom content has expanded quite a bit, EarthLink primarily offers you a connection to the Internet, the same as your phone company offers you a connection to its phone network. There are additional features, such as some very nice Help pages and a well-integrated Personal Start Page (which you can customize to provide direct links to your favorite features). But AOL goes beyond an Internet connection. AOL is an outgrowth of what are sometimes called "bulletin board services" or (BBS). It offers not only a connection, but has its own vast array of exclusive content available to members only. As you'll see (briefly) in the following pages, AOL has its own forums, chat rooms, discussion areas (message boards), software libraries, news centers, shopping centers, and other features that go way beyond just an Internet connection.

NEW TERM A *forum* is an online meeting place where folks of similar interests can get together, share information, and have discussions via their computers.

NEW TERM The *chat room* is the online equivalent of a meeting room, where you can "talk" to other folks or listen to lectures. The talking, in this case, is done by typing on your iMac and sending the message to the chat room where others can see it.

NEW TERM A *message board* is similar to the bulletin board in your local supermarket. You can use it to leave little statements or messages for others to see and reply to.

NEW TERM The *software library* is a place that stores files (such as software) that can be retrieved (downloaded) by others.

> Actually, AOL and EarthLink do share one other feature, instant messaging, which is the ability to communicate one-on-one with fellow Internet users. EarthLink is offering a special version of AOL's popular Instant Messenger software (it should be available by the time you read this book).

If you have children in your household, AOL has taken steps to make it kid safe. That is, it has special Parental Controls available to create a custom online setup for your children. This limits them to certain online forums and Web sites where the content is certified to be friendly for them.

EarthLink's kid safe feature is called KidZone, which provides a special online environment where children can find games and educational information (including homework help).

Making the EarthLink Connection

When you first set up your iMac (in Hour 1), you were "interviewed" by two setup Assistants from Apple. The second, Internet Setup Assistant, is used to let Apple find an Internet service for you.

But you don't have to take that route.

You already have software for an Internet provider (or ISP for short) on your iMac's hard drive, from EarthLink, a service that has gotten great reviews as being one of the best ones out there.

To get to it, just click on the Internet icon on your iMac's drive, where you'll see a folder labeled Total Access. That's the trade name for EarthLink's service.

Within that folder is its Registration & Utilities program. Just double-click on that program to get started.

> Before signing up with EarthLink, check the little inserts that came in your iMac computer's accessories box. You're apt to find a special offer for new EarthLink members. If it's not there, your favorite computing magazine may have it, too.

The first screen you see will be EarthLink's license agreement. You must agree to it to move on (it's not a multiple-choice option). After you've given it the OK, you'll see the setup screen (shown in Figure 3.1). Most of the options are grayed out because you haven't signed up with the service yet. That'll change later.

No matter what Internet service you want, be sure to have a credit card handy to enter your billing information. Some services can debit your checking account in payment instead, such as AOL and CompuServe. EarthLink will do it, too, but you have to call its customer service department to set it up.

FIGURE 3.1

This program is used to establish your EarthLink account.

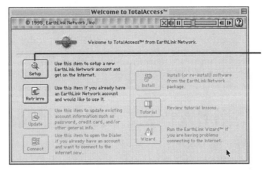

Click Setup to start the process

As you sign up for EarthLink, you'll hear a little audio presentation with up-to-date instructions. The buttons shown at the upper right of Figure 3.1 are similar to that on a cassette or CD player. Click the X button to stop the show.

If you're already an EarthLink subscriber, click the Retrieve button in Figure 3.1 to set it up to work with your account.

From here you'll be taken through a number of information screens where you can enter your setup information. Here's a summary of what you'll need to do to sign up. Click on the Next button to move on and the Previous button to recheck your information.

You'll notice that some of the navigation buttons in EarthLink's setup screen have a thick rectangle around them. Whenever you see this type of button (in any Mac program), you can press the Return or Enter keys on your iMac's keyboard to activate the function. It'll keep you from having to "mouse around" all the time.

▼ To Do

1. **Modem Setup**: On the next screen, EarthLink will select a modem for you. Most times it guesses right and chooses Apple iMac Internal Modem. Next...

2. **Setup New Account**: Give yourself a username here (see Figure 3.2). You can pick your own name, or something that sounds, well, nice. EarthLink puts up a notice if the username you've chosen is taken and gives you a chance to use something else. Next...

3

FIGURE 3.2
Establish your email address and password here.

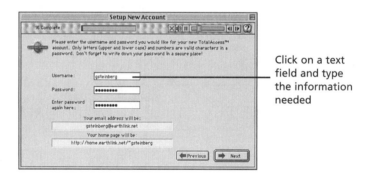

Click on a text field and type the information needed

3. **General Information**: Type your name and address information as shown in Figure 3.3.

FIGURE 3.3
The billing information you see here is, of course, not real.

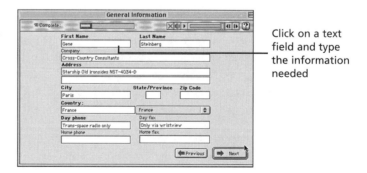

Click on a text field and type the information needed

▼

▼ We are getting close to the end now. So just hang in there as we continue with the last few steps to set up your EarthLink account:

4. **Phone Setup**: You'll see a screen where you can enter your long distance and dial-up prefixes, along with your local area code. Next...

5. **Communications Status**: EarthLink will open a screen showing the status of your connection to the service. If everything is okay, you'll see some more information screens, where you need to enter your credit card billing information. . Next...

It's a good idea to stay at your computer when the Connection Status screen is up. If the EarthLink's 800-service number is busy or there's a connection problem, you may have to OK a screen or two to continue.

6. **Phone Setup**: Based on the area code you're in, you'll see a list of local access numbers (see Figure 3.4). You can only pick one. Next...

FIGURE 3.4
Select the phone number nearest you.

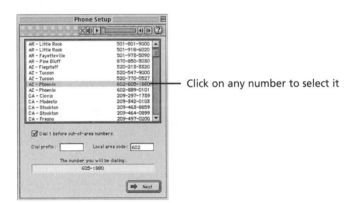

Click on any number to select it

7. **Installation**: Yes, you may already have your Internet software installed, but EarthLink needs to know about it. So click on the first option in the Installation screen (see Figure 3.5). After this has been done, click Install. In a few moments, you'll see a screen requesting you to Restart your iMac. Click Restart to finish the

▼ setup process.

FIGURE 3.5

Go through the formalities about picking Internet Explorer here.

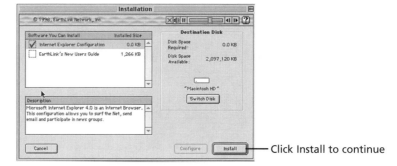

Click Install to continue

8. **Tutorial**: EarthLink provides a nice Tutorial video that can really help you get used to the service. After your iMac has restarted, you'll see a Tutorial screen giving you the choice of watching the video. Click Play to see it. Click Done to move on and begin your first connection to the service. The first video you see will help you get used to using a Web browser (see Figure 3.6).

FIGURE 3.6

Experience your computer's multimedia features with this video from EarthLink.

Click Next to see another video

9. **Welcome to TotalAccess**: Haven't we been here before? When you're finished looking at videos, click Previous over and over again to get to the first screen; then Done to open the Welcome screen. Unlike the picture shown in Figure 3.1, all the buttons are dark and cannot be used to perform their labeled functions. Click Connect to continue.

10. **Remote Access**: To log onto EarthLink (finally!), click Connect on the screen shown in Figure 3.7.

FIGURE **3.7**
The Status line will show you the steps taken to connect to EarthLink.

Status line

11. **Browse the Internet**: Okay, what to do here? You're logged in, with no place to go. Just look on the right side of your iMac's desktop for an icon labeled Browse the Internet. Double-click on it to launch your Web browser and open Earthlink's home page (see Figure 3.8). If it's not there, click on the Apple menu, choose Internet, and select Browse the Internet from the submenu.

FIGURE **3.8**
Earthlink's home page greets you when you first join the service.

Click once on any item to see more

Click on My Personal Start Page to make one of your own

NEW TERM   A *home page* is the introduction to a Web site. It will contain some brief information about the person or business running the site. You will find links to other
pages and (no doubt) a few ads, too.

▼ 12. **The Personal Start Page**: A great feature for EarthLink is the ability to create your very own, customized start or home page for the service. To set it up, click on the item labeled My Personal Start Page shown in the lower left of Figure 3.8. You'll be given a menu of choices as to what to include (not to worry, you can always change it whenever you want, over and over again). When you're done, you'll see a result similar to the Start Page I've created for myself (see Figure 3.9).

FIGURE 3.9

Yes, this is the author's real EarthLink Start Page.

Click once on any item to see more

▲

No doubt you'll want to spend a little time exploring the vast frontiers of the Internet with EarthLink. When you're ready to sign off, here's what to do:

1. Click on the File menu of your Web browser and choose Quit. This will turn the program off.

2. Click on the Application menu (as I explained in Hour 2, "Exploring the iMac Desktop").

3. Choose Remote Access.

4. Click on the Disconnect button.

5. Finally, click on the little square at the upper left of the Remote Access window, which will shut down (quit) that program too. In Hour 5, "Files, Folders, Windows, and Other Things," I'll tell you what all those little things on program windows are and how to use them.

▲

If you cannot find Remote Access in your application menu, no problem. Just click on the Apple menu, choose Control Panels and select Remote Access from the submenu. After you open Remote Access, click the Disconnect button to end your EarthLink session.

How to Join AOL

AOL's software is located in the Internet folder on your iMac's drive. To get to it, just double-click on the Internet folder; then double-click on the folder labeled America Online 4.0 (version 5.0 was being developed when this book was written).

 Before you launch AOL's software, look for a little AOL insert card in your computer's accessories box. The insert has a special AOL "free time" offer and a sign-on registration and password number. If you don't find this insert, call AOL at 1-800-827-6364 for assistance. You'll also want to keep your credit card handy so you can enter your billing information when requested on AOL's sign-in screen.

First You Get Connected

When you see the America Online program icon, double-click on it. After about 10 or 15 seconds, you'll see the first of several setup windows (see Figure 3.10). They may be different from the ones shown here, but as long as you read the instructions offered, you'll be able to get through it like a champ.

FIGURE 3.10

This is the beginning of the AOL sign-up process. Choose Automatic Setup.

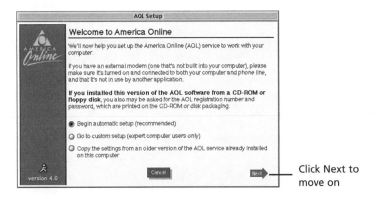

Click Next to move on

Remember, you can always cancel if you change your mind. If you decide to try it again later, no problem. It will start up right from the beginning.

There are three choices in your first AOL setup window, but the first, Begin Automatic Setup (Recommended) is the one to pick.

Before continuing, be sure your computer's modem is connected to your phone line (and that nobody else is using that line during the setup process). If the line is busy, the AOL software won't be able to complete the sign-up process.

On the next setup screen, AOL Setup, the program will take a few moments to test your modem to determine what kind it is (see Figure 3.11) and set up the software to get you the best possible connection. The software is designed to run on many different types of Mac computers, and there are lots of modems out there.

FIGURE 3.11

AOL's software will probe your computer's modem to set up the ideal connection profile for it. Be prepared to wait a couple of minutes for the process to finish.

The clever AOL software will soon get the message and report back to you that, yes, you are indeed using an iMac's internal modem (see Figure 3.12).

FIGURE 3.12

If this says it's an iMac internal modem, you're home free.

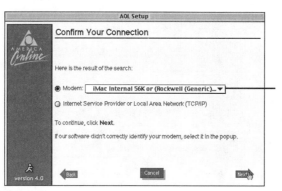

If AOL's software makes a mistake, click the pop-up menu and select the right type of modem from the list

Okay, I know you're anxious to get going, but the software needs to do a few more things before you make that first connection as an AOL member. Next up is a dialog box where you confirm the dialing options (see Figure 3.13).

FIGURE **3.13**

Read the screen carefully before moving on, in case you have to set it up for Call Waiting.

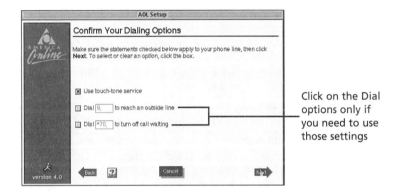

Click on the Dial options only if you need to use those settings

If you have Call Waiting service, be sure to click on the second Dial option. The numbers shown, *70, are used by most phone companies to disable Call Waiting for the next call; this will prevent your AOL hookup from being interrupted if someone tries to call you while you're online.

After AOL software has decided how to connect to your computer's modem, it needs to determine where you are, so you'll dial up through a local number. On the next screen, you'll be asked to enter your area code (see Figure 3.14). As soon as your modem setup has been completed, type in your area code in the appropriate text field so that America Online can hook you up to the closest and fastest (thus the cheapest) connection in your area.

FIGURE **3.14**

AOL needs this information to find a local connection number for you.

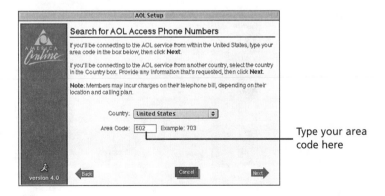

Type your area code here

After you've clicked Next, AOL's host computer will be called up to check its directory. And don't be alarmed at the connection noises you hear on your computer's speaker. They're normal.

If AOL can't find a number for you, you'll get a chance to enter a different nearby area code and have it try again. But for most cities, you'll be awarded with a result similar to the one shown in Figure 3.15.

FIGURE 3.15

Here's a list of AOL numbers in Arizona.

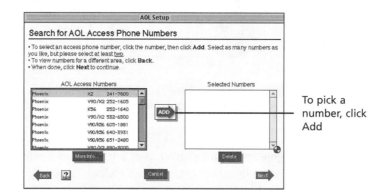

To pick a number, click Add

3

 If more than one number is available in your city, pick at least two. AOL's access numbers are apt to get busy in the evening, so this gives you a chance to connect at the alternate number (AOL will switch automatically if it cannot connect the first time).

When you add a number, you'll see a confirmation screen (I won't show it here). Just click OK to move on.

Create Your America Online Account Now

AOL will now dial up your local number and take you to a screen where you begin to set up your online account (see Figure 3.16).

 If you're already an AOL member, click on the second option in Figure 3.16 and place your present screen name and password in the text fields to pick up your account information.

FIGURE 3.16

The default option lets you sign on as a new member.

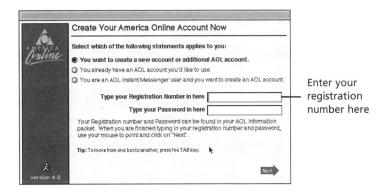

Enter your registration number here

Take out that insert from AOL (offering the free monthly trial) and enter the registration and password information where requested on your iMac's screen.

Click the Next button.

AOL will now guide you through a series of setup screens where you give them your name, address, and billing information. That's why I suggested you have a credit card ready.

AOL can also debit your checking account for your monthly charges at a slight surcharge, but you may have to wait a day or two to get online, so they can set up the paperwork.

After your billing information has been set up, AOL will ask you to agree to its Terms of Service. These are the rules covering the service, and you'll want to check them. They're a little more involved than the standard software license. But basically, AOL expects you to be a good citizen online, and not bother others, that sort of thing.

What Do I Call Myself?

Folks who join an online service don't have to use their real names. And sometimes they can't (because someone else is already using it). Instead you give yourself a "handle," as they used to say when CB radios were popular. That's a nickname, which AOL calls a *screen name.* It's the equivalent of what is known as a "username" on EarthLink.

After you've signed up, AOL will display a screen where you name yourself. At first, they'll suggest a name, based on your real name with perhaps a few numbers after it.

But feel free to change it and try something else. Just remember that because no two AOL members can have the same screen name, you may have to endure a few moments of trying out names until one "takes."

Please remember that you can't change your initial (master) screen name. So pick it with care. But you can add more screen names to your account (for your family or perhaps to give yourself another online "identity" like Superman and Clark Kent). As of the time this book was written, AOL was setting up their system to allow for six extra screen names, with up to 16 characters each.

The First Connection

In a few seconds, you'll see AOL's opening screen and hear a "Welcome" message from that little "man" inside AOL's software (see Figure 3.17). And then you'll hear another announcement (just like on AOL's TV commercials and that Tom Hanks/Meg Ryan movie), "You've Got Mail."

FIGURE 3.17

Welcome to AOL.

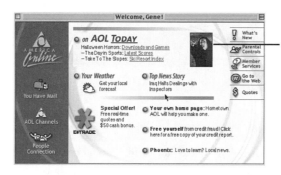

Click once on any picture or underlined title to see more

Yes, indeed, there will be mail in your AOL mailbox. Click on the You Have Mail icon, and you'll see a letter on your computer's screen direct from AOL's outspoken head, Steve Case, welcoming you to the service. Well, don't take it as a personal greeting; every new AOL member gets one.

The Welcome screen (with your name in the title) is your gateway to the day's major features on AOL. If you want to see more of their range of services, click on the AOL Channels icon (see Figure 3.18) to access a list of the various online departments.

AOL has several areas offering online help for new members, but if you really want to learn about the service on your own time, you may want to buy one of those AOL books. I've written three of them, by the way, *AOL 4.0 Quick Reference*, *Sams Teach Yourself AOL in 10 Minutes*, and *Using America Online 4.*

FIGURE 3.18
Change your AOL channel here.

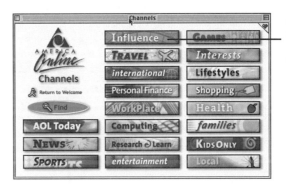

Click on a channel icon to learn more about that subject

AOL members get around with keywords. You can enter the name of the area you want to visit in the bottom text field on the AOL toolbar, click on the Go button, and you're off to that location. As a new member, try the keyword, well, New Members.

Summary

In Hour 3, I introduced you to the incredible global computer network, the Internet. You received instructions on joining an Internet service, such as EarthLink, and an online service, such as AOL. You learned the differences between the two, so you can make a decision about which to try (although many folks just use both).

In Hour 4, "A Look at Your iMac Software," I'll introduce you to the other software packages that were included with your new computer, and in Hour 8, "Teach Yourself AppleWorks," through Hour 10, "Faxing, Cooking, and Other Software," you'll learn about those programs in more detail.

Q&A

Q I'm already a member of AOL? Do I have to join again?

A Not at all. When you run the AOL software that comes on your iMac, you'll see a screen where you specify whether you're joining as a new member, or you're an existing member. If you're already a member, just type your present screen name and password (if you have more than one on your account, any will do), and your membership settings will be transferred. And you'll still be able to use the AOL software on your other computer (just not at the same time).

Q You really don't show us any advantages to EarthLink. Are there any?

A Actually, yes. First off, it's two bucks a month cheaper than AOL (at least as of the time this book was written) and EarthLink is less affected by busy signals during the evening prime time access hours. In addition, you have more flexibility in terms of running software other than AOL as part of your Internet connection. While you can use another browser and other Internet programs with your AOL connection, you cannot use other email software (except for Claris Emailer, a now-discontinued email program). And you cannot access AOL's Newsgroups feature with anything but AOL's software.

With EarthLink and other regular Internet services, you can choose from a number of different email programs. The same goes for such features as Internet news-groups. I'll tell you about these and other Internet features in Hour 11, "The Internet: Learning the Ropes," and Hour 12, "The Wonderful World of Email."

Q Do I have to join EarthLink or AOL? What about another service?

A Although Apple made a deal with these two to include them with your new iMac, you are free to join any service you like, or just copy over the settings from the service.

In addition to EarthLink (which was merging with MindSpring when this book was written), there are thousands of Internet providers. Some are local, some are national in scope. Even local phone companies and long distance carriers have gotten into the act (and they often give you special deals if you take Internet service as part of a special service package). When picking a service, you'll want to compare prices and services. If you travel, you'll also want to know if you can connect in other cities without paying long-distance charges.

Among online services, there's CompuServe, a service that's now owned by AOL, but it caters more to businesses and professional users. And there's Prodigy Internet, which tries to compete head on with AOL.

3

Q I already have a high-speed cable modem hookup. Can I use it with the iMac?

A Most likely, yes. Many cable modem services use an Ethernet port to connect to computers. And because you already have one with your iMac, hookups ought to be a piece of cake. But you'll need to contact the cable company directly about setting up your computer's Internet features to support their service.

The same holds true if you plan on trying out a DSL (Digital Subscriber Line) service, which allows you to get high-speed Internet connections direct from your regular phone lines.

If you are already using another item on the Ethernet jack, say a printer or another Mac, you'll need a "hub," a central connection device, to support multiple hookups (unless, of course, you already have one). Your computer dealer can help you purchase what you need. For a single hookup, a so-called Ethernet "crossover" cable can probably do the job.

Hour 4

A Look at Your iMac's Software

A computer is somewhat like a blackboard. You need to write something on the blackboard to have something to read. And you need to run software in order for your iMac to have something to do.

Fortunately, when you buy an iMac, you don't have to go out and buy some software to get it running. Some very nice programs are already installed on the hard drive, ready to run with a double-click of your mouse.

But, of course, if you want to expand your horizons, there are thousands of Mac programs out there, covering lots of different areas, from games to photo retouching.

In this lesson, I'll present

- The programs that came bundled with your new iMac.
- A quick guide as to what the programs do.
- Some suggestions on how to get software if your dealer isn't friendly to iMac owners.

Here's how to find the applications stored on your computer:

1. Double-click the Applications folder. This opens the directory showing what's available (see Figure 4.1).

2. To see what's inside another folder, double-click it.

3. If you see just an application icon of some sort, such as Simple Text, double-click that icon to launch it.

FIGURE 4.1

The Application folder's directory shows you the software installed on your iMac.

Double-click a folder icon
to see the program itself

▲

A Fast, Cheap Guide to Your iMac's Software

The programs that come with your iMac cover a wide range of purposes. But they have a few things in common, the first of which is that they are easy to learn and use.

In this Hour, we'll take a brief tour through the bill of fare, and in Hour 8, "Teach Yourself AppleWorks," Hour 9, "Managing Your Bucks with Quicken 98," and Hour 10, "Faxing, Cooking, and Other Software," you'll get more detailed information about how to use these programs.

Let's look at what resides inside the Applications folder:

- **AppleCD Audio Player**: It's like having an audio CD player in your iMac. This program (see Figure 4.2) mimics the features of the CD or DVD player you probably have hooked up to your home stereo. Click the right arrow to start playing; click the square box to stop. You can also do a limited amount of "programming" with this feature. The slider at the right side of the player window sets volume level.

FIGURE 4.2
A CD is already playing.

Click the down arrow at the lower left to see a track-by-track listing

You can install your applications elsewhere!

When you set up your iMac, you'll find your applications have been placed in the Applications folder. One of the beauties of the Mac operating system is that you don't have to install your programs all in one place. Over time, for example, you may decide to make new folders to cover different types of software. One example is Games.

• **Network Browser**: This program (see Figure 4.3) is used to connect to other computers on your network. After you've connected, the other computer's drive appears as a disk icon on your iMac's desktop.

FIGURE 4.3
The computer I'm connecting to here is my Apple PowerBook, which is on the same network as the iMac.

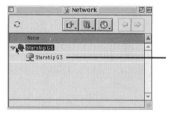

Double-click the other Mac to connect

4

If the user of the other Mac computer set up a password for network access (just as you did for your iMac in Hour 1, "Setting Up Your iMac"), you'll see a dialog box on your screen. You'll have to type in the username and password to connect to the other computer.

• **QuickTime**: QuickTime is Apple's multimedia software. The program inside this folder, MoviePlayer, is used to view QuickTime videos and (if you buy Apple's QuickTime Pro upgrade), do some simple editing, too. And beginning with version 4, you can even access streaming audio and video presentations direct from the Internet. I'll cover this subject in more detail in Hour 13, "Multimedia Is More than a CD-ROM Game."

- **SimpleText**: Almost every time you double-click a Read Me file, you're opening a program called SimpleText (see Figure 4.4). You only see part of it in this picture. The document itself takes up several pages. In order to see more, just take your mouse and click along that bar on the right side of the window (the scroll bar), or use the Pg Dn and Pg Up keys on your computer's keyboard. I'll tell you more about using all those little doo-dads on a document window in Hour 5, "Files, Folders, Windows, and Other Things."

FIGURE 4.4

This is a typical Mac Read Me file, which was made in SimpleText.

Press the Pg Dn key on your computer's keyboard to see more

- **Adobe Acrobat Reader**: As you noticed when you opened your iMac's accessory box, there isn't much printed literature there. Most of your help information is available via the Help menu. Other reading material comes in the form of Acrobat documents (see Figure 4.5), which are exact electronic copies of the original printed book. You can actually print out these pages with good quality, but then that sort of defeats the purpose of having an electronic, rather than hard copy, version of a manual.

- **Adobe PageMill:** If you want to create your own Web site from scratch, this program eases the way. You can use it in the same fashion as a word processor (such as AppleWorks, described next) to enter text and pictures. Before you know it, you'll have a ready-made Web site that you can make available on the World Wide Web by way of your Internet service provider (or AOL).

FIGURE 4.5

This online (electronic) manual is used to explain how to use Acrobat.

Click the right arrow key at the top of the screen to go to the next page

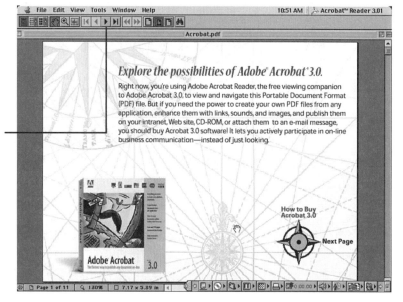

- **AppleWorks (ClarisWorks)**: AppleWorks is a great integrated program that serves the purpose of several separate programs (see Figure 4.6). It works as a word processor to handle your letters, novels, and so on. It can be used to draw pictures, set up business charts, and keep a database of business contacts. I'll give you a brief tutorial on how to use this program in Hour 8.

Some of the earliest iMac units shipped with the program still known by its original name, ClarisWorks, rather than AppleWorks. But the actual program is essentially the same, despite the name change.

NEW TERM An *integrated* program is one that includes the functions of several programs in one. That's different from a program *suite*, which involves a number of separate programs put in one box. Examples of program suites include CorelDraw and Microsoft Office.

FIGURE 4.6

Here's a personal letter I'm working on with AppleWorks.

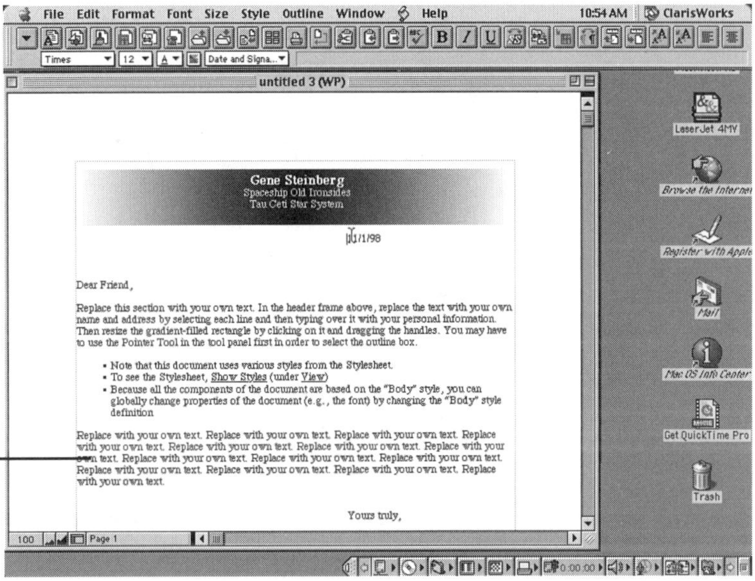

Click any text on the screen to add to it or change it

FIGURE 4.7

Use FAXstf to make your iMac double as a fax machine.

Click one of these folder icons to see the contents

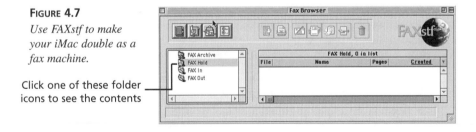

- **FAXstf**: Your iMac already has a built it modem. So wouldn't it be nice if you could also use the modem to work as a fax machine, too? That way the documents that you write could be sent to your clients without having to print a copy and run it through a separate machine. Well, it's possible, with FAXstf, a well-known Mac fax software package (see Figure 4.7). I'll give you a brief tutorial about sending faxes on your iMac in Hour 10. But briefly, the program also lets you keep an address book of your regular contacts, and you can print faxes after you get them.

- **Nanosaur**: What good is a multimedia computer without some games? Well, Nanosaur is a 3D effects game (see Figure 4.8) that appeals to young and old. You ride a virtual dinosaur and enter a thrilling prehistoric world where you confront many dangers. The game is enhanced with great sound effects. And you can record your score each time you play, to see how well you're mastering the obstacle courses.

FIGURE 4.8
Ride a dinosaur through a Stone Age environment of excitement and danger.

- **Quicken Deluxe 98**: One great use of your iMac is to manage your finances. Quicken Deluxe 98 (see Figure 4.9) is a popular program that serves both as checkbook and bookkeeper. You can also use it to print your personal or business checks, using special checks supplied by the software's publisher, Intuit, or other companies. You can also do financial planning and projections. I'll tell you how to set up this great program to manage your personal finances in Hour 9.

FIGURE 4.9
Track your personal or business finances with Quicken Deluxe 98.

Click the Record button to write a check

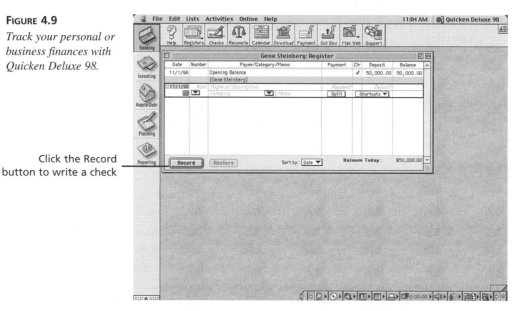

4

- **World Book Encyclopedia**: This program (which you have to install direct from the CD) gives you a handy research tool for education, business, and just plain fun. You can check out articles on a variety of subjects, consult a world atlas, or look up a word in the program's online dictionary.

- **WS Guide to Good Cooking**: Unfortunately, my poor efforts at cooking are usually limited to boiling water or warming up a TV dinner. But even a novice can learn to do lots of great things in the kitchen. I'll tell you more about this program in Hour 10.

 Apple Computer frequently changes the lineup of software included with its consumer computers, such as the iMac and iBook. So don't be concerned if you have software I haven't described, or if one program or another described here isn't part of your package.

Summary

In this hour, you got a brief look at some of the software that Apple thoughtfully included with your iMac. I covered the basics and showed you some illustrations. When you get to Hour 8, Hour 9, and Hour 10, you'll learn more about the great features these programs offer.

For now, you'll want to spend a little time with each one. Look over at the Help menu, where you will find online tutorials that will assist you in getting started.

In Hour 5, I'll show you how to traverse the highways and byways of your iMac, how to manage folders, what all those little controls are on document windows, and so on.

Q&A

Q I tried to open a program I retrieved from a friend. It had an .exe name at the end of it? But it won't run? What's wrong?

A Programs designed for the PC platform use different programming code than the Mac version. So they won't run without a little help. There are ways, though, to use them. Two programs, SoftWindows, from FWB, and VirtualPC, from Connectix, can turn your iMac into a real Windows machine. A third program, RealPC from FWB, emulates the DOS environment (though Windows can be installed, too). I'll tell you more about emulating Windows on your iMac in Hour 18, "Coping with the Windows World."

Q I keep reading about computer viruses in the daily paper. Should I really be afraid of such things?

A I don't want to scare you unnecessarily. But it's quite true that there are a number of computer viruses around. They are made by some nasty people who are playing practical jokes, or who just want to hurt people. Although some of them are not harmful, others are dangerous and can damage your personal files or even your programs.

Fortunately (for us, not them), most of the viruses infect users of that "other" platform. But there are a few of them on the Mac, too. If you plan on handling files from your friends and business associates, you'll want to get some virus protection software. I'll tell you more about that subject in Hour 24, "An iMac Safety Net."

Q I went to my local computer store to buy some Mac software. I couldn't find much. They tell me that there are only a few programs made for the Mac, and that I bought the wrong computer when I purchased a Mac OS computer. I want the truth!

A I think about Jack Nicholson's scene-stealing cry in that great movie, *A Few Good Men.* But the fact is, you can definitely handle the truth, and the truth is that there are thousands of Mac programs out there. You can find games, programs for retouching photos, programs for desktop publishing, programs to run a doctor's office, a dentist's office, and lots more.

CompUSA, Computer Town, and some other retailers have special Mac areas where you're bound to find a reasonable number of titles. But other dealers tend to give the Mac short shrift, and if they have any Mac software, it's just a few popular selections. However, dealers can order them for you. In addition, some programs actually come in on a CD that carries both a Mac and Windows version (check the box to see), but more often than not the package is in the Windows aisle.

You'll also want to check one of the Macintosh magazines on your newsstand for suggestions; for example, *MacAddict*, *MacHome*, or *Macworld*. And look at these magazines for ads from mail order houses that do stock Mac software. You'll be surprised at the variety of programs out there for your iMac. And some of them have no Windows equivalent, which means some of your friends who use the "other" platform can even envy you now. One interesting example is a very unusual word processing program known as Nisus.

When you get up and running with your Web browser, you'll find you can even order Apple products direct at its own online store, called, of course, The Apple Store.

Q **The iMac sounds okay to me, but I'd like something better. Can I buy better speakers for it?**

A Absolutely. There are lots of really good computer speakers out there. Some even include Dolby Surround Sound and special digital effects. The best products are the ones made by the well-known stereo speaker makers, such as Advent, Bose, Boston Acoustics, Cambridge SoundWorks, JBL, and Monsoon (to name just a few examples). As with regular home audio speakers, the more expensive models tend to sound better. Some are even good enough to do double duty as a small stereo system.

> The second generation "slot loading" iMacs have a higher quality "Odyssey" sound system from the well-known audio manufacturer Harman Kardon. If you want to give your iMac a little more oomph in terms of audio reproduction, you can consider the iSub, from Harman Kardon, which is designed to mate perfectly with your computer's onboard audio.

Strangely enough, I've even managed to get the widely advertised Bose Wave Radio to handle the sounds from my iMac, because it has convenient jacks for external audio sources. Just keep the radio at least a foot away from your iMac, because the radio's speakers are not magnetically shielded and may affect the color purity of the monitor.

PART II

Making it All Happen

Hour

HOUR 5

Files, Folders, Windows, and Other Things

In previous lessons, you discovered the neat, orderly iMac desktop, which is designed to mimic a typical office desk in terms of layout.

What you see is one of the great inventions of modern personal computing. Before the Mac operating system came out, the typical computer presented itself to you with a text interface. There were just letters and numbers there. White letters on black, black letters on white, and so on.

In order to tell that computer to do something, you had to type instructions on the keyboard and, usually, use the Enter or Return keys to send the command to the computer's brain or microprocessor.

With your iMac, you see a visual representation of what you want (an icon), and you use your mouse to select and click on that item. (You can even use the keyboard if you prefer for a lot of this.)

In this lesson, I'll tell you

- How to manage your iMac's files.
- What folders do and how to move from one to the other.
- How to work with document and directory windows and what the little doo-dads that surround them do.
- How to get rid of the files you don't want (with some precautions).
- How to use your iMac's keyboard to give the mouse (and your hand) a rest.

A Folder Is a Container

In the Mac OS, a folder is the computer equivalent to your file folder in your office, and it has a similar look (see Figure 5.1).

FIGURE 5.1

A folder on your iMac's desktop can hold a file or simply another folder (or many of each).

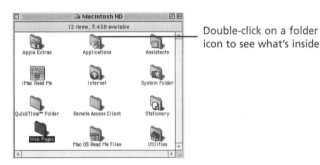

Double-click on a folder icon to see what's inside

A fast way to find the folder you want among those listed is to type the first letter of the icon's name on your iMac's keyboard. The first folder with that letter in it will be selected (highlighted) and will appear bright as day.

You can easily reorganize your iMac's desktop simply by clicking and dragging on a folder and putting it inside another folder (or pulling it out of one).

A Variety of Folders

No doubt you've noticed that some folders have different icons on them than others. Some of these are strictly custom jobs from the publishers of some programs who want to give their folders a special look.

But others are designed to reflect the special nature of their contents. In the following list, I'll show you some of the more common folder styles and what they're used for.

- **Apple Extras folder**: This folder is a grab bag of extra programs and instructional information that Apple tosses in.
- **Applications folder**: This folder stores all of your applications.
- **Assistants folder**: You'll find your Mac OS Setup Assistant here, along with an alias to the Internet Setup Assistant (the original is buried several levels deep inside the Internet folder).
- **Internet folder**: All of your Internet access software is put here.
- **Mac OS Read Me Files folder**: This folder contains the various information files that cover basic instructions and perhaps known problems and solutions for Apple's system software.
- **QuickTime folder**: This folder contains Apple's multimedia software, which you can use to view and (with limits) edit audio and video productions.
- **System folder**: The contents of the software required to operate your computer is in the System Folder.
- **Utilities folder**: This folder contains little programs that help you manage and fix things, such as Apple's Disk First Aid.
- **Alias to a file or folder**: The little arrow at the lower left and the italicized name indicate this is not the actual folder or file, but a reference to it. You double-click on this icon, and you'll see the contents of the original folder (like accessing your files via remote control).

5

It's so easy to move folder and file icons around that you can easily move things that shouldn't be moved. Don't move the files that are within an application's folder, as the program might not run when all its files aren't in place. And don't touch any of the files in the System folder until you've read Hour 15, "What's a System Folder and Why Do I Need One?" Moving the wrong file to the wrong place in the System Folder might prevent your iMac from running or starting properly.

Selecting and Opening Folders

Working with folders is simple. You click once on a folder and then drag the icon to move it somewhere. And you double-click on it to see its contents.

In addition, there are some neat ways to move things around by the keyboard, too.

Here are some of the things you can do without ever touching a mouse. The techniques work for both folder and file icons (way cool):

- Use the arrow keys on the keyboard to move from icon to icon. Movement is in the direction to which the arrow points (up, down, left, right).
- Use the Tab key to move from one icon to the next.
- Hold down the Shift key if you want to select more than one folder at a time.
- Hold down the Option key when you double-click on a folder icon to open that icon, *and also* close the parent folder the icon is in. So, if you double-click on an icon inside the Applications folder, while holding down the Option key, the Applications folder is itself closed.
- Hold down the Option key when you drag a file or folder icon to another folder's icon, and you'll make a copy of the original. The original will just stay where it is.
- Press the Return key to highlight the name of an icon you've selected. You can then rename the icon something else if you like. There's nothing to prevent you from calling your Applications folder "the den of inequity" instead, if you prefer.
- Press Command+M when you select an icon, and you'll create an alias to it (see Figure 5.2). You can also click on the File menu and choose the Make Alias command, or hold down Command+Option while dragging a folder, to accomplish the same thing. As I mentioned in Hour 1, "Setting Up Your iMac," an alias is a reference to the original file, folder, application (or disk, for that matter). It's a great feature that lets you, in effect, have a number of ways to get to a folder without having to make extra copies.

A fast way to know if an icon is an alias (other than the little arrow pointer at the lower left) is the label. It will always be *italicized.*

FIGURE 5.2

Not live, but "Memorex," or rather an alias or pointer to the original icon.

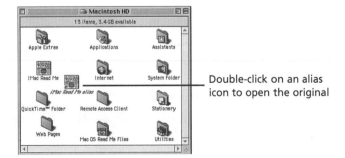

Double-click on an alias icon to open the original

- Press Command+Delete to move a selected item to the trash.

If you move the alias of a file to the trash, the original is not deleted, just the alias. If you really want to delete the original, too, you need to drag both icons to the trash.

A File Isn't a Container

Compared to a folder, the file icon actually does something rather than just function as a container. If you double-click on a program's icon, you open the program itself. When you open a file, it does two things: launch the program, and then open the file and bring it onto your screen. I'll cover the elements of a directory and document window a bit later on in this lesson.

The great thing about the Mac operating system is that many of the skills you use to handle folder icons work in the *very same way* with file icons, too. So you don't have to learn anything new to work with them. This is one of the wonderful features that makes the system so easy to master.

Be careful about renaming application icons. The Mac OS Finder keeps a directory of document and program links that lets you double-click on a file to open the program. But if you rename the program's icon (such as calling your "AppleWorks" software "The Great Starship" instead), it might upset those links. Nothing to prevent you from changing a document file's name, though.

5

Changing the Folder/File Viewpoint

In the previous sections, I covered file and folder icons in their standard state, as icons. But you don't have to view them that way. As I explained back in Hour 2, "Exploring the iMac Desktop," you can view your icons as a list if you prefer (see Figure 5.3), just by choosing the View as List option from the Finder's View menu. There are two advantages to this arrangement:

- You save space, which is great if you have lots and lots of icons to work with.
- It takes a little longer for your iMac's screen to display the fancy artwork in a regular icon, so things might slow down a bit if you have lots of icons in a folder.

FIGURE 5.3

With the list view, you sacrifice appearance for speed and convenience.

Name	Date Modified	Size	Kind
▷ Apple Extras	Fri, Oct 23, 1998, 3:12 PM	—	folder
▷ Applications	Mon, Oct 26, 1998, 7:19 PM	—	folder
▷ Assistants	Fri, Oct 23, 1998, 3:13 PM	—	folder
iMac Read Me	Thu, Jul 16, 1998, 12:00 PM	20 K	SimpleText read-only document
▷ Internet	Yesterday, 12:08 PM	—	folder
▷ Mac OS Read Me Files	Fri, Oct 23, 1998, 3:14 PM	—	folder
▷ QuickTime™ Folder	Wed, Jul 22, 1998, 11:12 AM	—	folder
▷ Remote Access Client	Wed, Jul 22, 1998, 11:13 AM	—	folder
▷ Stationery	Wed, Jul 22, 1998, 11:20 AM	—	folder
▷ System Folder	Yesterday, 12:04 PM	—	folder
▷ Utilities	Yesterday, 3:49 PM	—	folder
▷ Web Pages	Fri, Oct 23, 1998, 3:13 PM	—	folder

Macintosh HD — 12 items, 3.4 GB available

Click on the scrollbar at the right to see the rest of this long list

Click on the left arrow next to a folder to see the contents (it will point down). Hold down the Option key to open all the folders inside that folder (this can take a bit of time). If you click on the arrow again, it closes the folder (and with the Option key held down, all the open folders inside it). Isn't that Option key great?

The disadvantage: Well, it doesn't look quite as pretty.

To select all your files and folders at once, press Command+A.

Button, Button, Who's Got...

The third method of viewing icons is the button view, and it's also selected from the Finder's View menu (see Figure 5.4).

FIGURE 5.4

Button, button, who's got...

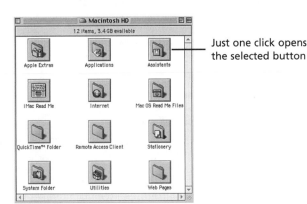

Just one click opens the selected button

The Button view saves you a click. A single click opens any of the icons. Of course everything is much larger now, so you use more screen real estate (and space is at a premium on your computer's screen).

Working with Windows, Doors, And...

For this section, it's just windows, and not the kind that you use on that "other" computing platform. To make a window active, you click on it (it makes the title black and brings it to the front). Every time you open a directory of any kind by double-clicking on it (a disk or folder) or a file, it brings up a display window (see Figure 5.5).

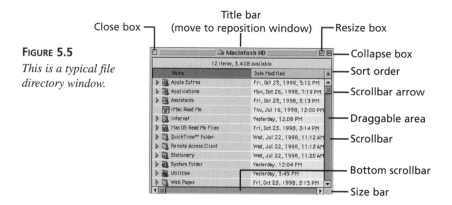

FIGURE 5.5

This is a typical file directory window.

The features I'll describe here apply to document windows also (although document windows might have a few more icons and displays to cover a particular feature). I'll get to the differences a bit later.

- **Close box**: Click on this box to close your document.

When you close a document window, you aren't closing the program. The program remains active till you choose Quit from the File menu (or press Command+Q) from within that application.

To close all open windows (whether two or 20) hold down the Option key when you click on the close box. This works with directory windows, but might not work with all programs (some don't recognize all the keyboard tricks).

5

- **Title bar**: This is the name of your folder list or document. Click on the title bar (or on any of the other three borders of the window) to move it around.

> If you're looking at an open Finder window, you can easily move it else-where by clicking on the icon next to its name and dragging that icon to another folder or disk.

- **Zoom box**: When you click on this box, either of two things will happen.

  One click of the resize box will change the size of the window to enclose its con-tents. If the size of your screen isn't big enough, the box will just be made as large as possible.

  A second click of the resize box restores the size to its previous setting.

- **Collapse box (sometimes called a WindowShade)**: The ultimate desktop space-saver. Click on this box to reduce the size of the window to just its title. Click again to restore the window to its former size (see Figure 5.6).

FIGURE 5.6

The ultimate way to reduce desktop clutter.

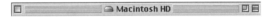

> If you cannot make the window collapse, try this: Go to the Apple menu, choose Control Panels and select Appearance from the submenu. Click on the Options tab at the top of the Appearance screen, and make sure the sec-ond option, Double-Click Title Bar to Collapse Windows is checked.

- **Change sort**: Click on this arrow to change the sort order of the contents (from top to bottom to bottom to top). If you click on one of the sort labels in the win-dow (Name, Date Modified, and so on), the contents of a directory will sort by that criteria.

- **Scroll arrow**: Click it to move up slightly (or down) through a directory or docu-ment window. Hold down the mouse when clicking on an arrow to get a continu-ous motion.

- **Draggable area**: This is the place where you can drag the scrollbar (see next item). If the area is white rather than gray (and the scrollbar isn't there), it means that the entire window is displayed on your screen and there's nothing to scroll to. You'll notice that there's both a horizontal and vertical draggable area.

Normally, you can only work on a window if you select it (to make it active).
But if you hold down the command key, you can move around a window
without bringing it to the front.

- **Scrollbar**: Click and drag on this square box to move back and forth through your
  folder list or document. The distance you can move depends on how big the listing
  or document is.

Click on the draggable area above the scrollbar to jump rapidly upward
through a list or document, a page or screen at a time. Click *below* the
scrollbar to move downward through the document at the same rate. This is
the equivalent of the Pg Up and Pg Dn keys on your iMac's keyboard.

- **Size bar**: Click on this bar and drag it to resize a document window the way you
  want (see Figure 5.7). It resizes in the direction you drag the mouse (up, down,
  sideways).

FIGURE 5.7

*Drag to the right
and the window gets
bigger.*

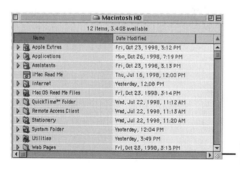

The window resizes in the
direction you drag the bar

5

- **Window options**: As I said earlier, some programs add a few features to the window to reflect special functions. In the picture shown in Figure 5.8, you'll see the
  extra options offered for AppleWorks (ClarisWorks). I'll tell you more about them
  in Hour 8, "Teach Yourself AppleWorks."

The ruler at the top of Figure 5.8 is used to show the width of the area where you enter
text. At the bottom left you'll see little icons that you click to change the way you view
your document or the size of the text on the screen. Each program will have its own
particular set of added features.

FIGURE 5.8

A document window offers additional features that control some program features.

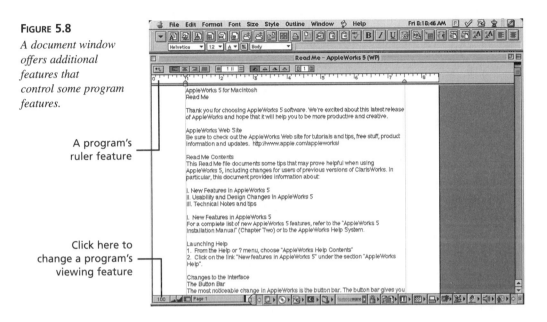

A program's ruler feature

Click here to change a program's viewing feature

Trashing It for Good

The final icon management feature I'll discuss is the trash can (see Figure 5.9). That's the place you send your files and folders when you decide you no longer need them. The first figure shows the trash is empty. The second (see Figure 5.10) shows the trash filled with one or more files.

FIGURE 5.9

This trash can is empty.

FIGURE 5.10

The trash is filled, and files are ready to be zapped.

To get rid of your files, simply follow these steps:

1. Click and drag a program's icon to the trash, which will be highlighted as soon as the icon is brought atop the trash. See Figure 5.11 for the effect.

▼ To Do

FIGURE 5.11

Release the mouse, and the file is placed inside the trash can.

2. Choose Empty Trash from the Finder's Special menu, which brings up this request for confirmation (see Figure 5.12).

FIGURE 5.12

Do you really want to zap that file?

When you OK the message, the file will be history.

Before you empty the trash, be sure you really want to get rid of those files. If you're not certain, click Cancel. When you dump those files, they are gone, probably for good (although there are a few programs that might recover them if you make a mistake).

The trash can works like a folder. If you're not sure what's inside, just double-click on it to bring up the directory list. If you decide not to trash something, click and drag that icon from it.

5

Summary

In this hour, you learned how to use the elements on your iMac's desktop. You worked with folders, files, and directory and document windows, and you discovered how your computer's Trash feature lets you remove items that you don't want.

In addition, you discovered how to use your iMac's keyboard to do many of the same tasks that the mouse is used for.

In Hour 6, "Making Documents, Editing Documents," we'll get deep into document management. You'll learn how to use your computer's file management and editing tools to create brand new documents and store them on your hard drive.

Q&A

Q How many folders can I place within another folder?

A You can nest hundreds of folders within folders. The practical limit is one of organization and speed. The more files you have to look through in the Open dialog box (something you'll discover in Hour 6), the longer it takes to display them. Just to be practical, I'd recommend you keep the number of items in a folder to 50 or less.

Q Can I protect my files from others who might have access to my computer?

Beginning with Mac OS 9, Apple has introduced a Multiple Users feature, which you can set up to allow limited access or no access by others who might want to use your computer. I'll cover this topic in more detail in Hour 21, "Backup, Backup, Backup...How to Protect Your Files."

If you haven't upgraded to Mac OS 9, you still have security software options that will provide equal or better protection. Your favorite software store can suggest some products for you. Some products to consider are DiskGuard from ASD Software, Private File from Aladdin Systems and DiskLock and OnGuard from Power On Software. If you haven't added a floppy disk drive to your computer, you might want to ask your dealer if the programs you're considering come in a CD version.

Q I installed a new program on my computer, but it wasn't put in the Applications folder. What did I do wrong?

A Those program installers don't always put things quite where you want them. When you install a new program, you might see a dialog box on your computer's screen where you can specify what folder you want them placed in. But sometimes you won't. In this case, the program's folder will sit on your hard drive (top level). But there's nothing to stop you from dragging that folder to the Applications folder to keep everything neatly organized. And, in fact, nothing to prevent you from moving the folders inside the Applications folder to another place on your hard drive. The great thing about the Mac operating system is that you can move some things around (except for things in the System folder) and the programs will run normally. Just be careful about the files inside an application's folder (as I explained earlier in this lesson).

Q I'm really impressed with all the great things you can do on the iMac with the keyboard. But what about all those pictures of the screen you have in this book? Did you sit in front of your computer with a camera to get them?

A I love photography, but there are very few real photos in this book—just the ones that show the exterior of the iMac's case in Hour 1 and, in Hour 22, "Giving Your iMac New Software, More RAM, and Other Things," where I'll show you how to install a RAM upgrade. You can make pictures of your computer's actual screen just as I did, without a camera. To "shoot" your screen, just press the following:

- **Command+Shift+3**: This keystroke combination gets you a picture file of the entire screen. When you type it, you'll hear a distinct camera "click" in your computer's speaker, and you'll see a file named **Picture 1** on your iMac's drive. The second picture will be **Picture 2**, and so on.

- **Command+Shift+4**: After you press this keyboard combination, just take the mouse and click on the screen. The cursor will change to a plus (+). Then move (drag) the mouse around the area of the screen you want to capture. When you release the mouse switch, the picture will be taken. Click.

- **Command+Shift+4+capslock**: This keyboard combination lets you take a picture of any open directory or document window. After pressing and releasing the keys, click on the window (or menu) you want to photograph. Click.

Q Help! My keyboard and mouse are dead? What do I do?

A First, make sure that both items are plugged into your iMac.

If they are, it might just mean that your computer has crashed because of a problem with a particular program. Although this doesn't happen too often, Mac OS computers can crash on occasion. Here's how you can get your computer to run again:

NEW TERM In computer-ese, a *crash* means that a problem with your software has caused your computer to freeze, or stop working. It doesn't mean you dropped it by mistake. There's also such a thing as a hard drive crash, which means something has caused the drive to fail. But that's a rare occurrence (see Hour 24, "An iMac Safety Net," for more troubleshooting help).

1. Press Command+Option+Esc. If this works, you'll get a message asking if you want to "force quit" the program you're using. With luck, the program will close gracefully. You should then restart your computer (using Restart from the Special menu) before you continue to use it because a force quit can leave your system a little unstable and might cause more crashes with other programs.

▼ To Do

5

▼   2. If the force quit fix doesn't work, you'll need to reset the iMac, which forces it to restart. So go grab a little paper clip and straighten it.

3. Open the jack panel at the right side of your iMac.

4. Slowly and gently insert the end of the paper clip into the hole marked with an arrow above it.

5. Press it in just slightly and release. You should see your iMac's screen darken and ▲   hear the startup chord sound.

For additional help on dealing with such problems, check Hour 24.

HOUR 6

Making Documents, Editing Documents

When you finished with Hour 5, "Files, Folders, Windows, and Other Things," you knew how to manage icons and windows on your iMac's desktop like a pro. Really, the Mac OS is simple enough to master really, really fast.

Now it's time to put all that information to work.

In this hour, you'll have the chance to work on a project on your iMac. You'll make a brand new document, containing the text of your first novel. Then you'll edit the document to make everything just perfect.

You'll learn

- How to open a brand new document.
- How to change the text style.
- How to move text around.
- How to move back and forth between one program and another, to work on more than one task (called *multitasking*).

NEW TERM *Multitasking* is the ability to run more than one application or function on your computer, such as writing a letter and printing another document at the same time.

Creating a New Document

For this lesson, I'll introduce you to Apple's integrated productivity program, AppleWorks (called ClarisWorks on some iMacs). You'll have a chance to create a brand new word processing document, perhaps your first novel. Then you'll see how to change things around to make the text flow better, or to remove parts you don't like.

> As I've explained, Apple rechristened ClarisWorks as AppleWorks around the time the iMac was first introduced, and that's how I'll refer to it. But several hundred thousand iMacs were sold with the program still called ClarisWorks (perhaps that's what you have). Not to worry. The programs are the same, but if you want to change it to AppleWorks, all you have to do is pay a visit to Apple's support Web site to retrieve a copy of an update that will convert your copy to a newer version. I'll show you more about navigating the World Wide Web in Hour 11, "The Internet: Learning the Ropes."

In short, you'll do some of the very same things I did when I wrote this book. And word processing is only one of the things AppleWorks does well; I'll cover more in Hour 8, "Teach Yourself AppleWorks."

To start your new document:

▼ To Do

1. Double-click the Applications folder on your computer's desktop.

2. Locate the AppleWorks (or ClarisWorks) folder and double-click that to open it.

3. The AppleWorks program icon ought to be right near the top. If not, look through the folder to find it; then double-click it. You'll see a little introductory screen (it's sometimes called a *splash* screen), which identifies the program and version number, and then you'll see a little dialog box asking what sort of document you want to create (see Figure 6.1).

FIGURE 6.1

Choose the kind of document you want to make.

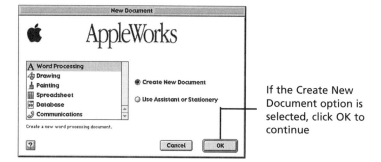

If the Create New Document option is selected, click OK to continue

AppleWorks has a setting that turns off the New Document screen when you launch the program. If it's not there, just press Command+N (or choose New from the File menu) to open it.

4. Select Word Processing from the list.

5. Click the little button labeled Create New Document.

6. Click OK. You'll see an empty document on your computer screen (see Figure 6.2)

FIGURE 6.2

Here's your blank word processing document, ready to be worked on.

Click here with your cursor to enter text

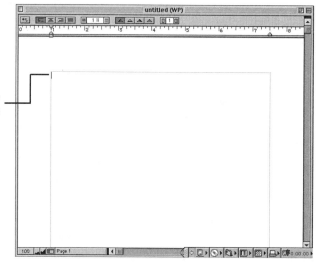

6

The second option in Figure 6.1, Use Assistant or Stationery, enables you to use AppleWorks' assistants to help you set up the style of your new word processing document. Go ahead and try it out; I'll tell you more about it in Hour 8.

Entering Text

The next step is simple. The text area of your document page is surrounded with a dotted rectangle. Click anywhere on it, and start typing (see Figure 6.3). You'll see the letters you type appear on your screen, and the mouse cursor will change to a blinking vertical line.

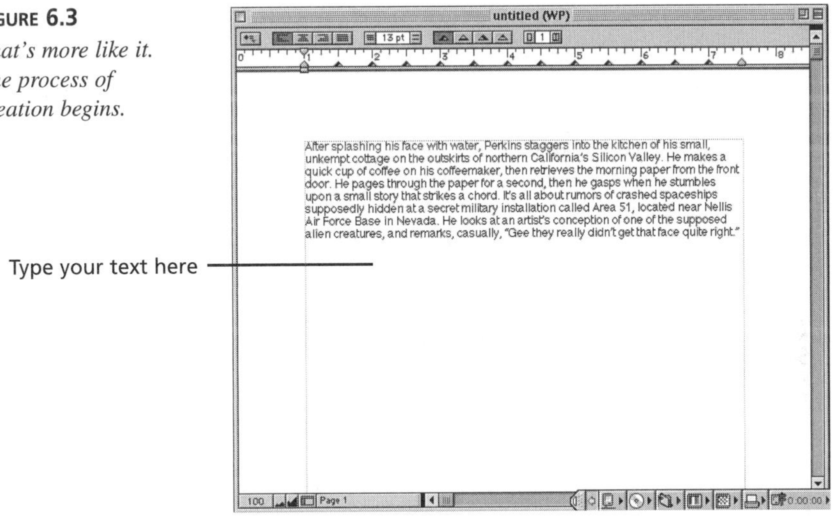

FIGURE 6.3

That's more like it. The process of creation begins.

Type your text here ——

After splashing his face with water, Perkins staggers into the kitchen of his small, unkempt cottage on the outskirts of northern California's Silicon Valley. He makes a quick cup of coffee on his coffeemaker, then retrieves the morning paper from the front door. He pages through the paper for a second, then he gasps when he stumbles upon a small story that strikes a chord. It's all about rumors of crashed spaceships supposedly hidden at a secret military installation called Area 51, located near Nellis Air Force Base in Nevada. He looks at an artist's conception of one of the supposed alien creatures, and remarks, casually, "Gee they really didn't get that face quite right."

There are some basic functions common to all Mac programs that involve editing text, and those are the ones I'll concentrate on here. So you'll be able to apply the things you learn in this lesson to other software, too, with a few changes.

Go ahead and write your material. For the purpose of this exercise, I'm going to include the text of an actual novel (one my son and I wrote), so you can get the flavor of a real writing session on your computer.

A computer isn't like a typewriter. You don't need to press the Return key after every line. Just continue to type in a single stream of words and only press Return at the end of a paragraph.

Formatting Text

After you've written a few words, maybe you've decided that some of this text ought to be different, or the words are too small. To start with, perhaps you want to make the next word in a bold text to have it stand out.

To make the next word or words bold, do the following:

1. Click the Style menu and choose Bold (or press Command+B).

2. Type the word or words you want to emphasize.

3. When you're done, click the Style menu and choose Plain Text (or press Command+T). The result is shown in Figure 6.4.

You can also restore plain text after typing bold text simply by pressing Command+B a second time.

FIGURE 6.4
You can make words bold for emphasis.

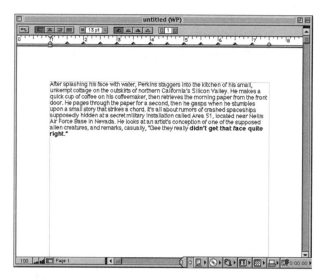

6

Here are some of the choices available to alter the look of the text in most word processing programs (you can combine two or more for a specific effect):

- **bold**
- *italic*
- ***bold italic***
- underlined
- ~~strikethrough~~
- double strikethrough
- Outline
- Shadow

No, wait a minute! Maybe the letters are just too small. So the next option is to change
the size of a paragraph or headline to give it emphasis.

Let's add a headline to the document and make it larger:

1. Click the Size menu and choose 24 Point.

2. Type the word or words you want to use as a headline.

3. Press the Return key to end the line or paragraph.

4. When you're done, click the Size menu and pick the previous size (in this case 12
   Point). The result is shown in Figure 6.5

FIGURE 6.5

*There you go. A big
headline to spruce
things up.*

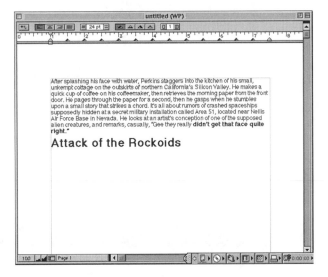

You can also style the larger text bold to make it stand out even better. Or you can even change the typeface (or font).

NEW TERM   A *font* is a collection of letters and numbers that come in a specific artistic style. There are literally thousands and thousands of fonts available for your computer.

Your iMac comes with a small number of fonts to pick from. As you get accustomed to using them, you'll begin to locate sources for other fonts. Some programs, such as those from publishers like Adobe Systems, Corel, and Macromedia, actually include a number of free fonts with their software. You can also buy fonts from your favorite software dealer.

To change the font you're using in your document, do the following:

1. Click the Font menu, which opens the screen shown in Figure 6.6.

FIGURE 6.6

Here are the fonts that came with your new iMac. The styled Font menu is a special feature of AppleWorks.

— Choose your font from this list

2. Pick the font you want to use by dragging the cursor and highlighting the one you want. The text you type next will be changed to the new face (see Figure 6.7).

You can also change the font or style of the words you've already typed by selecting that text and making your changes just as I described. I'll tell you more in the next section.

To Do

6

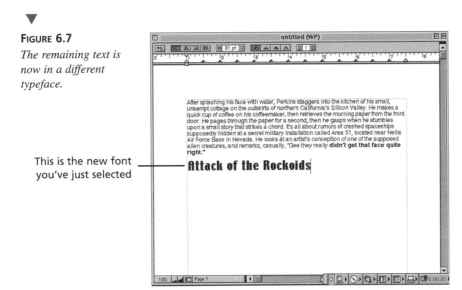

▼
FIGURE 6.7
*The remaining text is
now in a different
typeface.*

This is the new font
you've just selected

Text styles and size changes are designed to enhance the look of a document, but use the features with care. Putting too many styles and sizes together can make your letter or novel look like a ransom note.

Aligning Text

When you first start a new document, the usual setting for text is "flush left," which means the text is aligned at the left, and staggered at the right. Just like the text in this book.

Most programs offer a set of icons above a document's title bar (see Figure 6.8) to let you line up text different. Here's how they work:

- **Flush Left**: This is the standard format. The left side of text is aligned, the right side staggered.

- **Centered**: The lines are put smack in the middle of the page, and the right and left lines are indented identically. You'll usually center the text used for a headline.

- **Flush Right**: The right side of the text is aligned, and the left side staggered. This style is sometimes used for a photo caption or advertisement.

- **Justified**: This style commonly occurs just as you see it in your daily newspaper and many books and magazines. Both the right and left sides of the paragraph are aligned, except for the last line, which (if short) aligns at the left.

FIGURE 6.8
Here's the standard, four text alignment choices.

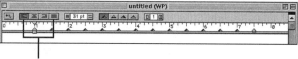

Click one of these icons to align text as shown

Editing Text

After you've written some material, no doubt you'll look it over and make a change. Perhaps you need to move some words around, or convert the regular text to bold and vice versa, or make it smaller. For this part of the lesson, I'll take you through the words you've already typed and show you how to select them for further changes.

Here's one way to select the text you want to edit:

1. Click the mouse key and move the cursor to the beginning of the area you want to select.

   Drag the mouse to the end of the area to highlight the text you want to select and release the key. The result is shown in Figure 6.9.

FIGURE 6.9
The highlighted text is selected, ready for you to edit.

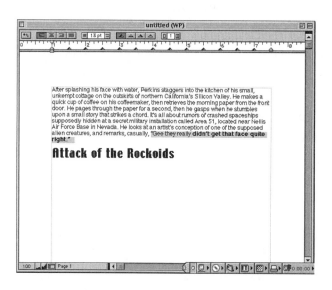

3. Change the style of your text as you want, and it will be applied to the selected area.

▲ To Do

6

As with many Mac OS features, there's more than one way to skin a cat, as it were. Here's another way to select an area of text:

1. Click the mouse button and move the cursor to the beginning of the area you want to select.

2. Press and hold the Shift key.

3. While holding the Shift key down, click the mouse cursor at the end of the area you want to select.

4. After making changes to the text, click again on the selected area to deselect it.

In addition, there are some mouse shortcuts for selecting specific amounts of text. Here are the common ones that apply to AppleWorks and similar programs:

- To select a single word, double-click anywhere on that word.

- To select an entire line, click three times anywhere on the line.

- To select an entire paragraph, click four times anywhere in the paragraph.

The options for selecting words, lines, and paragraphs I'm describing here apply strictly to AppleWorks. Some programs let you select an entire paragraph with three clicks, an entire document with four. You'll want to check the instructions that come with a program to see how such things may differ.

- To select all the text in the document, press Command+A or choose Select All from the Edit menu.

After you've selected text, be careful what you do next. You have only one chance to Undo what you've changed. If you press a single letter, that one letter will replace what is there on your screen (even if you selected an entire long document). That will constitute your single Undo option. Your only other choice, then, other than to manually edit the text, is to choose Revert from the File menu. This choice changes things to the way they were when you last saved your document (and that may just change too many things).

Using the Edit Menu to Adjust Text

In addition to selecting an item, you have several commands in the Edit menu that will work with all Mac programs. I listed them in Hour 2, "Exploring the iMac Desktop," so you'll want to recheck that text as a reminder.

But those are not all of the functions available. Some programs add the capability to insert special characters, numbers, or dates. Others let you check the spelling or fiddle with a program's settings (preferences).

In Hour 8, I'll cover some of the special Edit menu features that you'll find in AppleWorks. Because each program has a different range of choices there, you'll want to explore the menu bar commands of each program and try them out before getting to work.

Many of your iMac programs have common names for functions, but they may work differently. If you don't have the chance to read an entire manual, look over the Help menu for advice. Or consider getting a book from the *Sams Teach Yourself* line to get up to speed on new software as fast as possible.

Secrets of Moving, Dragging, and Dropping

There are several ways to move text around. One is simply to use the Cut and Paste commands from the File menu. Here's how it's done:

1. Select the text you want to move.
2. Choose Cut from the Edit menu to remove it from its first locale.
3. Click the area of your document where you want the text to be placed.
4. Choose Paste from the Edit menu to put it there.

6

The Mac's clipboard only holds one item at a time. That means if you Cut something else from your document before you paste the first item, the first item will be gone—history. There are some programs out there that make multiple clipboards, but that's not the standard way it's set up.

Many Mac programs, such as AppleWorks, offer still another great feature to move things around. And it makes it possible to bypass the cumbersome Cut and Paste routine.

It's called drag and drop.

And here's how you do it:

1. Select the text you want to move.

2. Click the text and drag it to the place where you want to move it. You will see (depending on the program) a small rectangle surrounding the mouse cursor.

3. Release the mouse key. Presto! The text is moved to its new location.

> You can also make a clipping of the text you want to move by dragging the selected text away from your document and clicking your computer's desktop. When you do it this way, the original text stays where it was. You can then take your desktop clipping and drag it to another document. Cool!

Switching Applications

When you are working in a specific program, its name will appear at the upper right of the menu bar. To switch to another application that may be open, just do this:

1. Click the application's name in the menu bar (it's also called the Application menu). This opens a list of all open programs (see Figure 6.10).

FIGURE 6.10
These are the programs you're now running on the iMac.

2. Select the name of the other program you want to work with (or the Finder if you want to use the features on your iMac's desktop).

Summary

You've now had an opportunity to create something all new on your computer, the beginnings of your novel or letter. You learned how to use the iMac's text editing tools (many of which are common from program to program) to manipulate the words in the document, to change things, to remove things, and to move things around.

In Hour 7, "Opening, Saving, Finding, Moving, Etc.," I'll show you what to do next—save the document. You'll also learn how to open new documents and locate other files on your computer's drive.

Q&A

Q I tried to open a document, but now I can't find it. What do I do?

A Call on Sherlock 2. Nope, not the dude who runs around with that Watson fellow on TV, but Apple's search program, which (among other things) locates files on your computer's drive (or any other drive hooked up to it).

To use it, just click the Apple menu and select Sherlock 2 (see Figure 6.11). Click the Files icon (the one at the left) and enter the name of the file you want to locate. This program is terrific, and it can find a lot more things than just file names. I'll cover Sherlock 2 in more detail in Hour 7.

FIGURE 6.11
Sherlock 2 is at your beck and call to find the files or information you want.

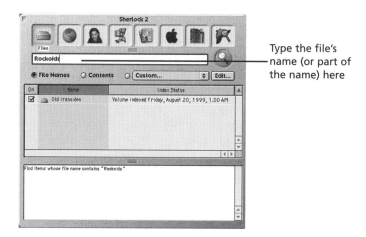

Type the file's name (or part of the name) here

6

Don't be alarmed if your version of Sherlock is different from the one I'm showing here. An earlier version of the program came with Mac OS 8.5, 8.5.1, and 8.6. I'll cover both in Hour 7.

Q I like this concept of multitasking, but whenever I try to type something while printing, everything is so sluggish. Why?

A Multitasking on an Apple computer is called cooperative. That means that the programs are set up to get out of the way or at least reduce their activities when other programs are working. But the process isn't perfect, and there are just so many ways to divide up tasks. It's normal for performance to be somewhat sluggish when two or more things are happening at the same time. Apple is working on a new operating system, Mac OS X (which may appear by the time you read this book), which will do multitasking a different way (it's called "preemptive") and make performance, well, snappier when many tasks are going on at once.

Q How many programs can I run on my computer at the same time?

A Each program you use takes a chunk of memory (or RAM). As you open a new program, you have less memory available for other programs. If you hit the limit, you'll see a warning on your computer screen that it needs to close another program to open the new one. In Hour 22, "Giving Your iMac New Software, More RAM, and Other Things," I'll tell you how you can easily (well, relatively easily) add more RAM to your iMac to allow you to run more programs at the same time or use some special programs that need lots of memory to work.

Hour 7

Opening, Saving, Finding, Moving, Etc.

If you've followed me so far, you now have a spanking new document on your iMac's screen ready to do—well—something with it. If you are satisfied with the document you re-created, you'll want to store it for safekeeping and later retrieval.

In this lesson, I'll show you how to open existing files, save files, and locate files on your hard drive (when you don't know where they are).

You'll learn

- How to use Apple's Open dialog box (the new and old versions).
- How to save files.
- How to use Sherlock, a great tool to find the files you want.

Using the Open Dialog Box

There are two basic ways to open a file. The first, discussed in previous lessons, is just to double-click on it. This process does double duty. It opens the application that made the document and then opens the document.

If you've already launched the program you want to use to work on another document, though, it's a little awkward to switch back to the Finder's desktop, locate, and double-click on another document.

Instead you can use the Open dialog box.

 There are actually two different types of Open dialog boxes available. There's the original version, used with older programs (and even some that come with your iMac). I'll be showing that one first. And there's a new style, called *Navigation Services*, which is designed to work better. I'll cover both in the following pages.

To open a file:

▼ To Do

1. Choose Open from the File menu. Or press Command+O. Either step will produce a dialog box similar to the one shown in Figure 7.1.

2. If the correct folder isn't shown, click on the pop-up menu at the top to locate the folder that contains the file you want to open.

3. Scroll through the file list to find your file. You can use either the scroll bar or Pg Up and Pg Dn keys.

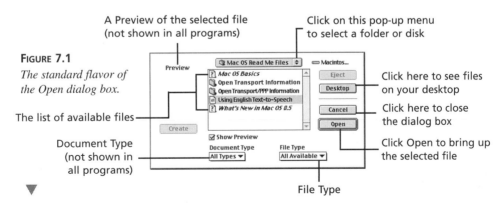

A Preview of the selected file (not shown in all programs)

Click on this pop-up menu to select a folder or disk

FIGURE 7.1
The standard flavor of the Open dialog box.

The list of available files

Click here to see files on your desktop

Click here to close the dialog box

Click Open to bring up the selected file

Document Type (not shown in all programs)

File Type

▼

Type the first letter of a file's name to move right to the files that begin with that letter. This is a great timesaver if the list of available files is very long.

4. Click once on a file to select it.
5. Click on the Open button to bring up the file. (Double-clicking on the filename itself does the same thing.) The result is shown in Figure 7.2.

FIGURE 7.2

Here's the file you chose to open.

Press Command+W or click the close box to close the open file

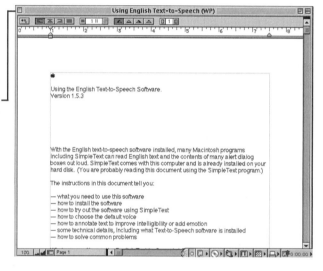

Apple has set up the Open dialog box so the folks who write the software can customize it for their own purposes. The example shown in Figure 7.1 comes from AppleWorks, and you'll see they've added Preview, Document Type, and File Type options. Other Open dialog boxes may have different options or show nothing extra.

Opening Files Via the Keyboard

You can perform many Mac OS operations from your iMac's keyboard, without lots of mouse clicking.

7

In addition to using Command+O to invoke the Open dialog box, here's a list of other keyboard timesavers:

- Use the Up and Down arrow keys to move to the item above and below the selected file.
- Use the End key to go to the bottom of the file list.
- Press Command+↑ to move up one folder level.
- Press Command+↓ to move down one folder level.
- Press Command+D or Command+Shift+↑ to switch to the desktop's file list.
- Press Command+O or Command+↓ when an Open dialog box is up to open a selected folder or disk.
- Press Command+Option+O to select the original of a selected alias file.
- Press the Return or Enter key to open a selected file. It works the same as the Open button.

Whenever you see a button surrounded with a thick rectangular line, it means that its command can be activated with the Return or Enter keys.

- Press Esc or Command+. (period) to close the Open dialog box without doing anything further.

And to think some folks believe you can't do anything on your iMac without a mouse or some alternative pointing device.

Navigating Through Apple's New Open Dialog Box

The Open dialog box I just described is the classic style, the one used by Apple for many years. As you work with your iMac's software, though, you'll begin to discover another sort of Open dialog box, one that will be appearing more and more frequently in the very newest software.

Let's take a look at this Open dialog box.

You can invoke it the same way as other dialog boxes. Choose Open from the File menu or press Command+O. But what you see is very, very different (see Figure 7.3).

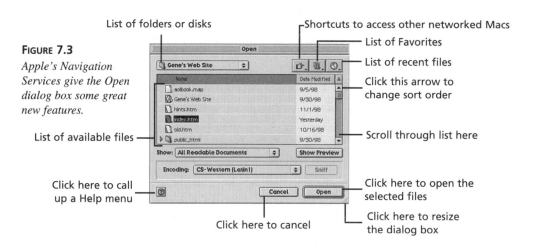

FIGURE 7.3

Apple's Navigation Services give the Open dialog box some great new features.

List of folders or disks

Shortcuts to access other networked Macs

List of Favorites

List of recent files

Click this arrow to change sort order

List of available files

Scroll through list here

Click here to call up a Help menu

Click here to open the selected files

Click here to cancel

Click here to resize the dialog box

Well, it sure looks different, although most of the functions are the same. But those new features are really great, after you get used to them. I'll focus on those in the following list.

Be careful about how many files you open in a program. Each open document may use a big portion of the memory available to the program. If you open too many files at once, the program may *seize* or stop working, or the computer may crash. A handful of files at a time is usually enough.

- **Shortcuts**: Click on this icon to bring up a pop-up menu showing your computer's desktop, hard drives, and fast access to a networked computer.

- **Favorites**: Use this pop-up menu to add the selected file or files to your list of Favorites (see Figure 7.4). After a file is on the list, you can call it up instantly (without having to know where it is) by a quick visit to this menu.

FIGURE 7.4

Use this menu to make a Favorite of the selected file.

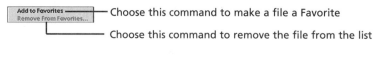

Choose this command to make a file a Favorite

Choose this command to remove the file from the list

7

When you make a file a Favorite, an alias to the file is automatically created and put in the Favorites folder (which sits inside the System Folder). You can also access those files from the Apple menu.

- **Recent**: This pop-up menu brings up a list of recently opened or saved files. It's the same list you see when you call up the Recent Documents listing from the Apple menu.

> You can make the new Open and Save dialog boxes larger. Just click on the resize bar at the bottom right and drag it to make the box larger (or smaller if it has already been enlarged). You can also drag the dialog box to another position in the screen (something you can't do with the older style).

New Open Dialog Box Shortcuts

You can still use your favorite keyboard shortcuts with Apple's new Open dialog box.

And there are some new ones, too. Here's the list:

- When you've selected a folder in the Open dialog box, press Command+→ to expand the folder to show its contents.
- When you've selected a folder in the Open dialog box, press Command+← to collapse the folder so it displays just the folder's name.
- To change the sort criteria, click on the label at the top of the Open dialog box. The standard setting is Name. Click on the Date Modified label to sort files chronologically.

Saving Your Files

When you make a new document, as I described in Hour 6, "Making Documents, Editing Documents," you have a file that lives only in your iMac's memory. When you shut down or restart your iMac, the file is gone, history.

If you want to keep that file, you need to save it first. This puts a copy of the file on your iMac's hard drive.

Here's how it's done:

1. If the file has not yet been saved, choose Save As (or Save) from the File menu, or press Command+S. This brings up the dialog box shown in Figure 7.5.
2. Choose the folder where you want to save your file from the pop-up menu.
3. If you want to put your file in its own folder, click the New Folder button, which brings up the dialog box shown in Figure 7.6. Just type the name of the folder where indicated.

▼

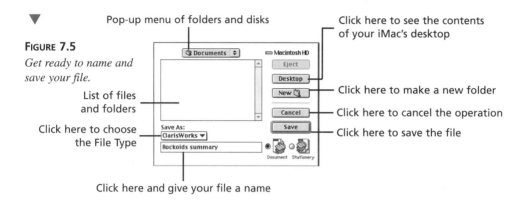

FIGURE 7.5
Get ready to name and save your file.

Pop-up menu of folders and disks

Click here to see the contents of your iMac's desktop

List of files and folders

Click here to choose the File Type

Click here to make a new folder

Click here to cancel the operation

Click here to save the file

Click here and give your file a name

FIGURE 7.6
Give your new folder a name.

Click the Create button after naming your folder

4. Type the name of your file in the highlighted text box. You'll want to give it a name that makes it easy to recall later on.

> Filenames are limited to 31 characters. If you give a file the same name as one already in the folder, you'll see a dialog box asking if you want to replace the other file. *Be careful!* If you replace the other file, that file is gone for good! It's best to give your new file a unique name.

5. Click the Save button to store your file.

> Before you save your file, double-check the name of the folder shown in the pop-up menu to make sure it's going to the right place. Otherwise, you may end up with little bits of pieces of a long project spread haphazardly around your computer's drive.

Save Dialog Box Keyboard Shortcuts

The Save dialog box has its own share of keyboard shortcuts. And, as you'll see, they are very similar to the ones I described for the Open dialog box. Consistency rules!

7

And here's the list:

- Use the Up and Down arrow keys to move to the item above and below the selected file.
- Use the End key to go to the bottom of the file list.
- Press Command+↑ to move up one folder level.
- Press Command+↓ to move down one folder level.
- Press Command+D or Command+Shift+↑ to switch to the desktop's file list.
- Press Command+O or Command+↓ when a Save As dialog box is on your screen to open a selected folder or disk.
- Press Command+Option+O to select the original of a selected alias file.
- Press the Return or Enter key to open a selected file. It works the same as the **Save** button.
- Press Command+S to activate the Save button.
- Press Command+N to create a new folder.
- Press Esc or Command+(hyphen) to close the Open dialog box without doing anything further.

A Tour of the New Save Dialog Box

Apple's new Save As dialog box mirrors the Open dialog box with its special features, so I'll just cover it briefly.

You summon it the same way, by choosing Save or Save As from the File menu in your unsaved document. The dialog box shown in Figure 7.7 will appear.

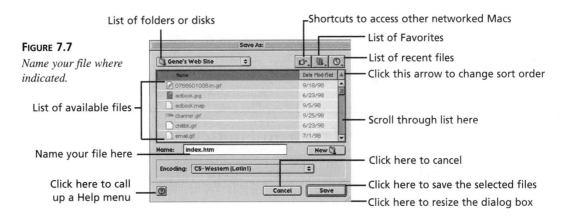

FIGURE 7.7
Name your file where indicated.

List of folders or disks

List of available files

Name your file here

Click here to call up a Help menu

Shortcuts to access other networked Macs

List of Favorites

List of recent files

Click this arrow to change sort order

Scroll through list here

Click here to cancel

Click here to save the selected files

Click here to resize the dialog box

Save, Save, and Save Again

After you've made a copy of your file on your computer's drive, you can go ahead and continue working on it.

But what you do on your screen doesn't change the file you're storing. To do that, choose Save from the File menu or press Command+S.

You should get in the habit of saving your document every 5 or 10 minutes or so. If your computer crashes, or there's a power outage, the only part of your file you'll be able to get is what you've saved (even if a later version is on your screen). Some programs even offer automatic saving options so a file is always saved at regular intervals. Check the manual or Help menu to see if that's available for you.

If you quit a program without saving, you'll see a dialog box asking if you want to save the changes. Unless you're absolutely sure you don't want to keep the changes, click the Save button in the dialog box to record the latest version of your file for posterity.

OS 9 Where's That File? Only Sherlock 2 Knows for Sure

When I first learned how to use a Mac, I quickly got in the habit of saving my work at regular intervals. But I always had a problem finding the stuff I'd saved. The files were all over the place, a real mess. Like the desk in my home office (which still looks that way).

Naturally, I could never find the files I needed when I needed them. So I had to keep searching for them and moving them all to the right place.

Fortunately, Apple has a great way to find the files you put in the wrong place (or just misplaced).

It's called Sherlock 2, and it puts the magnifying glass to your iMac to find the file.

To call up Sherlock, just choose that name from the Apple menu. Or, if you're in the Finder, press Command+F to bring up the screen shown in Figure 7.8.

7

FIGURE 7.8
Sherlock is your iMac's file detective.

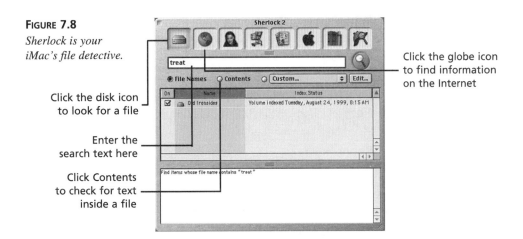

Click the globe icon
to find information
on the Internet

Click the disk icon
to look for a file

Enter the
search text here

Click Contents
to check for text
inside a file

Sherlock has three ways of locating something.

We'll start with the first, by filename. To locate the file by its filename:

▼ To Do

1. Click on the disk icon to select the proper function.

2. Enter the file's name (or part of the name) in the text field.

3. Click on Custom if you want to search for a file by date or some other criteria.

4. Click the Find button (the magnifying glass). Within seconds you'll see a screen like the one shown in Figure 7.9.

FIGURE 7.9
The game's afoot! Sherlock 2 has found your file.

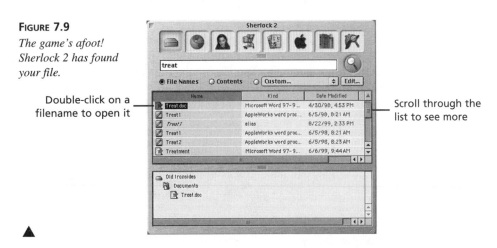

Double-click on a
filename to open it

Scroll through the
list to see more

▲

Click once on a file's name, and you'll see its exact location listed at the bottom section of the Sherlock 2 screen.

After you find the file you want, double-click on it to bring it up.

To select more than one file, do the following:

1. Click on the first file.

2. Hold down the Shift key and click on the last file in the group.

3. To open the selected files, choose Open Item from the File menu.

If you want to select two or more files that aren't consecutive, use the Command key instead of the Shift key while you select each and every one.

Locating Text Inside a File

Sherlock 2 can really dig down deep to find the stuff you want. For example, maybe you need to find a file with a certain word in it, but you can't recall the file's name. So you call up the second option in Sherlock's bag of tricks, Contents (see Figure 7.10).

FIGURE 7.10

Like a good detective, Sherlock has many tricks up its sleeve, such as finding the text inside a file.

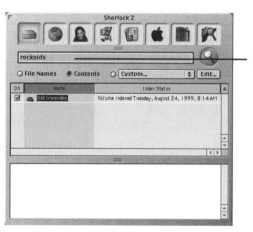

Enter the text you want to search for here

7

Sherlock needs to make an index of your computer's drive before it can search for the text inside a file. To make the index, click on the Find menu, and choose Index Volumes, and then select the name of the drive you want to index on the following screen. The cataloging process can take anywhere from a few minutes to an hour or two to complete, so you may want to be prepared for a long lunch break before you get started.

 If you've already selected Sherlock 2's file search option (the standard setting), you can press Command+G to pick to the Contents option and press Command+H to search the Internet.

Locating Material on the Internet

The next feature of Sherlock 2 is accessed by clicking the Globe icon (see Figure 7.11), which selects the Internet channel (we'll get to the others shortly). This great feature lets Sherlock log on to the Internet and then call up any of several search engines to find the information you want.

FIGURE 7.11
Sherlock can also surf the Internet in search of the material you want.

Click on a search tool to activate it

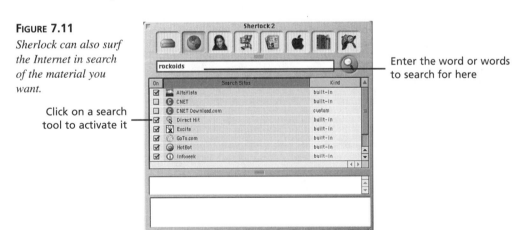

Enter the word or words to search for here

Sherlock 2's Internet search feature only works if you've signed up for an Internet account, as I described in Hour 1, "Setting Up Your iMac," and Hour 3, "Getting On the Net." In addition, if you're on AOL, you have to log on to that service first before invoking the Sherlock 2's Internet feature (it won't do it automatically).

The Internet has a huge amount of information on all sorts of subjects, and Sherlock 2 is tapping huge databases to find the information you want. Here's how it works:

▲ To Do

1. Open Sherlock 2.

2. Click on the Globe icon (or press Command+H).

3. Enter a word or phrase that describes what you want.

4. Click the Find (magnifying glass) button.

Within a few seconds, Sherlock 2 will dial up your Internet service and then seek out the information you want. See Figure 7.12 for an example.

FIGURE 7.12

Sherlock 2 is ranking its results to show which ones are the closest matches.

Click here to learn more about the item

Click on the underlined item to open it

If you find a likely match among the list, just click once on the item to see additional information in the bottom half of the screen.

Click once to open the actual reference (see Figure 7.13). The information will show up in a Web browser window.

7

FIGURE 7.13
At last! The information you sought, courtesy of Sherlock 2.

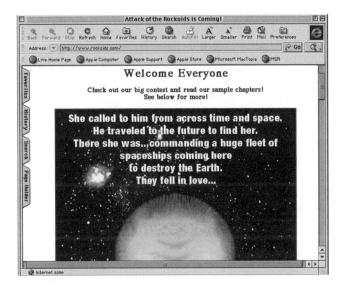

Some More Sherlock 2 Channels

In addition to searching for files on your hard drive and Internet sites, Sherlock 2 comes with an additional half-dozen channels that are used to seek out Internet information in various fields. To access any of these, just click the appropriate icon in the Sherlock 2 search screen.

These include

- **People**: You can look for email addresses and phone numbers for your friends and business contacts.
- **Apple**: This option brings up Apple's product information and support Web sites.
- **Shopping**: A handy choice. You'll be able to pick from a list of vendors and check products and pricing. In time, many online merchants will provide Sherlock 2 plug-in modules so you can search their offerings as well.

If you happen to receive a search plug-in for Sherlock 2, just drag the file to your closed System Folder icon, and it will be placed by the clever Mac OS Finder in the correct location (a folder called Internet Search Sites).

- **News**: Read the latest news and views from major news services around the world.

- **Reference**: A great place for you to do online research for homework or a special office project, or to simply to learn more about a topic.

- **My Channel**: Be creative. You can simply drag and drop search modules from your Internet Search Sites folder and build your own custom channel that searches the information you want.

What About Sherlock One?

The original version of Apple's Sherlock, which came with Mac OS 8.5, 8.5.1, and 8.6, didn't have all the fancy graphics at the top of the screen. Instead, there were three tabs that were used to access the Find File, Find by Content, and Search Internet features (see Figure 7.14).

FIGURE 7.14

This is the version of Sherlock that shipped with Mac OS versions 8.5 through 8.6.

Despite these differences, these three features work about the same as the newer version. The older version of Sherlock, however, doesn't have the ability to divide search sites into channels, and is not quite as speedy in retrieving information for you.

If you haven't upgraded to Mac OS 9 yet, contact your dealer. If you're a recent iMac purchaser (and got Mac OS 8.6 instead), Apple may be able to save you a big chunk of money with a low-cost upgrade to the latest system version.

Just contact Apple at 1-800-335-9258 and ask about their Mac OS "Up-To-Date program." The upgrade price, at the time this book was written, was $19.95 plus local sales tax.

Summary

Traversing Apple's two flavors of Open and Save dialog boxes isn't always easy. There are lots of detours, and it's very easy to put a file in the wrong place. With this lesson, you learned how to deal with those detours. And you discovered handy keyboard shortcuts to get around those dialog boxes in quick order.

In Hour 8, "Teach Yourself AppleWorks," you'll learn about one of the best productivity programs out there. With it, you'll be able to write letters, keep a database of business contacts, make simple charts, and draw pictures. It's called AppleWorks, the program I've been using so far to demonstrate your computer's file-handling features.

7

Q&A

Q **After I saved my new document, I used the Save command again, but I didn't see the dialog box. Where is it?**

A It's not necessary after your file has been saved the very first time. Each successive Save command will simply update the file that's on your computer's drive. You only need to bring up that Save As dialog box when you want to make another copy of the file with a new name. Then you use the Save As command instead.

Q **I use the Save command over and over again but nothing happens. What's wrong?**

A The Save command works only if something is changed in your document (even one single letter or number). Otherwise, well, nothing happens. Some programs will give forth a beeping sound if you attempt to save a saved document without making any changes.

Q **I looked, and looked, and I can't find Sherlock or Sherlock 2 on my iMac. Where is it?**

A Apple's Sherlock search program first came out as part of Mac OS 8.5. If you have an earlier system version (and the first few hundred thousand iMacs used 8.1), you won't find it.

But you don't have to go without. You can easily upgrade to the latest version of the Mac operating system. Just contact your dealer for details.

Q **I tried to open a file from the Favorites list of that newfangled Open dialog box, but it didn't work. What happened?**

A Could be that you deleted the file. After a file is gone, there's no going back (unless you follow the steps I will describe in Hour 24, "An iMac Safety Net").

Q **I need to work on some files from my office. But they come on floppy disks. Can I install a floppy drive on the iMac?**

A Yes, you can. There are external drives for your computer that will do the trick. These include Imation's and Winstation's SuperDisk drives, which read the floppy disks with the HD label on them. These drives can also read a special type of floppy, the SuperDisk, which holds 120MB of data (about the equivalent of 85 regular floppies). Other manufacturers have introduced regular floppy drives as well. I'll tell you more about the various extended storage options in Hour 21, "Backup, Backup, Backup...How to Protect Your Files."

But there are ways to get those files without buying another product. If you have another Mac on the network, you can use file sharing to exchange files. Hour 21 will cover that, too. You can also exchange files via modem, if both you and the other Mac user have an Internet or AOL connection. I'll cover the technique of attaching files to email in Hour 12, "The Wonderful World of Email."

Hour 8

Teach Yourself AppleWorks

There are literally thousands of programs available for your iMac. They cover the gamut from games to financial management programs. You can explore the stars, run a doctor's office, and learn how to cook.

But most often the sort of things you'll be doing can be accomplished with just a very few programs. This lesson is devoted to one of those programs, considered the best of its kind. It does several things quite well, and best of all you don't have to buy it. It's already available as part of the software bundled with your computer.

It's AppleWorks.

In this lesson, you'll get a fast and dirty (well not too dirty) tutorial on

- How to put together a simple brochure in AppleWorks.
- How to make drawings for your documents.
- How to make business reports and charts.
- How to create a database of business and personal contacts.

Introducing AppleWorks

AppleWorks is a "Swiss army knife" sort of program. It serves in place of several programs. But more important, it does those functions well—well enough to make professional looking documents without having to spend lots of time to paging through a long, complex manual.

 Just to remind you, on a number of first-generation iMacs, AppleWorks was known by its former name, ClarisWorks. But the program, past the label, is the same.

The Bill of Fare

You can consider AppleWorks to be the functional equivalent of six different programs. You can also combine the functions, providing an even greater variety of potential uses. Here's what AppleWorks does:

- **Word processing**: Creates text-based documents for ads, brochures, letters, novels, reports, and more.
- **Drawing**: Does simple line drawings, using lines, circles, and rectangles.
- **Painting**: It won't help with the garage or the den, but the AppleWorks paint module lets you add color and shading to your drawings. It's great for making simple illustrations for your documents, and when you get the hang of it, you may discover you have a flair for computer art.
- **Spreadsheets**: Creates a document with numerical data, useful for business reports, financial summaries, or charts. The program even does the calculations for you (so you can put the pocket calculator back in the closet).
- **Database**: Makes a record of your business and personal contacts. Then uses the information for a computerized Rolodex, customer or billing records, or to print out mailing labels.
- **Communications**: Okay, there has to be a dud in the group, and this may be it. Now that Internet access and email is so very easy to get, you probably won't find much use for this module, unless you need to make a modem connection to another computer user who doesn't have email capability. That's one of the primary things it's good for. If you want to try it out, just check the Help menu and enjoy.

Making Your First Document

I already covered the basics of making and formatting a word processing document in Hour 6, "Making Documents, Editing Documents." So for this lesson, I'll cover the document creation process from a different angle. Rather than have you build your document from scratch, we'll let the computer do most of the work for you. You just have to make a few choices and click a few buttons (of course, you still have to write the content of the newsletter; computers haven't quite gotten around to replacing writers yet, thank heavens!).

To guide you along, we'll call upon one of the AppleWorks Assistants.

Here's how it works:

1. Double-click on the AppleWorks program icon to launch it (see Figure 8.1).

FIGURE 8.1
What sort of new document do you want to create?

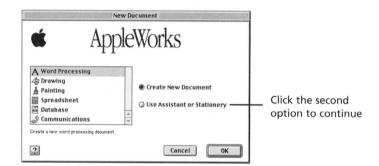

Click the second option to continue

2. Click the small button labeled Use Assistant or Stationery, which brings up the choices shown in Figure 8.2.

FIGURE 8.2
Let AppleWorks help you set up your new document.

This label tells you more about the Assistant selected

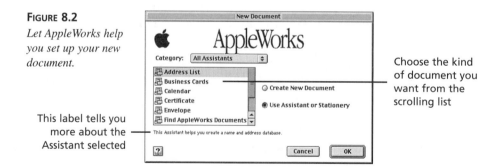

Choose the kind of document you want from the scrolling list

▼   3. For this lesson, we'll create a newsletter, and that choice requires that you scroll down through the list (because it's near the bottom).

4. Click OK to open the Newsletter Assistant screen shown in Figure 8.3.

FIGURE 8.3

AppleWorks will walk you through the process of setting up the style for your newsletter.

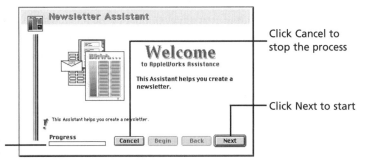

Click Cancel to stop the process

Click Next to start

Bar showing progress of setup process

5. To continue, click the Next button and make your choices from the options shown in Figure 8.4.

FIGURE 8.4

What is your document going to be used for?

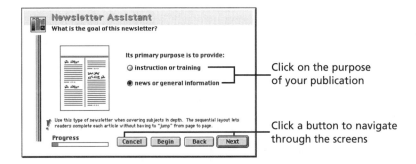

Click on the purpose of your publication

Click a button to navigate through the screens

6. Let's set up a newsletter that's suitable for a club or religious institution. So click on the News or General Information option.

7. Click the Next button to continue, which brings up the screen shown in Figure 8.5. Here you need to decide what size paper your document will be printed on. Notice that the progress bar is advancing. We're getting somewhere now.

Feel free to toggle between the Next and Back buttons to review your work before you finish it.

▼

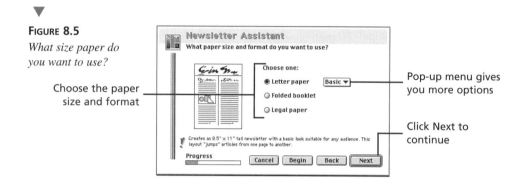

FIGURE 8.5

What size paper do you want to use?

Choose the paper size and format

Pop-up menu gives you more options

Click Next to continue

8. To keep things simple, choose Letter paper.

9. Click on the pop-up menu next to Letter paper and choose New Age. This is one of several basic styles offered.

10. Click Next to move on, which brings up a screen where you give your newsletter a title.

11. Enter the title in the text field.

12. Click Next to continue through our journey. This will open a screen where you choose how often your newsletter will appear and what issue number you're working on.

13. Choose your date and numbering options and click Next. I selected November, 2001 (I like to think ahead and also show you the Mac isn't affected by the so-called Y2K problem) and made it issue number 99. Now that's really being optimistic because I've never published an issue before.

14. Select the number of pages you want your newsletter to have and then click Next.

15. Choose whether it will have a table of contents and click Next. Select no for the sake of simplicity. This will bring up another screen, shown in Figure 8.6, where you decide whether to have an editorial or not.

16. We are very close to the finish line. If you don't believe me, check the progress bar. Because I will express an opinion at the drop of a hat (make that a keyboard), I'll pick Yes for the editorial and then click Next to continue.

17. If you want to have a self-mailer (with a mailing label attached), you'll say yes to the next option. Click Next.

18. Wow, we're just about there. The screen in Figure 8.7 shows we're at the finish line. And you'll also have the choice of having AppleWorks make a "Tips and Hints document" to help you along the road to a great newsletter.

FIGURE 8.6

If you want to express your own views in the newsletter, you'll want to have an editorial.

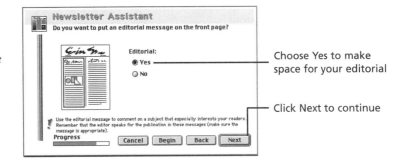

Choose Yes to make space for your editorial

Click Next to continue

FIGURE 8.7

Okay, hold your breath and get ready to see the results of your creation.

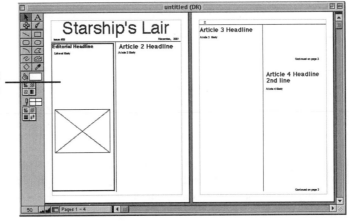

Click Yes here

Click Create to finish

Within seconds, AppleWorks will make two documents for you (you can switch between the two from the Window menu). The first is a blank template, with space for you to insert your articles and editorial (see Figure 8.8). The second, shown in Figure 8.9, gives you advice on how to set up your newsletter for best effect.

FIGURE 8.8

Just fill in the blanks to prepare your newsletter.

Click on an element and begin typing

FIGURE 8.9

This sample newsletter has advice on how to make a top-flight publication.

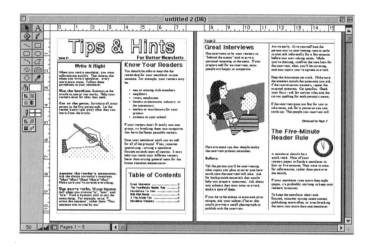

After your document has been finished, you'll want to make sure the spelling is perfect. To check spelling, do the following steps:

The spell check feature in AppleWorks isn't limited to the word processing module. You can use it with the other AppleWorks components, too. That's why I'm describing it in extra detail here.

▼ To Do

1. Choose Writing Tools from the Edit menu.
2. Select Check Document Spelling from the submenu (see Figure 8.10).

FIGURE 8.10

Check your spelling first before you publish.

▲

Save mousing around and use the keyboard shortcut Command+= to bring up the spell check screen.

Spell checking isn't perfect. It won't pick out a word that is spelled differently to convey a different meaning, or one that is incorrectly used. So you still want to read over your newsletter carefully before you print it.

Here's what those little buttons in the spell check window do:

- **Check**: Click here to find the spelling for the selected word.
- **Skip**: Don't bother checking this word; move to the next one.
- **Learn**: If the spelling is correct, but it's not in the program's dictionary, click this button to record it.
- **Cancel**: Click here to stop the spell check.

You can use the keystroke shortcut Command+. (that's Command+[period]) to stop your spell check. You'll be pleased to know that this very same shortcut is the standard command to halt an operation (though it doesn't work in all programs or all the time).

The numbered buttons at the left in Figure 8.10 let you quickly select a word to replace the one selected.

The Assistants feature I've described here is used to create many forms of documents; it's not just limited to word processing.

Now that you've gotten a brief start in creating a fancy document in AppleWorks, we'll move on to the next module.

Learning to Draw in AppleWorks

The phrase "a picture is worth a thousand words" is such a cliché that I hesitate to use it. Better to say that you don't have to be an artist to do a creditable job of drawing pictures with your computer.

Let's begin by creating a new document, just as shown way back there in Figure 8.1. But this time, you'll choose the second option, Drawing, which will produce the screen shown in Figure 8.11.

FIGURE 8.11

This is your canvas for your homegrown artwork.

Click on one of the tool icons to begin

Format menu

Arrange menu

Options menu

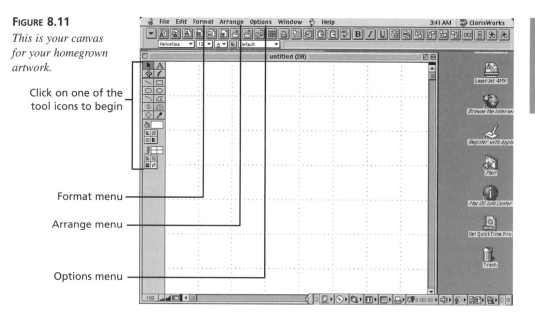

You'll notice the menu bar changed when you went to the AppleWorks draw module. Feel free to look over the new set of commands and try them out.

And don't worry if you can't draw a straight line with pen and ink; I have trouble with that also. But drawing illustrations on a computer is different in many ways. For example, making simple shapes is easy because the basic tools require just a click and a drag.

I don't want to mislead you about doing computer art. Doing simple drawings may be seem very easy, but complex artwork, whether on a computer or an ordinary canvas, requires imagination, talent, and training. But you can certainly get by with the basics. In addition, AppleWorks offers some packaged artwork (called *clip art*) that you can adapt to your needs.

Before you begin, take a look at AppleWorks' bag of tricks, the toolbar; there's not a screwdriver or wrench in the bunch. But take a look at Figure 8.12, and you'll see what that toolbar can do for you.

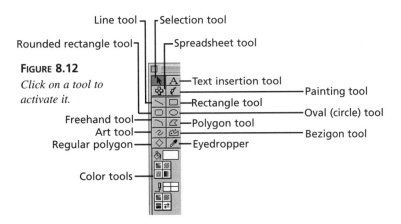

Line tool ⌐ Selection tool

Rounded rectangle tool ⌐   ⌐ Spreadsheet tool

FIGURE 8.12

Click on a tool to
activate it.

Text insertion tool

Painting tool

Rectangle tool

Oval (circle) tool

Freehand tool —

Art tool —

Regular polygon —   Polygon tool

Eyedropper

Bezigon tool

Color tools —

I know that you're anxious to start. But I just want to add a couple of bits of information first about the pieces of artwork you're going to create:

- Each element of your artwork is called an *object.*

- When you draw one object atop another, it's stacked, like putting some sheets of paper atop a desk (graphic artists call it "layers"). To switch the stacking order (to get at something underneath), you use the commands in the Arrange menu, such as Move Forward, Move Backward, and so on.

- You can size up objects as you desire on your computer's screen, but use the Object Size command in the Options menu to specify them exactly.

- To change the thickness of a rule or border, use the little tool with the stacked rectangles on it as shown in Figure 8.12 previously.

> You can open a big floating color palette this way: Click on a color tool in the toolbar and drag it away from the toolbar. Presto! You have a floating palette. To choose a color, just click on it and then click on the object on which you want to insert the color. Just close the close box at the upper left of the palette to send it away.

Now let's draw something, a simple shape:

1. Click on the rectangle tool to select it

2. Then click on the blank canvas shown in Figure 8.11 and drag the mouse to the right. You'll see a small rectangle, getting larger as you continue to drag it to the right.

▼   3. To make the rectangle longer, drag it downward.

4. When it's the size you want, release the mouse button. See Figure 8.13 for the result.

8

FIGURE 8.13

If I can draw, you can draw.

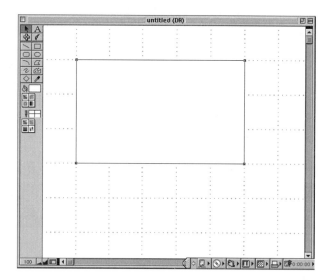

▲

After your object is drawn, you can click on it and move it around your screen. When the object is selected, you'll see little dark squares at each corner. If it's not selected, just click on the selection tool (shown back in Figure 8.12). Then click on the object itself to move it where you want.

> When drawing a shape, hold down the Shift key to keep it in proportion. This gets you a perfect circle or square, depending on the tool you're using.

Using the Paint Module

After you've become accustomed to drawing in AppleWorks, you'll want to give painting a try. First, you'll bring up the New Document window; then choose Painting, which produces the screen shown in Figure 8.14.

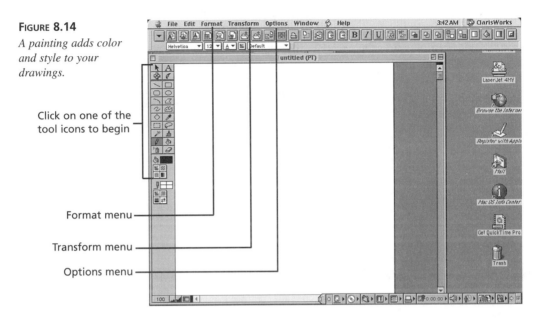

FIGURE 8.14

A painting adds color and style to your drawings.

Click on one of the tool icons to begin

Format menu

Transform menu

Options menu

Okay, it's very close to the drawing module, but no cigar. There are a few differences, such as the addition of the Transform menu, which adds a set of commands to manipulate your illustrations.

The other is the toolbar (see Figure 8.15), which resembles the drawing toolbar, but adds a few extras.

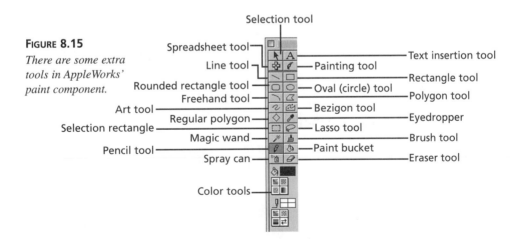

FIGURE 8.15

There are some extra tools in AppleWorks' paint component.

Selection tool

Spreadsheet tool

Line tool

Rounded rectangle tool

Freehand tool

Art tool

Regular polygon

Selection rectangle

Magic wand

Pencil tool

Spray can

Color tools

Text insertion tool

Painting tool

Rectangle tool

Oval (circle) tool

Polygon tool

Bezigon tool

Eyedropper

Lasso tool

Brush tool

Paint bucket

Eraser tool

The new tools do precisely what their labels say they do. You can use the pencil tool to perform some of the same functions as a regular pencil, although it takes a little while to make your mouse act like one. The eraser tool can be used to wipe out the element you drag it over.

To see the difference between the drawing and paint functions, first make a rectangle just as you did in the previous section. The result, shown in Figure 8.16, shows a big difference.

Figure 8.16

A painting adds some color to your drawings.

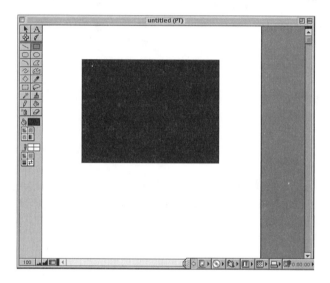

This rectangle is filled with black. To change the color, just click on one of the color tools before you make your drawing. You can also insert elements of color by using the paint brush tool.

The possibilities are almost endless.

Creating a Spreadsheet

AppleWorks' spreadsheet component lets you track financial information and prepare business reports and charts. Let's do one and see how easy it is to set up.

First, open your New Document window and choose Spreadsheet (see Figure 8.17).

FIGURE 8.17

Enter your financial information here.

Format menu

Calculate menu

Options menu

Spreadsheet column

Spreadsheet row

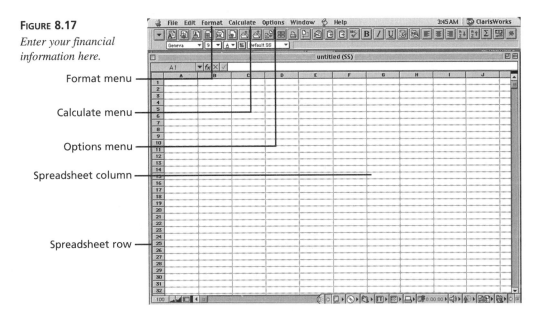

As you see, your AppleWorks spreadsheet document somewhat resembles graph paper. Here's the components you'll be working with:

- **Cells**: A cell is the compartment in which a bit of information is placed. Each rectangle shown in Figure 8.17 is another cell, and AppleWorks lets you work with thousands of them. Whew!
- **Grids**: The dotted lines between the cells are grid lines.
- **Rows**: The horizontal lineup of cells is called a row.
- **Columns**: The vertical lineup of cells is called a column.
- **Headings**: The letters across the top of the spreadsheet are column headings. The numbers at the left are row headings.

 When you make a printout of your spreadsheet, you have the option to remove the headings and grid lines.

Now that the preliminaries are out of the way, here's how to get started with your spreadsheet:

1. Click on the first cell in your spreadsheet to select it.
2. Click on the text entry field above the column levels to enter your information.

3. After entering the information, press the Tab key on your computer's keyboard to move to the next horizontal cell. Press the Return key to move to the cell right below it.

4. When you're finished entering your horizontal numbers, click on the first cell in the second row.

5. Click on the text entry field to insert your information.

> If your spreadsheet cell is too narrow, just put your mouse between any two columns. The mouse cursor will change to a horizontal line with an arrow at each end. Click and drag the mouse to the right to make the cell at the left larger. You can do the same trick between rows.

After you've entered all your data, here are some of the things you can do with it:

- **Calculate the Math**: Check the Calculate menu for the various choices.
- **Decorate It**: Use the options in the Format menu to make it look the way you want.
- **Make a Chart**: This setting is available from the Options menu. You have a choice of pie charts, scatter charts, and more. Check out Figure 8.18 for a sample.

FIGURE 8.18
This chart is built from a few rows and columns of numbers.

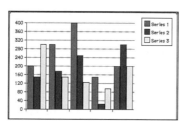

Your Computerized Rolodex File

I used to keep information about my business contacts on index cards, and I used a typewriter to update the entries. (Now this dates me a lot, I suppose.) With AppleWorks, you can create your personal index card file with your computer, using the database component. And you don't just have a set of cards (or records).

You can do lots of interesting stuff with them, such as

- **Sorting**: You can organize your records by date, name, location, and so on.
- **Mailing Labels**: You can set up and print out labels for business promotions, or to send out that newsletter you made earlier in this lesson.
- **Invoices**: You can use the information to send bills to your clients.

To get started with your interactive Rolodex file, you need to make a new database document. Just invoke that New Document screen and then choose Database. This opens a new database document window and one labeled Define Database Fields (see Figure 8.19).

FIGURE 8.19

Wait a minute! What are these fields for?

Field name and type appears here

Field creation buttons

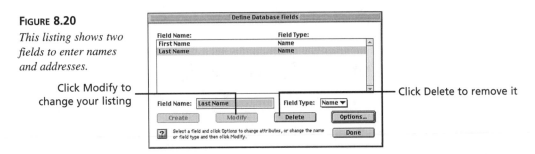

Enter field name

Choose field type

To create your little Rolodex file, you need to first tell AppleWorks what sort of information is going to appear on the index card. We'll start with a simple list of names. Here's how it's done:

1. Choose Name from the Field Type pop-up menu.
2. Type **First Name** as the Field Name.
3. Click the Create button. You'll see the label and type of field entered on the list.
4. Type **Last Name** as the second Field Name.
5. Click the Create button again. This adds the second field to the list (see Figure 8.20).

FIGURE 8.20

This listing shows two fields to enter names and addresses.

Click Modify to change your listing

Click Delete to remove it

6. When you're finished, click Done to create your simple index card. See Figure 8.21 for the result.

FIGURE 8.21

There you have it, the beginnings of your address book.

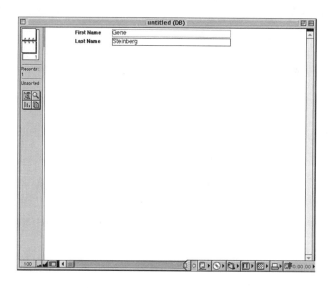

> To change the design of your database, simply choose Layout from the Layout menu. Then you can click and drag elements around as you prefer.

This is just the beginning of what you can do with your database. There are a wide variety of setups you can make for your records. And a single set of records can be used for a number of purposes, from that address book, to complete business reports, along with a chart or two from your spreadsheet to enhance the appearance.

The Sum of the Parts

You can share data between components in AppleWorks. You'll notice, for example, that the ever-present toolbar (shown back in Figure 8.12) has a spreadsheet tool you can use to insert tables in all sorts of documents. In addition, you can use the program's Insert feature (available from the File menu) to bring the contents of one document into another. That way you can spruce up your newsletter with the illustrations you make yourself or with photos that you can bring into your iMac with a scanner. I'll cover scanners and other devices you can add to your iMac in Hour 20, "Adding More Goodies to Your iMac."

Summary

The great thing about AppleWorks is not just that it rolls a number of software packages into one program, or even that it's easy to use. The fact is that AppleWorks gets rave reviews from the computing magazines because it does so many things so well.

In Hour 9, I'll cover one of the premiere Mac financial management programs, Quicken 98.

Q&A

Q When I launch AppleWorks, I don't see the New Document screen. Where is it?

A No doubt somewhere along the line you (or someone using your computer) has changed the preference. When you choose the Preferences command from the Edit menu, there are a number of settings you can make to the program. The first option under General Preferences, at the left of the dialog box, is a list of options under the label On Startup, Show… and here's where you can decide whether to display the New Document dialog, an Open dialog box, or just do nothing.

The option you pick depends on your work habits. One specific setting isn't necessarily better than another.

If you don't see anything on your screen, just choose New from the File menu or press Command+N to bring up the New Document screen.

Q I'm already using another integrated program, Microsoft Works. Is there any reason to switch?

A If you're happy with what you have, just install it on your computer. You don't have to change, but you may want to check with Microsoft to be sure that the version you're using will work properly on the latest Mac computers.

And you still might want to give AppleWorks a whirl because it's already installed on your computer. However, there's nothing to prevent you from using both programs, if you feel one does something better than the other.

8

Q I notice you dated your sample newsletter for some time in 2001. What about all those problems I hear about computers and the year 2000? What's the real skinny on this one?

A The folks who created the Macintosh computer had great foresight about this. They set it up so it would work without a dating problem at least until the year 2040 (and in some respects, for hundreds of years thereafter). I suppose we could worry about a "2041" problem, but I rather doubt that you'll be using this sort of computer then (maybe it'll be a museum relic, I suppose).

On the other hand, it's possible some of your software may need an update. Best thing to do is double-check with the publisher about this.

Q Just one more question: Where's the manual?

A A friend used to say to me, "Manuals? Manuals? I don't need no -------manuals." Sounds like a line from a movie. Anyway, there really is an AppleWorks User's Guide folder on your computer. It's in Adobe Acrobat format (which is also installed on your computer already), so you can read it on your screen or make a printout.

Hour 9

Managing Your Bucks with Quicken 98

Financial transactions get more complex all the time. It's not just reconciling a checkbook or two. You have to keep track of monthly bills, figure out budgets, track your financial worth, and decide whether an investment is a good idea.

And even if you're just a working stiff like me, you need more accurate tools than ever to keep up with the world of personal finance.

In this lesson, I'll introduce you to a program that works fine, not only with your personal finances, but also with small businesses. It's another great program included with your iMac—Quicken 98 Deluxe.

In this lesson, you'll discover

- How to set up your own checkbook on your iMac.
- How to track your monthly expenses.
- How to get started with financial planning.
- How to make reports and charts showing your financial picture.
- The advantages of online banking.

Getting Started with Quicken 98 Deluxe

Quicken 98 Deluxe begins with a simple checkbook and adds to that the capability of keeping a wide range of financial records. You can even keep both business and personal accounts, and use your Internet service to track your finances while online.

Here's a brief look at the things you can do with Quicken 98 Deluxe:

> If others have access to your computer, you may want to buy a security program so that your financial information cannot be accessed without entering the right password. You will want to check with your Apple dealer or favorite mail order catalog for such products. I'll cover the subject of security in more detail in Hour 21, "Backup, Backup, Backup...How to Protect Your Files."

- **Bank accounts**: Manage your personal and business checking accounts, and automatically reconcile your checks as they are written. You can also print checks if you have a printer attached to your computer.

- **Investment tracking**: Whether it's one stock or a large portfolio, Quicken 98 Deluxe helps you keep tabs on all of your investments. You can track transactions, compare market values, and see just how much profit you've earned.

- **Track your net worth**: Keep a complete record of all your debts and assets. You can record loan transactions, real estate loans, personal possessions, and more.

- **Financial planning**: This feature isn't just for your business. You can use Quicken 98 Deluxe to examine your personal finances, help you figure out where your money is going, assist you in making plans for the future, and track your possible tax liabilities.

- **Online banking**: If your financial institution supports this feature, you can log on to your Internet account and use Quicken 98 Deluxe to handle your transactions.

> Intuit, publisher of Quicken 98 Deluxe, also publishes a tax preparation program, called *MacInTax*, which can help you prepare your return with professional results. It can also read your financial information from Quicken 98 Deluxe to simplify the process.

- **Reports and charts**: You can use Quicken 98 Deluxe to make detailed reports and charts to give you a far-ranging picture of the present status of your finances, and how things might change in the future if you try different approaches.

Managing Your Bank Account

Because most of you will probably use a program such as Quicken 98 Deluxe to handle your checkbook, I'll begin with that feature.

> Before setting up Quicken, it's a good idea to insert the program's CD. That way you will be able to listen to the program's online guide as you begin to prepare your financial information.

9

To get started with Quicken:

1. Locate the Quicken application inside the Quicken folder on your computer (it should be in the Applications folder).

2. Double-click on the Quicken 98 Deluxe folder to launch it. The first time it opens, you'll be asked to personalize your copy. Enter your name in the text field and click the OK button.

3. After you've personalized the program, you'll see a prompt to register Quicken 98 Deluxe (see Figure 9.1).

FIGURE 9.1

Choose your registration option.

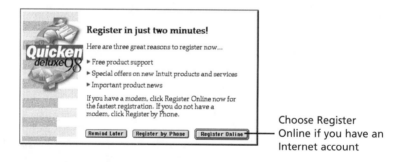

Choose Register Online if you have an Internet account

> I recommend that you register Quicken 98 Deluxe as soon as you can. That way you can contact the publisher for support if you run into a problem using the program.

4. After you've registered Quicken 98 Deluxe, the next prompt will give you a fast, guided tour of the program (see Figure 9.2). Click the New User button to continue.

FIGURE 9.2

*Quicken will guide you
through the process of
setting up your
account information.*

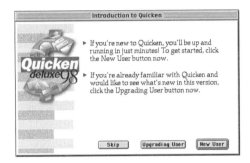

5. Your first step is to specify the type of account you want to create (see Figure 9.3). Let's start with the Home Categories option. Click OK to continue.

The little box at the lower left is what's called an Apple Guide Help menu. You can click on the right arrow for added assistance.

FIGURE 9.3

*Choose the category
you want and
click OK.*

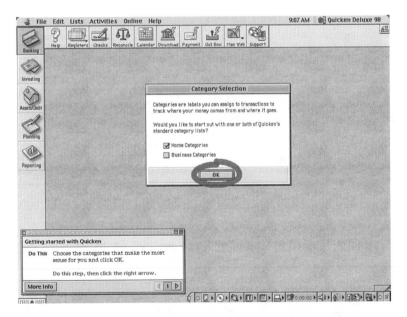

6. You'll see a Set Up Account screen (see Figure 9.4). Choose the Account Type you want; then enter the Account Name in the text field. For this lesson, we'll choose a regular bank account. Click Create to continue.

FIGURE 9.4

What sort of account do you want to create?

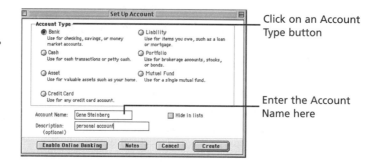

Click on an Account Type button

Enter the Account Name here

9

If you're going to bring over the transactions from your existing checking account, you'll want to dig out your checkbook for the remainder of the setup process.

7. Now's the time to enter the transactions in your Quicken 98 Deluxe account register. Notice it looks very much like a regular checkbook register and it's filled out in a similar way (see Figure 9.5). Place the ending balance from your checkbook in the Balance field to get started. If you're starting with a fresh deposit, use the Deposit category instead.

FIGURE 9.5

Enter your checkbook transactions here.

Click on the pop-up menus for entry shortcuts

Click Record to store the information

You must click the Record button to store a transaction before you can move on to the next one.

8. The first time you enter a payee's name, you'll be asked to give it a category. From then on, the information will be stored in the program for quick recall. Click the Tab key to move through the entry fields and the Record button to store it.

> If you just want to add a simple checkbook entry, you can speed things up by using the QuickEntry program. It's in your Quicken 98 Deluxe application folder.

9. Continue to enter your transactions until your account register is finished. Notice that your balance is adjusted automatically every time you enter a new transaction. You can tuck away that calculator. Reconciling your checkbook couldn't be easier.

> Press the plus key (+) in the Number field to enter the next consecutive check number. You can also use that keystroke in a date field to move to the next date or the minus (–) key to move to previous dates. Pressing t will return you to today's date.

Other Quicken Checkbook Features

You can easily access other Quicken 98 Deluxe features simply by clicking the appropriate labels on the program's toolbar (see Figure 9.6).

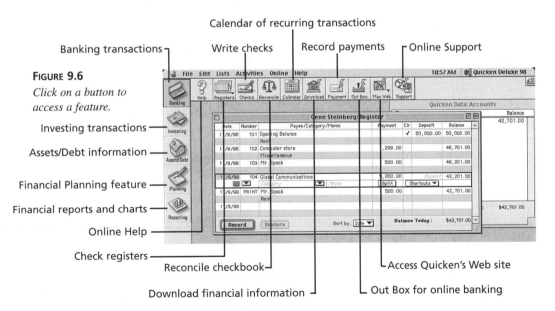

FIGURE 9.6
Click on a button to access a feature.

Banking transactions
Calendar of recurring transactions
Write checks
Record payments
Online Support
Investing transactions
Assets/Debt information
Financial Planning feature
Financial reports and charts
Online Help
Check registers
Reconcile checkbook
Download financial information
Access Quicken's Web site
Out Box for online banking

Writing a Check

Not only can you keep a checkbook register with Quicken 98 Deluxe, you can write checks, too. All you need is a set of special checks from Intuit, publisher of Quicken 98 Deluxe, and a printer to make checks that look as good as those made by large companies.

Here's how to write a Quicken 98 Deluxe check:

9

1. Click on the Check icon on Quicken 98 Deluxe's program toolbar, which brings up the blank check screen shown in Figure 9.7.

▼ To Do

FIGURE 9.7

Here's a blank check, ready to enter your information.

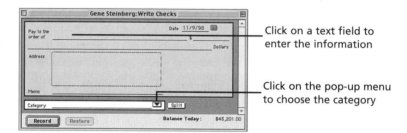

Click on a text field to enter the information

Click on the pop-up menu to choose the category

When you write a check in Quicken 98 Deluxe, the information is automatically recorded on your account register. No more need for double entries.

2. Click on a text entry field to enter the payee and the amount. Use the Tab key to move through the fields.

Quicken 98 Deluxe will automatically insert the information from the last transaction with the same payee, to save you time, but you can change it if necessary.

3. Click Record to store the transaction and bring up another blank check screen.
4. Close the Write Checks window to finish writing checks.

You can manage your finances in many ways with Quicken 98 Deluxe. For example, some folks prefer just to write checks directly from the check register.

▼

5. After your checks are written, you can use the Print Checks command in the File
 menu to get your completed check.

> Quicken 98 Deluxe includes a special feature, Billminder, which gives you an onscreen reminder about payments that are due. To set it up, choose Preferences from the Edit menu and scroll through the list to the Billminder option.

Tracking Your Investment Portfolio

In addition to managing your checkbook, Quicken 98 Deluxe can also keep tabs on your investment portfolio. That way you can track whether the money you've spent on those investments is really helping your bottom line, or reducing it.

To set up a financial portfolio in Quicken 98 Deluxe, first click on the Investing button on the program's toolbar (refer to Figure 9.6). You'll see some new button options across the top; click on the one labeled Portfolio (see Figure 9.8).

FIGURE 9.8

Enter your investment accounts in this register.

Enter current security information here

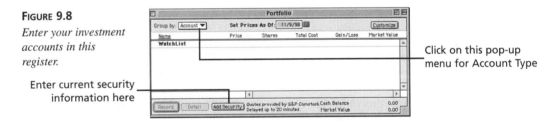

Click on this pop-up menu for Account Type

After you've typed all the information, Quicken 98 Deluxe will dial up your Internet service and receive the latest price information. That way you can easily see where your money is going, or how much you've profited from the investment.

Checking Your Net Worth

After you've set up your checkbook and investment portfolio, you'll want to consider setting up a complete financial statement. Whether you just want to see how much money you have, or you need the information for a business or personal loan, you'll find that Quicken 98 Deluxe can help guide you through the rough spots of recording the information in short order.

To set up your Net Worth statement:

1. Click on the Assets/Debt icon on the Quicken 98 Deluxe program toolbar (it's at the left).

2. This will change the icons at the top. Choose the one labeled Net Worth, which will bring up the screen shown in Figure 9.9.

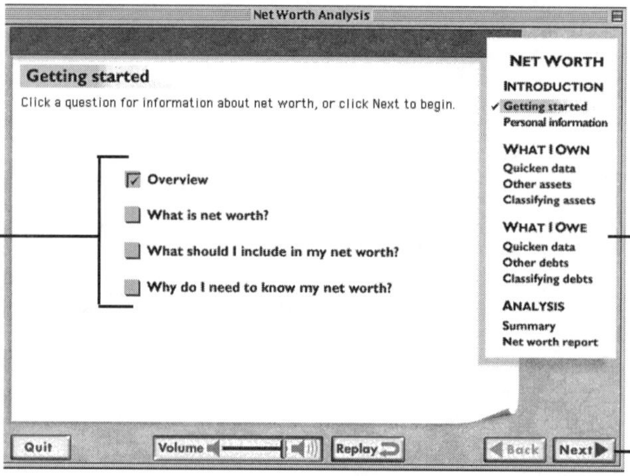

FIGURE 9.9
The Net Worth Analysis screen will guide you through the preparation procedure.

Click the check box to specify category

Choose the topic from here

Click Next to continue

When you first open the Net Worth Analysis screen, you'll see a short video describing what you'll be doing to create the Net Worth report.

3. Click the Next button to move through the process. An online narrator will help you along the way.

When you're done, you'll be able to open a graphic display of your financial picture and print a copy for your review, or to hand over to your financial analyst.

Creating Financial Reports

Now that you've set up a checkbook, done your monthly payments, and tracked your investment portfolio and net worth, no doubt you'll want to see what all this means to you.

Quicken 98 Deluxe can make a professional report and set of charts to show you your entire financial picture.

To Do ▼

To use this feature:

1. Click on the Report icon on the Quicken 98 Deluxe program toolbar. This will open a different set of icons across the top of the screen.

2. To make a financial report, click on the Reports icon, which opens the Reports screen shown in Figure 9.10.

FIGURE 9.10

Tell Quicken what sort of financial report you want.

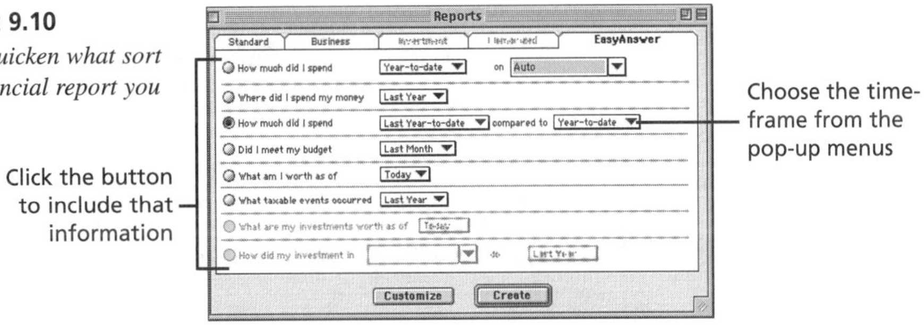

Click the button to include that information

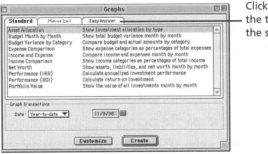

Choose the time-frame from the pop-up menus

3. When you're finished customizing the information, click the Create button to make your report.

▲

To Do ▼

You can also create a professional caliber chart showing your financial information. To access this feature:

1. Click on the Graphs icon on the Quicken 98 Deluxe program toolbar (see Figure 9.11).

FIGURE 9.11

Choose between a Standard business graphic or the EasyAnswer variety.

Click on the tab at the top to change the setup option

2. Choose the range of information you want to provide in your graph.

3. When you're finished, click Create to open the chart.

Your completed graph can be viewed on the screen or printed for later review. After a few hours of this, you'll feel like an expert.

▲

It's never a bad idea to have a backup copy of your financial data, in case something goes wrong with your original file. To make one or more backups, choose Preferences from the Edit menu and scroll to the File Backup icon.

Online Financial Transactions

More and more financial institutions have set up an online banking feature, so you can handle your bank transactions without ever visiting a branch.

Online banking enables you to do the following:

- Update Quicken 98 Deluxe with information received directly from your bank.
- Pay your bills electronically and regularly. No more envelopes, stamps, or having checks get lost in the mail. And no more past-due statements from your creditors.
- Transfer funds between one account and another at the same bank.
- Get up-to-date account balances for your checking account and your credit accounts in seconds.
- Handle scheduled payments, such as a car payment or mortgage, automatically.

The online accounts you establish with a financial institution are encrypted. That way, they are kept secure from prying eyes and potential thieves. You may want to contact a financial institution about the safety measures you're using before you set up your online account there.

In order to set up an online account, you need Internet access. Please check Hour 1, "Setting Up Your iMac," and Hour 3, "Getting On the Net," for information on how to get connected with an online service.

Summary

I don't want to pretend that I've done much more than scratch the surface of financial management possibilities you can explore with Quicken 98 Deluxe. As you can see from the brief tour in this lesson, the program has a surprising array of features.

If you want to learn more about the program, check the online manual in your Quicken 98 Deluxe CD. It's located in a folder called Onscreen Docs. You'll also want to check the Help menu for more assistance. The publisher also includes some neat videos in that Help menu. It's almost like having a support person at your beck and call to provide guidance.

Q&A

Q I got the hang of writing my checks on my computer. But what do I do with checks that I write at my supermarket?

A I often wonder what it would be like if folks went and unpacked their computers and printers at the checkout counter (well, I guess it's not too difficult with an iBook). But all you have to do is write a check by hand and then enter it in Quicken 98 Deluxe's account register when you get back home.

If you're printing your checks through Quicken 98 Deluxe, you can just prepare checks made out to the stores you're visiting, leaving the figures blank. Then you can reconcile your register later on (but don't forget to do it).

Q You say I can use Quicken 98 Deluxe to print checks. How's that done?

A Well, first you need a printer, and then you need to order checks from Quicken 98 Deluxe's publisher, Intuit (or through one of the check vendors you see in the computing magazines). I'll tell you more about connecting your computer to a printer in Hour 17, "Now That I Wrote It, How Do I Print It?"

Q I deleted Quicken 98 Deluxe by mistake. Can I reinstall it without having to restore all my other software?

A Yes, there's a separate CD for Quicken 98 Deluxe in your iMac's accessory box. And it has an installer application on it, so you can reinstall this program all by itself. It just requires double-clicking on the installer icon, clicking a few buttons, and it will be done in short order. You'll have to restart your computer to complete the process, though.

Q What's "Deluxe" about Quicken 98 Deluxe?

A The CD-ROM that comes with it. It contains additional financial information resources.

Q I have another computer here. I own the software, right? Why can't I install Quicken 98 Deluxe on that one too?

A When you purchase software, whether bundled with a computer or separately, you're not buying the software itself, but a license to use it. Most software licenses limit you to installing the program on a single computer, and maybe making a backup copy for safekeeping.

Some programs let you install one copy on a desktop computer and another on a laptop, so long as both copies aren't being used at the very same time. That would mean, if the license allows it, that you could install the same program on both an iMac and iBook.

The best thing to do is to read the software license that comes with the software to see what is covered. If you need to run more than one copy, you'll want to contact the publisher about additional software licenses. Usually, additional copies cost less than the first.

Q   I have been hearing about a newer version, Quicken 2000. Why did I get the older, 98 version?

A   Apple often changes the bundled software, so it's possible later generation iMacs will include Quicken 2000. But you shouldn't feel left behind. If you want to upgrade, pay a visit to Intuit's Web site at `http://www.intuit.com` and check out the news about Quicken 2000 for the Macintosh. The upgrade includes an Insights feature for improved financial management, and more tools to customize the look and feel of the program. What's more, when you upgrade from an older version, they give you a rebate.

9

HOUR 10

Faxing, Cooking, and Other Software

There's almost no limit to the things you can do with an iMac. As you've seen in previous chapters, you can use it to connect to the Internet, do word processing, draw pictures, prepare financial reports, assemble a Rolodex file, manage your checkbook and investment portfolio, and figure out your net worth.

In this lesson, we'll look at some of the other programs that came packaged with your iMac.

> Don't be surprised if the software you get in your iMac differs from what is
> described here. Apple may occasionally change the software package that
> ships with its consumer models.

One of those programs will turn your iMac into a fax machine, another program will
show you how to cook (yes, even someone like me), and another will help you edit the
photos you scan with a desktop scanner.

In this lesson, you'll discover

- How to fax your documents without having to make a printout first.
- How to take an interactive cooking lesson.
- How to use Soap (a really cool program) to retouch photos.
- An introduction to making your own Web site with PageMill.
- How to use find information with the World Book Encyclopedia.

Getting Started with FAXstf

If you've signed up with an Internet service or joined AOL, no doubt you've spent a little
time seeing how the modem inside your computer can open up a new world to you, a
world filled with possibilities for communication.

That modem can do more than surf the Internet. It can double as a fax machine, using a
clever program from a company known as STF Technologies, FAXstf.

> A number of modems come equipped with Faxstf, but the version that
> comes with your iMac has been tested to work with your computer's inter-
> nal modem. There is, though, a more elaborate version, FAXstf Pro, which
> adds extra features, such as drag-and-drop faxing, multiple address books,
> caller ID support, and more. You'll find a special upgrade offer to the
> enhanced version among the online documentation in the FAXstf folder on
> your computer's drive.

Here are a few of the things you can do with FAXstf. After this you may just want to give up on that old-fashioned fax machine:

- **Fax directly from almost any program**: Using a simple keyboard shortcut, you can call up FAXstf from within the program you're using and then fax your documents directly to one or more recipients.

- **Assemble an address book**: You can store information about your personal and business contacts, making it easy to send them a fax when you need to.

- **Receive and print faxes**: So long as your iMac is running, it can be set to receive faxes, just like that regular fax machine. The received fax can be viewed on the screen or printed.

- **Custom cover pages**: You can create a page that identifies you and your business and provides information about the fax that you're sending.

- **Scheduled faxing**: You can send your fax at a special time, to avoid busy signals.

Sending Your First Fax

Before you send your first fax, you'll want to set up the cover pages for your faxes.

To do that:

1. Pay a visit to the FAXstf 5.0 folder, located inside your computer's Applications folder.

2. Double-click the Fax Browser application.

3. Choose Settings from the Edit menu.

4. Scroll to the Cover Page icon and click it.

5. Enter your cover page information, as I've done in Figure 10.1.

FIGURE 10.1

Type your cover page settings here. They'll appear on every fax you send.

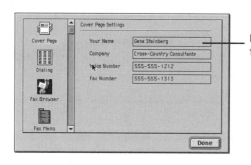

Press the Tab key to move from one line to the next

▼

> As you know, the Tab key is used to move from one text field in a dialog box to the next. To move to the previous text field, press Shift+Tab instead.

6. Click Done to finish; then quit the Fax Browser program. You won't have to open it again unless you want to change the settings or view or print a received fax.

Now you're ready to send your first fax. As a test, perhaps you can have a friend or business colleague who is willing to serve as guinea pig for your little experiment. You'll want to ask that person if he is willing to receive a fax and then send one right back to you. Just be prepared to offer a lunch or dinner as payment for that person's time.

With the preliminaries out of the way, open up a word processing document you've made with AppleWorks (as described in Hour 8, "Teach Yourself AppleWorks"), as I've done in Figure 10.2.

> If you haven't gotten around to writing a full-fledged document with any of your computer's software yet, you can open one of your Read Me files instead and fax that. Remember, this is only a test.

FIGURE 10.2

This is the actual document I wrote in AppleWorks.

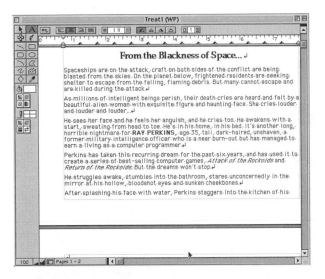

As you'll see from the following steps, sending a fax with your iMac is a piece of cake.

1. Hold down the Command and Option keys and choose Fax One Copy from the File menu, which opens the FaxPrint dialog box (see Figure 10.3).

FIGURE 10.3

Use this dialog box to begin the faxing process.

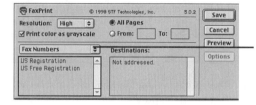

Click the pop-up menu to change the information displayed

 I know, I know, it usually says Print in that location on the File menu. But you can establish a special shortcut with FAXstf to invoke the faxing feature instead from the File menu (the Settings panel I introduced earlier in this lesson can be used to change the shortcut keys).

10

2. Now wait a minute! I bet you're going to ask me whether I intend to send that fax to someone over at STF. No, you can send it to almost anyone with a regular fax machine or fax modem. To do that, click the pop-up menu labeled Fax Numbers and choose the Temporary Address option, which opens the dialog box shown in Figure 10.4.

You can skip the pop-up menu and press Command+N to open the Temporary Address window without the preliminaries.

FIGURE 10.4

Enter the address information here.

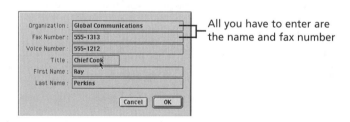

All you have to enter are the name and fax number

3. After the contact information is entered, click OK to save it. You'll return to the FaxPrint screen, and your recipient's name will already be shown in the Destinations box (see Figure 10.5).

▼

FIGURE 10.5

The fax will be sent to anyone on the Destinations list.

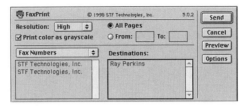

The contact you set in FaxPrint won't be added to your FAXstf software; it's just there temporarily, for use this one time. To add a permanent contact, open the Fax Browser program, click the phone book icon, and then click the New Contact button and type your information in the Fax Numbers directory. Now it will show up in the pop-up list of contacts when you prepare to fax your document.

4. Click Send to process your fax and get it ready to be transferred to your recipient.

To send a fax to a recipient in your FAXstf phone book, just click and drag the name to the Destinations field in your FaxPrint dialog box.

Depending on the size of the document, it will take a few moments for FAXstf to process it. Then you'll see a screen appear on your computer labeled *FaxStatus* that will display the progress of the faxing operation.

Receiving a Fax

To receive faxes automatically, you'll need to configure FAXstf to run in receive mode.

Here's how it's done:

1. Launch the Fax Browser program.
2. Choose Settings from the Edit menu.
3. Scroll to the Fax Modem icon and click it, which opens the screen shown in Figure 10.6.

FIGURE 10.6

Select the number of rings before the fax is answered from the Answer On pop-up menu.

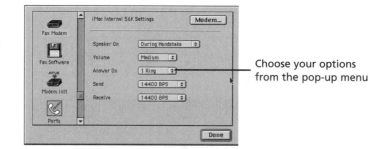

Choose your options from the pop-up menu

4. Choose the number of rings before the fax modem answers a call. From one to three rings is normal. Some fax machines give up trying after five or six rings, so don't set it that high.

> If your modem shares your voice phone line, you'll probably want to have the fax software answer after three or four rings, to give you time to pick up the phone.

▲   5. Click Done to put the settings in effect.

From here on, your iMac will be ready to receive faxes for you, so long as it's on when the call arrives. You can use the Fax Browser software to check the fax after it arrives.

Learning to Cook with Your iMac

For the rest of this lesson, I'll briefly touch on three of the other great programs that you'll find on your iMac's hard drive. The first is designed to help even clumsy-fingered folks like me learn how to cook.

It's the Williams-Sonoma Guide to Good Cooking from Broderbund.

To start working with this program:

1. Open up your iMac's accessory box and take out the Guide to Good Cooking CD.

2. Insert the CD into your iMac's drive. Be sure you press the CD tray in and wait a few seconds for the drive to spin up and mount the CD.

3. Locate the WS Guide to Good Cooking folder inside your iMac's application folder and double-click the WS Guide program icon. After a few credits roll by (and the theme song plays), you'll see the screen shown in Figure 4.7.

To Do

10

When you launch the WS Guide software, it may request that your color "depth" setting (the number of colors displayed on your screen) be changed. Go ahead and click Yes to the change. It will revert back to your previous setting when you quit the program.

FIGURE 10.7
Choose the sort of cooking information you want from the WS Guide's kitchen.

Click an icon to open the feature

4. For this exercise, click the Recipe Finder icon, which opens the screen shown in Figure 10.8.

FIGURE 10.8
Select your recipe here.

Click the icons at left to customize

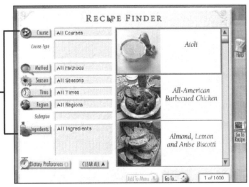

If you have special diet requirements, click the Dietary Preferences button shown at the lower left of Figure 10.8 to customize your selections.

To explore the program, just click the various buttons. To open a recipe, simply click the picture showing that dish.

Here are a few more WS Guide to Good Cooking features you'll want to check out:

- **Recipe Finder**: Search through more than 1,000 recipe cards, covering a wide range of choices from meat to fowl to vegetables.

- **A-Z Recipe Index**: The entire menu of recipes can also be examined in alphabetical sequence.

- **Favorite Recipes**: Create a scrapbook of the recipes you like from among those available in this program.

- **Menu Planner**: Organize an entire meal, using up to six separate recipe cards. You can also consult a set of recommended menus provided with the program.

- **Glossary**: If you're new to all this, you may just want to see what some of the terms really mean.

- **Online Videos**: The CD includes 66 videos showing cooking techniques. It's like having a chef at hand to guide you along the way to a successful meal. No more burned meat loaf.

10

Cleaning Up Photos with Soap

A decidedly different way to edit images is available in the form of Kai's Photo Soap from MetaCreations. It looks very different from the programs you've worked with so far (and in fact, it looks different from most Mac programs).

But unlike the other software I've covered so far, Kai's Photo Soap isn't on your iMac's hard drive when you set it up. You have to install it. Now don't worry about having to do anything really complex. Installation of this program is easy, and what you learn here applies to most of the programs you'll be installing as you expand the software lineup on your iMac.

Here's what you need to do to get Soap on your iMac:

▼ To Do

1. Locate the Soap CD in the CD wallet in your iMac's accessory box.
2. Insert the CD in the drive.
3. Double-click the CD's icon to bring up its directory.
4. In the directory, click the Soap icon labeled English.
5. Locate the item labeled Kai's Photo Soap SE Installer and double-click it, which opens the screen shown in Figure 10.9.

NEW TERM   The designation SE is commonly used to mean a "special" or limited edition of a program. Sometimes an advanced feature will be missing, but the program is otherwise fully functional. The LE designation is also used to identify this sort of product.

FIGURE 10.9
*Here's the Kai's Photo
Soap installer screen.*

Click Continue
to proceed

6. On the main screen, click the Continue button to move on.

7. The next screen will show the program's Read Me file, which offers some installation and setup tips. Click Continue to proceed.

 The Soap Read Me file can be saved to your iMac's drive or printed for later review, simply by clicking the buttons that have these labels.

8. Click the Install Location pop-up menu and select the Applications folder from the dialog box.

9. To install the program itself, click the Paint Brush icon on the next screen. You'll see a prompt informing you that other applications must be quit to install Soap. Click Continue to move on.

10. Over the next minute or so, you'll see a screen with a progress bar, showing you the status of the Soap installation process. When it's finished, you'll see a Restart prompt. Click the Restart button to restart your computer, so that you can use the program.

Of course, not all programs can be installed by pressing a paint brush. Most have a button labeled Install (now how's that for having a way with words?). But the basic procedure is the same.

Getting Started with Soap

Before attempting to run Soap, make sure that the program's CD is in your computer's drive. It won't work without it.

After your computer has restarted, locate the Kai's Photo Soap SE folder inside your Applications folder. Double-click the program's icon, which will produce an introductory screen, followed by Soap's unique IN Room (see Figure 10.10)—its main command center.

FIGURE 10.10
Soap takes over your computer's screen with a totally unique look.

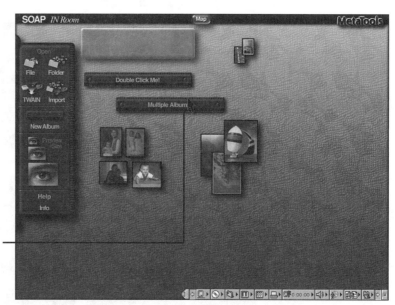

Click an icon to activate the feature

You'll see that Soap doesn't have a menu bar that resembles any other Mac program (or in fact programs on that "other" platform). It's almost like having a brand new operating system, but everything is clearly labeled and all you have to do is click here, drag there, and you'll be able to come up to speed on the program without much bother.

Each element of Soap is identified by a specific type of "scrubbing" room that you enter to do your work. Here's some of what the program can do:

- **Map Room**: This is your starting point, the gateway to the other features of Soap. Click a room's icon in the Map Room to move to the next function.

- **Prep Room**: Visit here to prepare your image for editing. You can resize the photo (make it bigger or larger), rotate it (so it's at a different angle), and crop it to select only a part of it.
- **Tone Room**: Adjust the tonal balance of your image, such as brightness and contrast.
- **Color Room**: Here's where you can actually adjust the colors of the image you want to work with.
- **Detail Room**: Enter here to make an image sharper or smoother (see Figure 10.11). If you're working with photos, you even have the option of removing that "red eye" effect. That's the effect you sometimes see in a photo when folks look like they haven't slept in a few days (or have had one too many the night before).

FIGURE **10.11**

As you can see, this sample photo needs a little work, well, more than a little work.

Click a button to
activate the feature

- **Finish Room**: Here's where you do the final touchups, change background colors, and apply special effects.
- **Out Room**: When you're finished editing a photo, you can save it to your computer's drive or make a print.

Creating Your Own Web Site with Adobe PageMill

When you set up an account on AOL or an Internet Service Provider such as EarthLink, you get a quick way to create your own Web site.

On AOL the feature is called 1-2-3 Publish, which you can reach by the AOL keyword of the same name. For EarthLink, the feature is called Click-n-Build, and you'll be able to access it direct from your Personal Start Page. Either way, you can create a simple Web page just by answering a few questions, typing in a paragraph or two, and choosing some artwork from the selections provided.

Over time, though, you might just want to do something better, more sophisticated. And the tools to do that come right on your iMac, in the form of a program from Adobe called PageMill. This is a program that creates documents in the language of the Web (called HyperText Markup Language or HTML), but hides it all behind a simple graphical interface. In fact, the program doesn't look all that different from a word processor, such as AppleWorks.

10

Some of the earliest iMacs did not come with Adobe PageMill. However the program is available from dealers, if your appetite is whetted by this brief description of what it can do. You can also get a demonstration version of the program from Adobe's Web site at http://www.adobe.com.

Adobe PageMill is a easy-to-use, yet flexible program for creating Web pages. You can start with a few simple paragraphs and a photo and end up with something quite sophisticated.

At the core, a Web site is just a collection of files, consisting of text and graphics. When you put them all together, they become your Web site.

To get started, you'll want to install PageMill. It's not placed on your iMac's drive when it comes from the factory:

▼ To Do

1. Locate the Adobe PageMill CD in the CD wallet in your iMac's accessory box.
2. Place the CD in the drive.
3. Double-click the CD's icon to bring up its directory.
4. Double-click on the icon labeled Install Adobe PageMill 3.0

▼   5. Click Continue at the opening screen to proceed.

6. On the next screen, select the country in which you reside (so the proper version is installed). The US and Canada is selected by default. Click OK to continue.

7. Read the software license (each program you use has a license that covers how the program can be used). Then click Accept to move on to the main installer screen.

8. Click Install to begin the actual process, which will take a couple of minutes to complete.

9. After installation you'll be asked to proceed through a small questionnaire, which is used to register the product. When you're done, you'll see the final installation

▲   screen. Click Quit to finish.

The Adobe PageMill 3.0 folder will be placed on the main directory of your iMac's drive. You can leave it there, or drag the entire directory to the Applications folder to keep it with your other programs.

As part of the regular installation process, you can actually specify a different location for the installation. But it's just as easy to put the program's folder there afterward.

A Fast Tour of Adobe PageMill

Once you've installed Adobe PageMill, you'll want to take a few moments to get acquainted with the program. There is a very good help system with the program, but if you want more information at hand, check out the installation CD, and look for a folder labeled User Manuals. Inside that folder are two electronic manuals for the program. The first, called "Getting Started," will guide you step-by-step through the process of setting up your first Web page and uploading the files to your Internet service provider.

Here's a brief overview of how to get your Web page started:

1. Locate and double-click on the Adobe PageMill icon. This will bring up an empty document screen (see Figure 10.12).

2. Type your message in the text entry window (see Figure 10.13). The toolbar above the text window can be used to style your text.

You are limited in how accurately you can adjust styles on your Web page, since Web browsers work differently in interpreting a site. You'll find, for example, text sizes are relative, such as smaller or larger, or largest.

▼

FIGURE **10.12**

You can place text and pictures in your Adobe PageMill document and have it ready to go in short order.

Click on the text
window to enter text ——

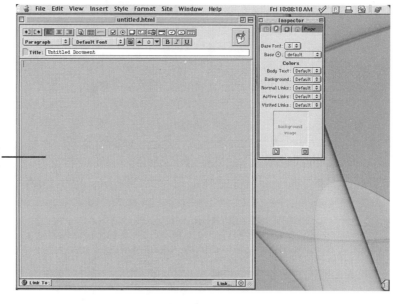

FIGURE **10.13**

This is the introduction to the author's Web site.

Use the toolbar to
style your text

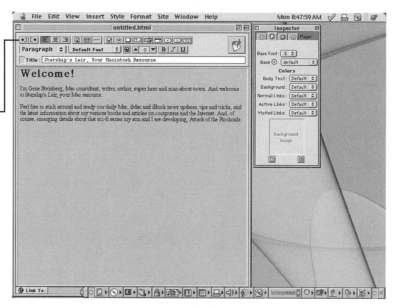

3. Before continuing you'll want to save your new document, so you won't lose anything should your iMac crash. Just choose Save As from the File menu and give the file a name. An introductory or home page for a Web site is usually called either index.html or index.htm. If you use something a little more creative, it won't be recognized by a Web browser as a home page.

▼   4. After you enter text, no doubt you'll want to add a photo or drawing to spruce up the site. To insert an image on your Web page, first click on the text window where you want the picture to be placed.

5. Click on the Insert Object toolbar button, which is located at the right of the text orientation buttons on the PageMill toolbar.

6. In the Insert Object dialog, locate and select the image you want to add.

7. Click Insert to include the image.

8. When you're finished creating your Web page, choose Check Spelling from the Edit menu to spell check your text.

9. Finished? Not quite. Now that you're Web site is ready, you have to actually upload it to your online service. In order to do that, choose Upload from the Edit menu and enter the information needed to access your service.

> Each Internet or online service has its own requirements for uploading your Web site. For example, on AOL, you'll want to use the keyword *My Place* to access the upload area. You'll want to check your service's help information for the proper upload method.

▲   10. Once your site is uploaded, you'll be able to access it via the address or URL your service has set for your Web site. Figure 10.14 shows how my Web site looks through a browser.

FIGURE 10.14

Yes, this is my real Web site, or at least the version that was set up at the time this book was written.

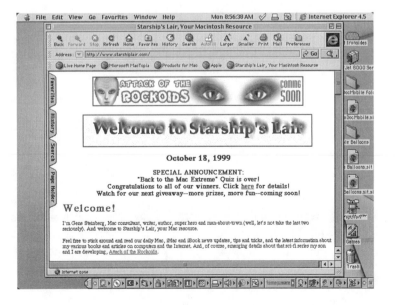

I've only scratched the surface of the program's capabilities here. In addition to adding text and images, Adobe PageMill is capable of professional-caliber work. It can easily handle a lot of complex Web features. These include animation, order forms, frames, sounds, tables and lots more. As you continue to work with the program, you'll be amazed how many cool things you can add to your Web site. The online help menus and the electronic manuals will guide you safely through the tasks.

Summary

In this lesson, you were introduced to the simple methods of making your computer function as a fax machine. You worked with some cooking software, you were shown a really clever way to retouch photos, and you learned how you can create your own Web site.

Each program shown here comes with an extensive set of instructions. They begin with the online Help menus. And some programs also include online manuals that you can read onscreen and print for further reference.

In Hour 11, "The Internet: Learning the Ropes," I'll focus entirely on the Internet. You've probably already had a chance to visit the World Wide Web, but there's a lot more for you to see, so check out the next lesson.

10

Q&A

Q I sent a fax of a drawing with the EPS label on it and the recipient complained that the quality was awful. What went wrong?

A EPS files come in a language called PostScript, which is used by publishers to get high-quality illustrations. But fax software doesn't support PostScript and can only send the low-resolution screen preview of the illustration. That's the limitation of this process. I've seen attempts to support PostScript in fax software from time to time, but so far, it hasn't succeeded.

But just about any other text or picture can be faxed without trouble with pretty decent quality.

Q I tried to send a fax, but nothing happened. I didn't hear the phone dial on my iMac. What went wrong?

A It's a good idea to double-check your modem hookup. Make sure that your phone cable is plugged into your wall jack and your computer's modem jack before you send a fax.

Q **There's a busy signal. Will FAXstf dial again?**

A Yes. The normal setting is to redial three times, five minutes apart. You can change this setup by using the Settings panel in your Fax Browser software.

Q **I turn off my iMac at night. How do I receive faxes then?**

A Okay, you've got me there. This is one limitation of a fax modem. Your computer must be on for it to work. Otherwise, you might really want to think about getting a regular fax machine (they aren't quite obsolete yet).

Q **I tried to run the WS Guide to Good Cooking, and I got an error message. What happened?**

A Try it again and check the error message. You may have just seen a prompt telling you that you need to use the program's CD to work with the software.

If your computer freezes when you try to run this program, or any program, check out Hour 24, "An iMac Safety Net," for some troubleshooting hints.

Q **I installed Kai's Photo Soap, but it's not in the Applications folder. Where is it?**

A If you missed the option to select your destination when you installed Soap, you'll find it at the top level of your computer's drive directory. You can leave the program where it is, or drag the program folder to the Applications folder icon and have it hang out with the other software you have.

Q **My iMac has some software you didn't discuss in this book. Why?**

A Apple Computer, naturally, reserves the right to change the software package as it wants, for special promotions, or because they've made new agreements with software publishers.

The programs I'm covering in this book came along with the original iMac packages. Over time you'll see other programs added to the list. For example, some iMacs come with Palm Desktop, a program that lets you work with 3Com's line of Palm Pilot handheld computers.

And, though I hate to say it, some of those changes may mean that some of the software packages I'm describing won't be there at all. But there's nothing to stop you from visiting your software dealer and buying a copy of any of these programs if you like what you see.

In addition, some dealers may offer custom software packages at a slight additional cost. The possibilities are endless.

HOUR 11

The Internet: Learning the Ropes

When you connect to another computer or a networked printer, you're on a network. The Internet is a network, too, only much larger. To the tune of millions of computers, sending and receiving information all day long, every day, all across the world.

And I suppose when humans are regularly exploring the far reaches of the universe, the scope of the Internet will be similarly expanded.

In this lesson, you'll get a chance to exercise your Internet surfing skills. You'll discover

- What some of that weird Internet jargon means.
- How to change your home page.
- How to make a list of favorite sites.
- How to search for information on the Internet (with a little help from Sherlock 2).
- How to download files.
- Whether Internet "cookies" really are something to be feared

Getting Started on the Internet

The first time you open your Web browser on your iMac, it goes to a special location, a home page. For this lesson, you'll need to have your Internet connection established to be able to take advantage of the information.

 NEW TERM   A *home page* is like the cover of a book. It's the introductory page at a Web site. A typical home page will tell you about the site and offer fast access to other parts of the site (or to other sites with similar content).

> If you're using America Online instead of a regular Internet service, you can still take advantage of the information here. A Web browser, based on Microsoft's Internet Explorer, is built into AOL's software. I'll cover some of the minor differences as we continue.

To run your Web browser, just do the following:

▼ To Do

1. Go to the Apple menu and choose Internet Access and select Browse the Internet from the submenu. This will launch the Microsoft Internet Explorer browser and start your Internet connection. If everything is set up properly, you'll see Apple Remote Access, your iMac's Internet dialing machine, doing its thing and connecting you to your net provider. Once connected, your home page will appear (see Figure 11.1).

FIGURE 11.1

Here's the author's personal EarthLink Start Page.

Click a button or underlined title to bring up another page

▼ 2. Click any underlined title or button to see another page. For this example, I'll select EarthLink's Entertainment channel (see Figure 11.2).

FIGURE 11.2

A single click takes you to another Web page or even another site altogether.

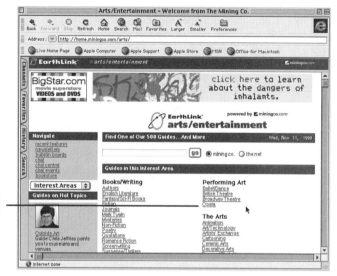

Click any underlined title to see more

3. To return to the previous page (whatever it is), click the Back arrow on the toolbar. The Forward arrow takes you to the next page (if there is one). Click the Home ▲ icon to go back to the home page you selected.

Feel free to spend a little time clicking here and there to see whatever information suits your fancy. A quick click of the Home icon on the toolbar gets you back where you started. Your browser will track your visits via a history file.

If you've visited lots of sites during your session, you can access any one of them quickly by clicking the Go menu and selecting that site from the list. You can also access the history and other features by clicking the tabs at the left of your browser window.

 A *history* file simply records the sites you visited with your Web browser during your session, so you can get to them again.

Making Sense of URLs

The clever folks who designed the World Wide Web devised a way to summon a site quickly without knowing the exact route. Unfortunately, it's not in plain English, so it might seem a little confusing. You call up a Web site by its URL.

NEW TERM   *URL* is short for Uniform Resource Locator, and it's the syntax used to identify a Web site so that it can be accessed.

Let's see what all those little letters and numbers mean by calling up a common, garden variety Web site—Apple's. You can access it this way:

1. Click the Address field below your browser's toolbar.

2. Enter the following: http://www.apple.com (do it exactly as I have written it).

3. Press the Return or Enter key on your iMac's keyboard. Your Web browser will send the request for the site across the Internet and then retrieve the information to display in your computer. In a few seconds, you'll see Apple Computer's home page, just as you see in Figure 11.3.

FIGURE 11.3

Welcome to the home of the "Think Different" folks, Apple Computer, Inc.

Click a picture to see more

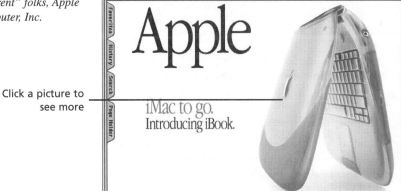

When you open your Internet Explorer browser, you'll find there's already an icon for Apple Computer right below the Address field.

▼   4. To see more information at Apple's site, just click any of the colorful pictures.

> Not all pictures you see at a Web site can be clicked to take you to another destination. You'll know you can access such a destination (or link) with a picture when your mouse cursor changes to a hand whenever you point it over the picture.

▲

Let's dissect Apple's URL to see what the information means:

- **http://**   This prefix tells the browser that you're asking for a Web site. If it has an **ftp://** prefix, it means you're accessing a file transfer site instead (it stands for "file transfer protocol").

- **www**   This information tells the browser this is the URL for a Web site, though a number of URLs don't have it.

> If a site's URL has the telltale www letters in it (and not all do), you can skip the http:// prefix and just enter the rest of address. The Web browser is clever enough to know what you want.

- **apple**   This is the first part of the site's domain name.

NEW TERM   A *domain* is the online equivalent of the street address of the Web site. It tells the browser where to go to get what you want.

> Each part of a URL, except for the prefix, is separated by a period or a slash. Don't forget to enter the correct character where needed to get to the right place.

- **com**   This identifies the site as commercial. The suffix **edu** means the site is an educational institution, **org** represents an organization of some sort (usually a charitable organization or club). If you see **be** as the suffix, the site is located in Belgium. When the suffix is **ca**, the site is located in Canada, and **uk** represents the United Kingdom (and **co** identifies a commercial site from that country).

If you've visited a site before, you'll notice your Web browser will try to fill (or autofill) the missing information when you begin to enter the URL. If it's correct, just stop typing and press Return or Enter to get to where you want. Otherwise continue to enter the proper address.

URLs are not case sensitive, so it really shouldn't matter whether you enter the address with upper- or lowercase letters. But if a site has a password as part of a URL, you'll need to type that perfectly (upper- and lowercase, as required).

Making Your Own List of Web Favorites

Over time, you'll visit Web sites you'd like to return to again and again. But you'll find out that the Go menu's history file is only good for a few dozen sites. The older sites are automatically removed from the list.

What to do?

Fortunately, your browser has a way to store the URLs of sites for quick retrieval. You can take advantage of this feature by using the Favorites menu. It's the best trick this side of *Star Trek's* "Beam me up, Scotty" routine to quickly get where you want to go. Here's how it works:

1. Access the site you want to revisit regularly. For this lesson, I've chosen my regular business Web site, Starship's Lair (see Figure 11.4).

2. Click the Favorites menu (see Figure 11.5) and choose the first option, Add Page to Favorites. The site you've opened will immediately become a part of this menu. Real neat!

You can save a trip to the Favorites menu by typing Command+D to add the page to the list.

3. If you want to check the sites you've added in order to change or remove them, choose the second command in the Favorites menu, Open Favorites, or choose the Favorite button on the toolbar.

FIGURE **11.4**

If you like this place, you can make it a Favorite for quick return visits.

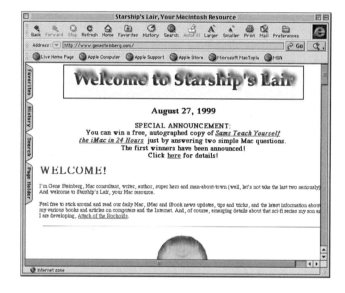

FIGURE **11.5**

Your Favorites menu can be quickly customized to your taste.

4. To remove a site, simply select it from your Favorites directory and press the Delete key. Acknowledge your decision to delete on the next screen and zap—it's gone. Once again, you can also access your Favorites by clicking the tab at the left of the browser window.

AOL members have a different way to store sites for fast retrieval, and it works with any area you access on that service. It's called a Favorite Place. If the area or site can be added to your Favorite Place directory, you'll see a small, heart-shaped icon at the upper right of the title bar. Just click it to add that location (or insert the location in your email).

11

Searching the Internet

There are literally millions of sites on the Web. Some are run by large commercial enterprises, such as Apple Computer, or government institutions, such as the CIA or IRS (yes, really!). And each and every site might have hundreds or even thousands of pages to access.

The possibilities are almost mind-boggling. Fortunately, with easy Web access and easy ways to make sites, there are also easy ways to find the information you want.

In Hour 7, "Opening, Saving, Finding, Moving, Etc.," I introduced you to Apple's clever Sherlock search tool. To briefly recap, Sherlock 2 lets you:

- Find files on your computer's drive.
- Find text inside a file.
- Search for information on the Internet.

Sherlock 2 is a great way to automate Web searching. It works behind the scenes to access huge Web search tools to locate something.

But you'll often find that a direct visit to those search sites can provide a more leisurely way to explore the Internet. To see the possibilities, click the Search icon on your Web browser, which will open a screen similar to the one shown in Figure 11.6.

FIGURE 11.6

I've set my Web browser to access Yahoo! (http://www. yahoo.com) as the search locale, but you can pick another if you want.

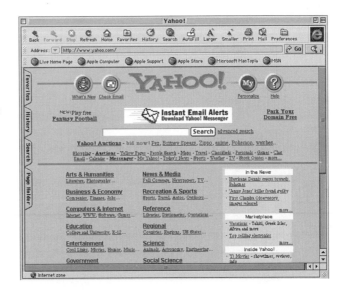

When you set up your Web access, you might find that a different search site is selected. No problem. You can try that site or change it to another site by entering that site's URL in your Internet Control Panel. I'll tell you more about making such settings in Hour 16, "Using Control Panels to Customize Your iMac."

You'll see that Web search sites do a lot more than just search. Here are other things you'll often find at these locales:

- **News and financial information**: The search site links to a news service, such as CNN or Reuters, to offer hourly updates on the day's events.

- **Recommended sites**: The search site's management reviews new places, often every day, and will recommend popular watering holes for further review.

- **Ads**: You can often place personal and business ads at a Web search site or find fast links to such places.

- **Free email**: Sites such as Yahoo! let you create your own personal email account (although you received one when you joined an Internet service).

- **Custom settings**: You can set up a search site front page to look the way you want (very much like EarthLink's Start Page). When you click the My icon at Yahoo!'s home page, for example, you'll see a sample Front Page that you can tailor to your own needs (see Figure 11.7). Check the Personalize This Site screen to customize the page.

FIGURE 11.7

This is my personalized front page at Yahoo!'s Web site.

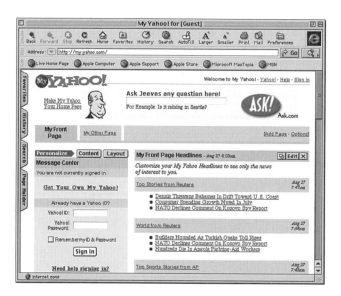

There are several large Web sites that basically compete with Yahoo!. The best thing to do is to try out a few for size and see which one works best for you. Here are some of the others:

- **AltaVista**: `http://www.altavista.com`
- **Excite**: `http://www.excite.com`
- **AOL NetFind**: `http://www.aol.com/netfind`. Nope, you don't have to be an AOL member to use this search tool (although it's similar in many respects to Excite because it uses Excite's search capabilities).
- **HotBot**: `http://www.hotbot.com`
- **Infoseek**: `http://www.infoseek.com`
- **LookSmart**: `http://www.looksmart.com`
- **Lycos**: `http://www.lycos.com`
- **Netscape Netcenter**: `http://home.netscape.com`

The Web search sites shown use different techniques to ferret out information, so what you find at one site might be different from what you find at another. And don't forget, Apple's Sherlock 2 search program can check a number of search engines to find what you want.

Downloading Files from the Internet

The Internet is not just a place for information. It's a place where you can get pictures and software, too. As you explore various sites, you'll find "download" areas and other places where you can retrieve files and transfer them to your computer.

Before I show you how to download a file from a Web site, here are two points to consider:

- **Compatibility**: If you're downloading software, check the information at the Web site on whether the software can run on your iMac. Look for something that specifies compatibility with a Macintosh. If it says Windows or DOS, you won't be able to use the program, unless you buy one of those PC emulator programs (see Hour 18, "Coping with the Windows World").

- **Computer Viruses**: Movies such as *The Net* and *Independence Day* have romanticized the unlikely notion of using a computer virus to beat the bad guys. But in our real world, a computer virus is something vicious. It can cause your computer to crash, or even damage your files. Although major online areas will check their files to be sure they're virus free before putting them up, you should arm yourself with virus protection software before you attempt to get these files. See Hour 24, "An iMac Safety Net," for advice.

With the preliminaries out of the way, let's find a file to download and see how it's done:

1. For this lesson, first access Apple's support Web site, at `http://www.apple.com/support`, which opens the screen shown in Figure 11.8.

2. Look for the Mac OS CD icon, place your mouse cursor above it and choose Software Updates from the list that appears to the left of the CD icon. In a few seconds, you'll see Apple's software updates page (see Figure 11.9).

FIGURE 11.8

Apple's support Web site has files and troubleshooting information for all users of their products.

3. Locate a file title under Featured Software and click the Get button.

4. On the next window, click the name of the file you want to retrieve. In a few seconds, you'll see the Internet Explorer Download Manager window (see Figure 11.10). If you want to stop the download, just click the filename, press the Delete key, OK your decision on the following screen and the process stops.

FIGURE **11.9**

Get software for your iMac and other Apple products from this site.

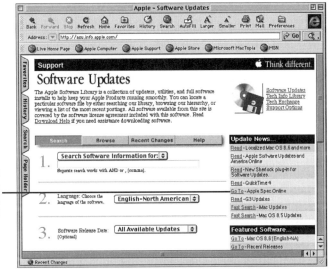

Click any item to bring up information or start a download

FIGURE **11.10**

This file transfer is now in progress.

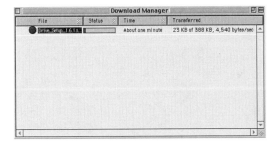

In addition to the actual file you want to download, most sites will offer a link to an instruction file or a page that explains how to install the software. Look for telltale references to such titles as Instructions, Read, or Text for this information.

The Low-Down on Internet Cookies

You've heard the warnings. When you visit a Web site, they are apt to send you a dangerous thing called a *cookie* that can ferret out the secrets of your hard drive, damage your files, or just cause general annoyance.

NEW TERM In the online world a *cookie* is not something that tastes better with milk. It's actually a small file that is sent to your computer when you visit a Web site. It saves information about the places you visited at the site so that you can access them more efficiently next time you go there.

When you visit a Web site for the first time, perhaps you signed a guest book or you took a certain route through the various pages that made up the site. Maybe you had to establish a password to get in.

When you visit that site, it sends a little file to your computer. This file, the cookie, is designed to track that information, so the folks who run the site can see which areas are visited most frequently (it helps them sell ads, frankly). The cookie also helps you get where you want quickly.

I suppose that it's possible to imagine there's some insidious purpose behind those cookies, and that someone out there really wants to steal your financial information or whatever. But in the real world, cookies aren't really anything to worry about.

Now death and taxes—well, that's something else again.

11

The words "It's a jungle out there" were never more true where the Internet is concerned. Although most sites are safe, there is a lot of content out there that might offend you. And if your kids access the Internet, you'll want to put some safety measures in place. With Internet Explorer, just choose Preferences from the Edit menu and select the Ratings option. You'll then be able to set custom settings to stop access to sites with unacceptable content. AOL members can also use a feature called Parental Controls.

Summary

This lesson offered you a tutorial on Internet use. You learned how to change your browser settings to point to a different Web site when you start up, how to locate information, and how to transfer files to your computer. You also discovered how to store a list of your favorite Web sites, so you can get back to them in seconds.

Many of you join an Internet service just to send email, and I'll cover that subject in Hour 12, "The Wonderful World of Email."

Q&A

Q I tried to access a Web site. But the attempt to load it failed. What's wrong?

A There are several reasons why you won't be able to access a site. Here's what to check:

- Make sure that you are still connected to your Internet service. Sometimes a poor connection will result in getting disconnected, but usually Apple Remote Access, your connection software, will report that after a short time.

- Double-check the URL to that site. If you enter even one letter or number incorrectly when specifying the address, you won't be able to connect to the site (or you'll get the wrong place).

- Web sites might be run by no more than a single computer, perhaps one not much different from your iMac. If that computer crashes (or is down for maintenance), you won't be able to connect. There's nothing you can do but try again at a later time.

Q I notice you're using Microsoft's Internet Explorer for this lesson. Do I really have to use Microsoft's product? Is there any alternative?

A Absolutely. You do have a choice, and the choice is Netscape. You'll find a copy of the program is already installed on your iMac. Just check the folder labeled Internet Applications, inside the Internet folder, and a recent version of Netscape will be there for you to try. You can run that instead of Internet Explorer if you prefer. Just remember that Netscape calls its Favorites feature Bookmarks, but the function is the same.

Q I started downloading a file from the Internet, but then I got disconnected. How do I get it back?

A If you're using Internet Explorer, you can sometimes resume the file download (but it's not 100 percent dependable). Just choose Download Manager from the File menu and double click the listing for the file you tried to retrieve. Then choose your downloading option. You'll be connected back to that site and, if all goes well, the file download will continue where it left off. But as I said, the process isn't perfect, and sometimes it'll just try and try and not succeed. In that event, you'll just need to start the file download from scratch.

Q Okay, I downloaded a file. Now where is it and what do I do with it?

A Your iMac comes with a little program, StuffIt Expander, that can process the file after you get it and convert it to a form that you can use. After that's done, take a look at your computer's desktop. You'll see the file there. If you double-click it, it'll either open the file or start the installation process. If you're not sure what to do, go back to the site and see if there's a text or instruction page there with further instructions.

Q It didn't work. I got the file but I didn't see any StuffIt Expander or anything like that. What happened to it?

A Use Sherlock 2's file search feature to locate StuffIt Expander on your hard drive. If it's not there, you might need to go back to your original system CD. You'll probably be able to locate a copy on that CD (just look for it with Sherlock). After you find the file, click the folder that contains StuffIt Expander and drag it to the Internet folder on your computer's hard drive. In a few seconds it'll be copied over. Your Web browser will know what to do with it after you download a file.

11

Hour 12

The Wonderful World of Email

Have you noticed your letter carrier's "pouch" looking a little lighter these days? It's not because folks have stopped sending mail. Far from it. It's the result of sending mail via a different method.

In this lesson, you'll learn how to use email to communicate quickly with millions of people around the world.

You'll discover

- How to address your email so it gets to the right destination.
- How to send files over the Internet.
- How AOL's email setup differs from the rest of the world.
- What email spam is all about and how to deal with it.
- The truth about those email hoaxes.

Learning How to Send Email

You don't need an envelope, a stamp, or even a piece of paper. After you set up your Internet account, sending email is really quite simple. And you don't need to buy any special software. Your iMac already has a program that will do the job just fine for you: Microsoft's Outlook Express.

> If you've opted to use Netscape rather than Microsoft Internet Explorer as your Web browser, you'll be pleased to know that it has its own email feature, called Messenger, that has pretty much the same features I'm covering in this lesson. In addition, there are two nifty commercial programs, Eudora (from Qualcomm) and Mailsmith (from Bare Bones Software) that you might wish to check out.

Here's how to get started with Internet email:

▲ To Do

1. Click the Mail icon on your iMac's desktop. If it's not there, choose Internet Access from the Apple menu and select Mail from the submenu. Either result will launch Outlook Express (see Figure 12.1).

FIGURE **12.1**

Use Microsoft Outlook Express to send and receive email.

Click an icon to
activate that feature

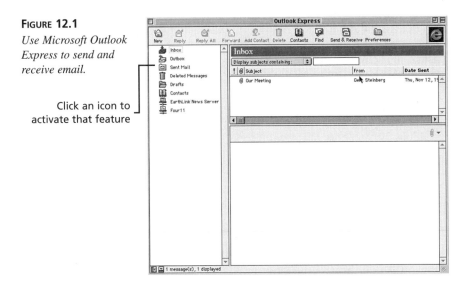

> If you prefer to use the keyboard to bring up a new message window, type Command+N instead.

2. To send a new message, click the New icon, which brings up a blank message window (see Figure 12.2).

FIGURE 12.2

Write your email on this form.

Click tab to move through the text fields

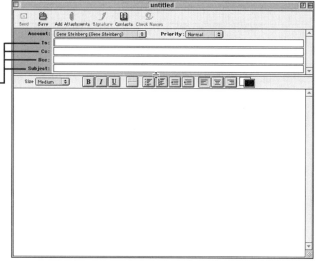

3. If you don't know of anyone to send a message to, just enter your own email address in the To field. This is, after all, only a test.

> The Cc field is used to send a courtesy copy (or carbon copy) to someone else. The Bcc is a blind copy, which means that the recipient won't know who else got a copy.

4. Use the Tab key to step through to the subject line and give your message a topic name.

5. Click Tab to move to the message window and write your message.

12

> The toolbar in the message window is similar to the one you saw in programs such as AppleWorks. It's used to format your email document.

6. When you're finished writing your message, the Send button will darken. Click Send to mail it. Your Internet provider will be dialed and, when you're connected, your email will go on its way.

> Be careful about applying text formats to your email message. Unless you know for sure that the person who gets your message is using Outlook Express, expect that any of the formatting you set so diligently may look like plain, old, unvarnished text when opened. While other Internet email programs may interpret the text with reasonable accuracy, AOL's email feature may not.

> After your email is sent, click the Remote Access icon on your Control Strip (the little toolbar at the bottom of your computer's screen) and choose the Disconnect command to log off.

A Fast Guide to Internet Addresses

As you saw in Hour 11, "The Internet: Learning the Ropes," Internet communications have to follow a strict format to work. And the same is true about email. Here's how to address your email so that it gets to the right place without any problem.

For this example, I'll dissect an email address I use with my AOL account, **gene@aol.com** (cards and letters welcome):

> If you're on AOL and you're sending email to another member on the service, you don't have to add the domain information (@aol.com). AOL's email system will figure that out automatically.

- **gene**: This is my Internet name or screen name.

- **@aol.com**: This is the domain name, the location where the email account is located. As I explained in Hour 11, a designation of **com** means it's a commercial site, **org** refers to an organization, and so on. You'll also find the suffix net for some Internet services, such as **@earthlink.net**. My EarthLink address, by the way, is gsteinberg@earthlink.net.

- **Don't use the spacebar!** The Internet doesn't recognize an empty space, and will ignore everything before it. If the email address has two names in it separated by a space, use an underscore (_) instead, such as **gene_steinberg**. Quite often eliminating the space entirely will work just as well.

- **Caps don't matter!** Uppercase, lowercase, makes no difference.

Sending Files with Your Email

Your email isn't limited to just a message. You can transfer files that way, too. If you want to include a file with your email message, just follow these steps:

1. Address and write your email as described previously. Before sending it, click the Add Attachments button on your Outlook Express email form, which opens the dialog box shown in Figure 12.3.

FIGURE 12.3

Choose the file or files you want to send.

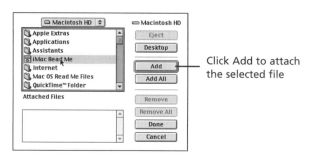

Click Add to attach the selected file

12

2. Locate the file you want to send in the dialog box (using the information you learned in Hour 7, "Opening, Saving, Finding, Moving, Etc.") and click Add. The file you've attached will appear in the bottom pane (half) of the dialog box.

To attach all the files in the opened folder, click the Add All button instead.

3. When you're finished, click Done to return to the email form (see Figure 12.4).

FIGURE 12.4

Your completed email with a file attached is ready to ship.

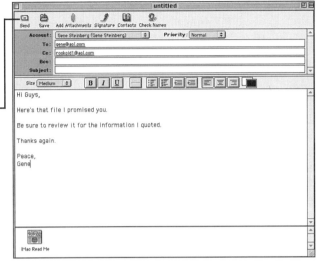

Click Send to mail it ⎤

If you add a file by mistake to the Attached Files list, just select it and click the Remove or Remove All button (if appropriate) to detach the file. Also please bear in mind that Internet services often restrict the size of file attachments to a few megabytes (check with the service to see). If files are too large, the email will be bounced (returned) back to you without reaching its destination. If you need to send a large file, you may consider buying a program that can compress files to make them smaller, such as Aladdin's StuffIt Deluxe.

Some More Great Email Features

As you saw back in Figure 12.4, there are some other features in your email software you'll want to use from time to time.

Here's what they do:

- **Save**: If you don't want to send your email right away, click this button to keep a copy for later shipment. If you have a lot of email to write, you may want to build up a collection (queue) and send them later on in one operation. The email will be stored in the Drafts folder in Outlook Express. In order to send it, you'll need to open it from there after you are connected.

- **Signature**: This feature lets you add your personalized signature to all your email (automatically), by the click of a button.

- **Contacts**: This feature lets you store the email address and other contact information for your friends and business associates (see Figure 12.5 for a sample). The New icon is used to add additional contacts to the list.

FIGURE 12.5

Here are a couple of contacts added to my address book (the first isn't real).

Click an icon to activate that function

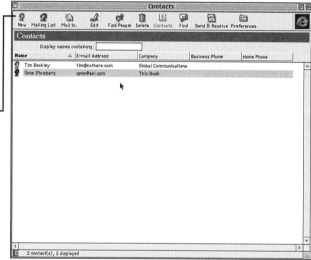

- **Check Names**: This feature is used to look for duplicate email addresses (so the recipient doesn't see the same thing twice).

12

> If you're not sure what an icon in Outlook Express does, simply hold the mouse cursor over it for a second. A label briefly describing its function (a *tooltip*) will soon appear. Many programs with toolbar icons have a similar feature.

How to Receive Email

That's the exciting part. After you write some email to your friends and business contacts, you'll probably want to check your Internet mailbox regularly to see what's there. And unlike the postal service, deliveries occur at any hour of the day or night, even on weekends and holidays and when it sleets, snows, and rains.

Here's how to access your email:

1. Launch Outlook Express.
2. Click the Send and Receive button. This operation will log you on to your Internet service (if you're not already connected), ship the email you've written and then retrieve the email that's waiting for you.
3. If there's email awaiting you, you'll see it displayed in the inbox (see Figure 12.6).

> You can also configure Outlook Express to automatically check your email at a regular interval. The option, under Outlook Express 4.5, is available when you choose Preferences from the Edit menu, and select the screen showing General Preferences.

FIGURE 12.6

You've got mail! No, wait, that's the announcement from the "other" online service.

Click the email listing to see the message

The little paper clip icon means a file is attached

4. To read the message, just click once on the listing (see Figure 12.7).

FIGURE 12.7

Here's my first email message (to myself).

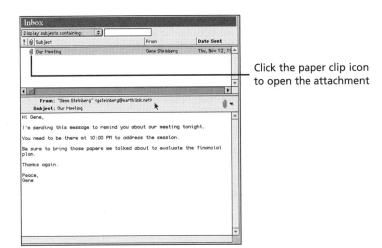

Click the paper clip icon to open the attachment

Replying to Email

If you want to answer the message, just follow these steps:

1. To reply to a particular passage in the message, click and drag on that passage to select it; then click the Reply button, which brings up the screen shown in Figure 12.8.

To Do

FIGURE **12.8**

Enter your response below the quoted text.

This is the text you selected when you clicked Reply

If the email was sent to multiple recipients, use the Reply All function if you want your response to go to the same people.

12

It's customary on the Internet to quote the relevant portions of a message when you respond. That way a busy recipient knows what you're talking about without having to refer to an older message. If you want to just say you agree to something, only quote enough of the message to show what you're agreeing to (not all of it, which just wastes everyone's time). You quote a portion of message simply by selecting it before you click the Reply or Reply All button. If you quote too much, you can always delete the extra text in your response before you send it.

▲ 2. Type your message; then click Send to ship it.

AOL Email Is Different

If you're an AOL member, you'll find that the same email features described previously (except for stored signatures) are there, but they look rather different.

To send email on AOL:

1. Log on to AOL.
2. Click the Mail icon on the AOL program toolbar (which brings up the screen shown in Figure 12.9).

> At the time this book was written, AOL didn't support separate email pro-grams, except for one, Claris Emailer. But that program has been discontin-ued, and may be hard to get (but it works really well if you're lucky enough to locate a copy).

FIGURE 12.9

AOL's email form may look different, but you can generally use it the same as you use Outlook Express.

Click an icon to activate that feature

3. Address your email.
4. Enter the subject.

> If you fail to enter a subject in the proper field, the email will usually go out with (no subject) in the subject line, but that may be confusing to the recipi-ent. Best thing to do is enter a subject description that applies to the mes-sage being sent, so the recipient can organize it properly if lots of messages are being received.

▼

▼ 5. If you want to attach a file, click the Attach Files icon and locate the file or files
      you want to send.

   6. Click the Send button to ship it.

> AOL users can take advantage of a special feature, Automatic AOL, to send
> and receive email and other messages at predetermined times (so long as
> your computer stays on). To set up the feature, click the Mail Center icon
> and choose the Set up Automatic AOL (FlashSessions) command.

▲

When you receive email on AOL, you'll hear that famous "You've Got Mail" announcement when it arrives (yes, just as in that movie with Tom Hanks and Meg Ryan).

Accessing the email is simply a matter of clicking the You've Got Mail icon, and selecting the messages you want to read. Piece of cake!

How to Combat Internet Spam!

When I was young (definitely in prehistoric times), Spam referred to a sort of lunch meat
of mixed composition. I actually remember putting it on a sandwich, but the flavor
eludes me, not to mention the ingredients on which it was based (hey, maybe I'm better
for not knowing).

Today, spam is the term for the Internet variation of the junk mail that fills your regular
mailbox. It comes in the form of offers for get rich quick schemes, porn sites, cheap
software, and more.

While no doubt some of it may consist of legitimate offers from real companies trying to
generate business on the cheap (and sending bulk email costs a fraction of what it costs
to mount a real direct mailing campaign), most of it is downright annoying.

Here are some tips on how to deal with this growing torrent of annoying material:

- **Don't respond to it!** Even if the message contains an address where you can ask
  to be removed from the list, ignore the message. When you send them email,
  you're only confirming that your email address is correct, and you make yourself
  vulnerable to getting more of it.

- **Complain to the Internet provider who sends it!** It's true that many of the
  addresses you see are forged, but that's your first line of attack. Forward the message (using that function in your email program) to the service from which the
  email may have originated. The usual address would be postmaster@*[domain]*

12

(the material in the bracket would represent the part of the address that follows the @ symbol, such as aol.com). Another is abuse@*[domain]*. Even if the email address is a fake, the major Internet services can examine the email for telltale information to see where it originally came from.

- **Don't expect miracles!** Services such as America Online have legal eagles on staff to combat this problem. They've even gone to court to get injunctions against the worst abusers. The reality is that spam won't stop completely. But if you report the problem to the appropriate parties, it can be reduced.

- **Look for compliance messages!** Legitimate bulk emailers are supposed to include their actual contact information in response to proposed government regulations. If you see this information, you'll have a source to whom to complain if you want to stop those mailings.

> When this book was being prepared, Microsoft announced a new version of its email software, Outlook Express 5, which will incorporate a Junk Mail Filter that can check your incoming email for the telltale signs of spam. If the incoming message fits the pattern, it will be marked "read" without you having to be bothered with it. Check Microsoft's MacTopia Web site at http://www.microsoft.com/mac for information on the latest updates to their Internet software.

The Low-Down on Email Virus Hoaxes

After you've been exchanging email for a while, no doubt you'll receive messages warning you not to open certain messages because they'll destroy your computer. You are asked to forward the email to everyone you know, to inform them of this great danger.

One infamous example of this sort of tomfoolery was the fake warnings about the so-called Good Times virus, which was forwarded to millions of people. Similar fake threats come from time to time. Here's some advice to consider:

- **Don't forward the message!** Spreading fear and confusion to others may itself be the actual virus here. And besides, sending chain letters (the ones that say to pass it on to someone else) is not allowed on AOL, EarthLink, or most other Internet services. If you forward those messages, you may only cause problems between yourself and the service you subscribe to.

- **Opening an email message won't give you the virus!** Aside from a rare bug that appeared in email programs a while back, you cannot get a computer virus just by reading a message. A virus can only be spread by a file that you can launch.

- **Watch out for unsolicited files from strangers!** You get them from time to time. A message from someone who says "Here's that photo you asked me for" with a few enticing lines. And then you see that there's a file attached to your email. Fortunately (for us, not them), most of the dangerous files sent this way only work with users of the "other" platform. They'll have .exe or .shs file extensions (to cover two examples). The folks who run those files (and again they're Windows-based files) can risk activating a real virus, or a program designed to steal the password they use for their online service.

- **Practice safe computing!** An old friend used to say in his public pronouncements, "Practice safe hex." But the meaning is the same. If you do lots of Internet visiting, you should definitely buy a virus protection program for your computer. Check out Hour 24, "An iMac Safety Net," for more information about this subject.

Summary

You may never use a stamp again after you get the hang of email. It lets you communicate to millions around the world without worry of rain, sleet, snow, or time of day. In fact, this entire book was written using email to transfer the completed manuscript files between my publisher and me.

In lucky Hour 13, "Multimedia Is More Than a CD-ROM Game," I'll introduce you to the wonderful world of multimedia, Apple style. And it's a lot more than just a fancy CD-ROM game, so stay tuned.

12

Q&A

Q Every time I try to send someone email from AOL it gets bounced back to me by some dude called MAILER-DAEMON@aol.com. Who is that person and what does he want with me?

A That's just AOL's automated notification name. You need to read the message to see why your email couldn't be delivered. Usually, it's because the email address was incorrect, or the recipient is no longer an AOL member.

Q I know the email address is correct. I've sent email to that recipient before and the account is still current. But the email gets rejected. Why?

A Internet services will, from time to time, shut down their service for maintenance. Sometimes there's an equipment failure that prevents email from getting to its destination. By virtue of its huge size, AOL handles more Internet email transactions than anyone else, and they've had some notable, well-publicized failures of the system on rare occasions. If your email is returned to you, just send it again. More than likely, by the time you sent it, the problem will be fixed, and it will get through.

Q Every time I send email to someone, I keep getting an angry response that I've reached the wrong party. Why is that person mad at me?

A Email addresses are very literal, and it's possible you've just got the wrong number there. Please remember to check the address carefully before you send the message. A single character or number incorrectly entered will send it to the wrong party (just as you press the wrong number on your phone dialing pad).

One of the consequences of having an easily remembered email address (such as the one I use on AOL, Gene) is that you become a target for misdirected email. I cannot tell you how often I get mail from folks thinking I am their long-lost uncle, brother, or son. Some have even sent me their resumes, tax returns, and more (really!).

Fortunately, a gentle reminder that they have made a mistake is enough to deal with the situation.

HOUR 13

Multimedia Is More Than a CD-ROM Game

Multimedia is an overused term. At its heart, it means the marriage of animation, audio, and video. Just about every personal computer is advertised as having multimedia capabilities, so I'm going to focus this lesson on what multimedia means to you and how the iMac can exploit this great capability.

In this lesson, you'll learn about the Apple technology that's so good it's being used by professional movie studios to create their products. It's called QuickTime.

You'll learn

- What QuickTime is (and isn't).
- How to view videos on your computer.
- How you can actually edit the pictures and sounds with QuickTime and iMovie.
- What QuickTime TV is.
- How to listen to an audio CD on your computer.

What QuickTime Can Do for You

First and foremost, QuickTime (by itself) isn't a program that you run. It's a set of tools that Apple developed that lets you create, edit, and view multimedia presentations on your Mac. There's even a Windows version, so your friends using the "other" platform don't have to feel left out in the cold.

The actual viewing and editing are done with programs that support the QuickTime technology. They range from the simple QuickTime Player application I'm going to cover here to sophisticated video editing software that commercial broadcasters use to create the programs you see every single day on TV.

Very briefly, here's what the current version of QuickTime provides for you:

- **Digital Video**: QuickTime offers techniques to compress video productions so they don't overwhelm your computer with their storage space needs. Without this compression, long video files (such as a movie or even a TV commercial) would be perfectly huge, far bigger than most computers could handle on any ordinary drive.

  NEW TERM *Compression* is a technique designed to make things smaller. The usual way is to find redundant data and reduce it to a shortcut that identifies the original. There are two types of compression: *lossless*, which means that the data compressed is not altered in any way, and *lossy*, where the information needed the least is removed. The new DVD video format uses a lossy compression technique that reduces the file size to a fraction of the original with minimal loss in quality.

- **Audio**: QuickTime gives you the capability to view, process, and edit audio presentations.

- **Streaming Audio and Video**: Working with your Web browser, QuickTime TV can deliver live audio and video on your iMac. You can watch programs delivered by major entertainment and news services such as ABC News, Disney, HBO, and more.

The descriptions in this hour are based on QuickTime 4. Older versions of QuickTime didn't include the streaming audio/video feature and had a different look and feel. You can download the newest version of Apple's QuickTime from its Web site at http://www.apple.com/quicktime.

Viewing QuickTime Movies

If QuickTime is just a set of tools, what do you use to see a movie? Fortunately, your computer has several programs that are QuickTime-aware and let you see such productions. These include AppleWorks (described back in Hour 8, "Teach Yourself AppleWorks") and even the SimpleText program you use to check out the program ReadMe files.

But for this lesson, I'll introduce you to Apple's QuickTime Player application, which not only lets you view QuickTime productions and image files in such formats as GIF and JPEG (common on Web sites), but lets you do some very basic sound and video editing.

> If you have an iMac DV, you'll also have a copy of iMovie, which can work with your digital camcorder to record and edit video productions that are close to professional grade. I'll introduce you to iMovie later in this chapter.

▼ To Do

In order to view a QuickTime movie

1. Locate the QuickTime folder inside the Applications folder.

2. Open the QuickTime folder and locate the file labeled Sample Movie. Double-click this file to launch QuickTime Player and open the picture shown in Figure 13.1.

FIGURE 13.1

This is Apple's sample QuickTime movie.

QuickTime 4 Sample Movie

QuickTime™

Play control —

Volume control —

Scrollbar for fast forward/rewind

Click here for more information

Click here for more options

13

3. Click the Play button (the one with the forward arrow) to begin playing your movie. You'll hear the audio and see the motion picture begin (see Figure 13.2).

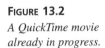

FIGURE **13.2**

*A QuickTime movie
already in progress.*

Click the Pause button
to halt the production

You can play a movie clip over and over again without stopping. Just open
the movie file and choose Loop from the Movie menu before you play it (or
press Command+L). Next time you play the movie, it will continue over and
over until you stop it.

Finding a Movie to Edit

Playing movies on your iMac is fun and instructive (particularly when it's an educational
movie, such as the ones on your Quicken 98 CD). You'll find lots of movies on the
World Wide Web (such as Apple's QuickTime Web site) or in shareware CDs to enjoy.
But if you want to get more involved in editing, you'll find a few additional features in
the QuickTime Player program (so long as you unlock the program, as explained in the
note about QuickTime Pro).

In order to unleash the full capabilities of the QuickTime Player program,
you need to upgrade to QuickTime Pro. When you register your computer
(or your Mac OS upgrade) with Apple, they will send you a serial number
(usually via email) that you can use to open up the additional features of
QuickTime Player. If you don't see any information on the QuickTime Pro
upgrade on your computer, a call to Apple's customer support line will get
you the right information. I'm writing this lesson using the Pro version of
QuickTime Player.

For this lesson, we're going to do some very simple editing with Apple's famous *Think Different* commercial.

First, you need a copy of the QuickTime movie version of this award-winning commercial. And here's how to get it:

1. Connect to your Internet service by using your Web browser, as explained in Hour 11, "The Internet: Learning the Ropes."

2. Summon up Apple's QuickTime Web site (copy this exactly because the path is a little complicated):

   `http://www.apple.com/quicktime/samples/stream/index.html#video`

3. Click the *Think Different* title, which will take you to a screen where it will play on your computer (after some data is downloaded).

4. After the production is finished, click the movie window and hold down the mouse button. This will open a pop-up menu with the option Save as QuickTime Movie. Choose that option.

> In order for you to save the QuickTime movies you download, you'll need to upgrade your version of QuickTime to Pro status, following the steps I've described in this hour.

5. You'll see a Save As dialog box, and you'll be asked to select a location on your computer's drive to save the file (see Hour 7, "Opening, Saving, Finding, Moving, Etc.," for more assistance in navigating a Save As dialog box). Save the file to your drive.

6. Log off your Internet service.

> If you're not connected to the Internet yet, no problem. You'll find more QuickTime samples to work with on your Mac OS CD. Just look for the folder labeled CD Extras and navigate to the one titled QuickTime Samples.

13

Editing a QuickTime Movie

Now that you have Apple's famous commercial at hand, you're ready to edit your copy. You can edit any QuickTime movie by using the very same steps that I'll describe next.

The first thing we'll do is separate the audio track from the video track, so that you have a separate sound file to play when you want. Here's how it's done:

1. Locate your QuickTime movie and double-click the file.

2. Double-click the movie file to open the screen shown in Figure 13.3.

> If you can't locate your file, no problem. Just launch Sherlock 2 (as described in Hour 7) and use its Find File feature to seek out the file. After you see it in the Sherlock window, double-click it to launch it.

FIGURE **13.3**
This is Apple's Think Different *commercial, ready for editing.*

> Movie presentations, such as Apple's *Think Different* movie, are protected by copyright. You are free to play with the file at your own leisure for your own amusement and education, but don't attempt to distribute an altered version of that or any other copyrighted file to anyone else. That would be a violation of the copyright and could get you in legal trouble.

3. Choose Extract Tracks from the Edit menu (see Figure 13.4).

> The editing operation I'm about to describe isn't actually going to change the file itself because we're going to generate a separate file. Just don't save the actual file you're working on; you want to leave it as it is.

FIGURE 13.4

Which portion of the video do you want to extract?

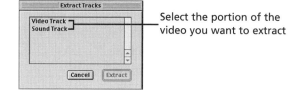

Select the portion of the video you want to extract

4. Select Sound Track and click the Extract button. This will open a little Untitled window with play buttons (see Figure 13.5).

FIGURE 13.5

This is just the sound portion of the movie.

5. If you want to save the file, choose Save or Save As from the File menu, which opens the dialog box shown in Figure 13.6.

FIGURE 13.6

Name the file from this screen.

Choose file format option here

When you save a file in QuickTime Player, the first save option, Save Normally, means that the file requires a player program to work. The second option, Make Movie Self-Contained, makes the file much larger but embeds a player program inside it.

13

You can use the very same technique to extract the video portion of the movie. You can also create a brand new movie, assembled from clips you've copied from other movies.

Here's how it's done.

1. Make a new movie document by choosing New from the File menu. Or press Command+N.

2. Open the movie from which you want to copy.

3. Click a frame you want to edit.

4. Choose Copy from the Edit menu.

> The first thing you see when you create a new movie document is just a title bar and the player buttons. Don't worry. When you put a picture in there, it will expand to show the picture, too.

> If you want to edit more than a single frame, just click the picture, hold down the Shift key, drag the scrollbar to the end of the part you want to edit, and release the key. When you choose Copy from the Edit menu, this entire sequence will be copied.

5. Click the empty movie document window and choose Paste from the Edit menu. This will copy the selected frame or frames to the new document.

6. Continue to copy and paste the frames you want to include in your new movie (you can move them out of sequence for fun, but remember that the sound track will be out of sequence too).

7. When you're finished, click the Play button on your new movie window to make sure it's OK. You can cut and paste portions of the new movie if you want to fix an error or change the order of presentation.

8. If you're satisfied with your work and want to save a copy, choose Save or Save As from the File menu and give your new production a name.

Go ahead and explore the options offered in QuickTime Player. Here are a few more features you'll want to try:

- **Import (File menu)**: This feature enables you to grab the picture or sound from a file.

- **Export (File menu)**: This option lets you save your movie or sound file in another format, if you want. It's useful if you want to send a file to a user on that "other" platform, which doesn't have QuickTime. There is, though, a QuickTime for Windows version available from Apple.

- **Present Movie (File menu)**: Use this command to select the way you show the movie—the normal way or as a slide show (where the entire screen, other than the movie area, is darkened). You can also choose to make the size of the picture larger or smaller, but when you go up in size, you will lose quality.
- **Delete Tracks (Edit menu)**: Remove either the sound or video from a movie clip.
- **Play Selection Only (Movie menu)**: This option will restrict the playback to the portion of the movie you selected. Combined with the Loop option, it will play that portion over and over again until you stop it.

As they say in show business, that's a take!

Introducing QuickTime TV

Streaming audio and video might be the wave of the future, but a lot of it is here right now. Using QuickTime TV, you're able to actually view a broadcast on your computer, direct from the Internet.

> In order for you to actually use the QuickTime TV feature, you need QuickTime 4 or later and an Internet connection. QuickTime TV works with your Web browser to deliver streaming audio and video content to your computer.

Here's a brief look at how to turn your iMac into a television set:

1. Log on to your Internet service and fire up your Web browser.
2. Access Apple's QuickTime TV Web site at `http://www.apple.com/quicktime/showcase/live`, which will open a screen similar to the one shown in Figure 13.7.
3. When you see the listing for a station you'd like to receive, click the icon.
4. You'll probably see a screen announcing that the broadcast is ready to be received. Click the Click to Begin Streaming icon to start receiving the broadcast. Within a few seconds your QuickTime player program will launch, and you'll see the show (see Figure 13.8 for an example).

13

> On some QuickTime TV programs, you might have to click an icon or title on the QuickTime Player screen for the actual show to begin.

FIGURE 13.7
Access live audio and video shows courtesy of QuickTime TV.

FIGURE 13.8
Your QuickTime Player program is now presenting the latest broadcast from the station you've selected.

Click any item to receive that station

Click the Stop/Pause button to end the show

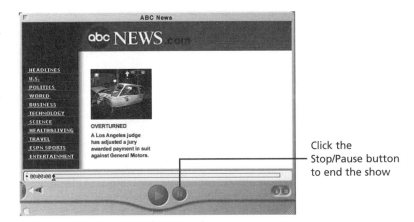

5. Click the slider below the picture and drag the mouse cursor back and forth and, after a small delay, you'll see different parts of the program (unless it's coming to you live, of course).

If additional programs are available, click the titles to see them.

When you're finished viewing your program, you can click the Pause/Stop button to end it and return to Apple's QuickTime TV Showcase Web site for more selections.

Check your Favorites menu in the QuickTime Player program for a list of popular programming sources. After you have a new channel on the screen, you can quickly add it to the list of Favorites simply by choosing the Add Favorite option in the Favorites menu.

Streaming audio and video is a great achievement, but it's still quite sensitive to the speed and quality of your Internet connection. If the pictures seem jerky and the sound is not as clear as you like, you can try logging off your Internet service and logging on again to see if it improves. Also, don't even try to do any Web surfing while you're watching a program, because you'll probably lose your QuickTime TV connection or quality will suffer seriously.

Edit Your Videos with iMovie

If you have an iMac DV or iMac DV Special Edition, you have a terrific tool to edit videos and give them a professional look. iMovie is located right on your iMac's drive, in the Applications folder, and it works with the DV models' FireWire ports to capture videotapes from your digital camcorder and place them on your hard drive.

Once you record the video, you can use iMovie's simple drag-and-drop editing tools to cut and move portions of your video. That way you can put scenes in a different order, or remove them entirely.

Here's a fast guide to help you get accustomed to editing your videos.

1. Locate the iMovie software, located in the iMac DV's Applications folder, and double click on the program. This will bring up the editing screen (see Figure 13.9)

2. First, you'll want to give your production a name. So go to the File menu, and choose New Project. Give your production (let's call it project from here on, as the pros do) a name.

3. To capture a clip from a digital camcorder, make sure it's hooked up to the FireWire port (and set up in the proper playback mode), then click on the Camera Mode button, which is located just below your preview window (see again Figure 13.9).

▼ To Do

13

▼

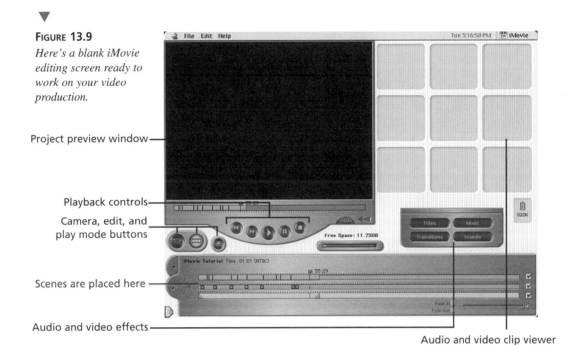

FIGURE 13.9
Here's a blank iMovie editing screen ready to work on your video production.

Project preview window—

Playback controls—

Camera, edit, and play mode buttons—

Scenes are placed here—

Audio and video effects—

Audio and video clip viewer

4. Click the Play button and it'll play back the video from your digital camcorder (an Import button will appear above these controls).

5. When you've located the scene you want, click the Import button to start recording to your iMac DV's drive.

6. When the scene is over, click the Import button again to finish recording the sequence.

7. Repeat these steps for each element of your video production. And you'll want to save the project regularly, to make sure that all the changes have been recorded.

Video clips use a huge amount of disk space. You shouldn't try to import more than a very few minutes at a time or you might end up filling your hard drive to its capacity. If you want to edit a very long production (more than 10 minutes or so), you might find it more convenient to do it in segments, and record each segment after deleting the project files for the previous segment.

▼   8. Just as the pros do, you can cut and remove scenes from the video, then copy them in a different location. Or just remove them altogether.

      9. Once you've finished moving things around, you can use one of the special effects tools to add sounds, narration, transitions (such as fading in and out of a scene, or overlapping it for a cool effect), and titles.

     10. When your production is ready, you can copy it back to your camcorder. Or save it as a QuickTime movie, so you can just email it to your friends or business contacts. You'll use the Export Movie command in the File menu, then choose the
▲   format to which to copy your video.

I've covered the raw basics of using iMovie here. There's a convenient Help menu that will guide you from beginning to end. In addition, you'll find a tutorial project, in the iMovie application folder, so you can assemble clips together for practice and see how the program runs before you get to work on a real project.

> Before you work with iMovie, I suggest you consult the iMovie Read Me file that is placed in the iMovie folder. This file will give you lots of hints and tips to get the best possible performance. For example, you'll want to quit all other programs, and eject DVDs and CDs and any removable disks (such as a SuperDisk or Zip disk) before you work on a project. Even the process of keeping tabs on a mounted disk can effect the quality of your video project.

Playing Audio CDs on Your Computer

I've focused so much on watching and editing movies that I almost neglected to mention that the CD player on your computer is perfectly capable of working with audio CDs as well.

It even includes a program that mimics the controls you have on a normal audio CD player.

Here's how to play a CD on your iMac:

▲ To Do

      1. Open your CD player tray and insert your favorite audio CD in it.

      2. Close the tray. Within a few seconds, the CD will *mount* on your computer's drive, and the CD will begin to play.

      3. If you want to control the playback process, open the AppleCD Audio Player
▼   application from the Application folder (see Figure 13.10).

13

FIGURE 13.10

Apple's CD player program resembles the setup of a regular home CD player.

Click the down arrow to move to a specific track

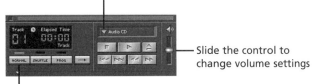

Slide the control to change volume settings

Click the down arrow at the bottom to see a track-by-track view

The normal CD playback option is *autoplay*, which means that the audio CD will start to play soon after it is inserted. You might want to turn off this option by clicking the CD icon on the Control Strip and selecting AutoPlay (which toggles the setting). That's because an infamous computer virus, AutoStart, is triggered by autoplaying an infected CD. Check Hour 24, "An iMac Safety Net," for information on how to protect yourself from such viruses, but remember that regular audio CDs won't be infected.

4. To jump to a specific track, click the down arrow (to the left of the words Audio CD in Figure 13.9) and select the track number you want.

5. To stop playback, click the Stop button on the AppleCD Audio Player program screen.

6. To remove the CD, choose Eject CD from the File menu or press Command+E.

Summary

In this lesson, you discovered Apple's QuickTime technology. And you learned to do some very simple editing of a video production, to get an idea of its capabilities using Apple's QuickTime player and iMovie software. You also learned about QuickTime TV and how to set up your computer to play perfectly ordinary audio CDs.

If you're used to the talking computers from *Star Trek* and other shows, you'll be pleased to know that, at least within some limits, your computer can also talk to you. You'll find out more in Hour 14, "Using the iMac Speech Recording Features."

Q&A

Q I love the clear and sharp pictures, but this is supposed to be a multimedia computer. Why are the sounds so, well, *tinny*?

A As I mentioned in Hour 4, "A Look at Your iMac Software," you can easily hook up another set of speakers to your computer to get better sound. There's only so much you can do with the tiny speakers that came with most of Apple's computers.

Q I notice that there's another program in the QuickTime folder, PictureViewer. How does it differ from QuickTime Player?

A PictureViewer is designed for still pictures; QuickTime Player is for movies.

Q Every time I start my computer, I get the message that QuickTime couldn't load because it is already installed. What's wrong?

A The message signifies that you have two copies of the QuickTime extension in the Extensions folder (within the System Folder). The solution isn't hard. Simply open the System Folder and then open the Extensions folder. You might want to change the Extensions folder window to the View as List option to allow you to quickly check for multiple copies.

Don't worry about all those strange files with strange-sounding names. I'll cover that subject in Hour 15, "What's a System Folder and Why Do I Need One?" If you see more than one copy of QuickTime, you'll want to trash one of them. But first you want to make sure that you have the latest version installed, so select one copy of QuickTime, choose Get Info from the finder's File menu, and see what the version is. Keep the latest one, toss the other, and restart your computer.

Q I double-clicked a QuickTime or sound file, and it won't open. The message says the application isn't available. What do I do?

A QuickTime supports more than 50 multimedia formats. It doesn't cover just Mac multimedia formats but Windows formats, too. They include such formats as WAV, AVI, and BMP files (all of which are part of that "other" platform). If you can't open a multimedia file, simply drag its icon to the QuickTime Player application icon and it should work.

You can automatically convert files from the "other" platform this way: Go to the Apple menu, select Control Panels, and choose QuickTime Settings from the sub-menu. Select QuickTime Exchange from the pop-up menu and make sure that it's checked.

13

Q I began to play a movie, but the sound is suddenly gone. What's wrong?

A First, check the Volume icon on the movie player screen and make sure that the dial is moved all the way up. If it is, take a gander at the Speaker (volume) icon on your Control Strip and check to be certain it's turned up, too. If you've attached a speaker system to your computer, make sure that the system is connected properly, that it is on, and that the level control is turned up.

Bear in mind that some QuickTime movies just don't have a sound track. To be certain your sounds are working, just click the sound slider on the Sound Level Control Strip, and it should produce a sound.

Q I keep hearing about another audio and video player, called RealPlayer. What's the difference? Is it better than QuickTime?

A RealPlayer is a competing streaming audio and video format from a firm called Real Networks. Because the formats aren't compatible, you cannot use QuickTime Player to run a RealAudio/Video production, or vice versa. If you want to try RealPlayer, you can download the latest version from the publisher's Web site at `http://www.real.com`.

In addition, if you've ever installed the full version of Netscape, called Netscape Communicator, you might find a copy of RealPlayer already in that program's folder.

Q QuickTime Player is nice, but it's rather limiting. I'd like to be able to do more with my movies. Are there better programs?

A Indeed there are; QuickTime Player is at best a beginning. When you get accustomed to checking the Internet for software, look for such products as Player Pro (a sound editing/sequencing program) and MovieWorks (which lets you create an entire multimeda presentation). If you have an iMac DV or iMac DV Special Edition, you'll also be able to work with iMovie to do near professional grade videos. I've decribed the program briefly in this chapter.

Hour 14

Using the iMac Speech Recording Features

"I'm sorry, Dave, I cannot do that."

How many of you remember Hal, the evil talking computer from the movie *2001: A Space Odyssey*? Or the more cooperative talking computer that you find in the various *Star Trek* TV programs and movies?

Well, those clever, verbal computers aren't quite here just yet. But, after a fashion, you can definitely make your computer talk to you; you can also use it as a dictation machine. Within limits, you can even give it simple commands to follow.

In this lesson, you'll learn

- How to use Apple's speech software to make your iMac talk.
- How to make your iMac's "voice" sound better.
- How to change your iMac's alert sounds.
- How to add (and record) new alert sounds.

Introducing Apple's Speech Manager

If you're a fan of talking books, no doubt you appreciate the fact that there are times you just don't want to actually read something. You'd rather have it read to you, so you can sit back and rest your eyes. Or maybe you have a visual impairment that makes it difficult to look at the screen for long periods.

Fortunately, the folks at Apple recognize the fact that it isn't always possible to sit there and read the text on the screen. Every iMac comes with speech software already installed, so it can actually read text back to you.

Not all Macintosh software supports speech technology. For example, both AOL and SimpleText can read text back to you. But AppleWorks can't. You'll want to check a program's menu bar commands or documentation as to whether such a feature is supported.

Let the iMac Do the Talking

I'll give you an example of just how the iMac can handle speech. You'll be able to hear the iMac's Read Me file (or any text document you want) read back to you. And it requires just a very few steps.

Here's how it's done.

1. Locate your iMac Read Me file (or any of the Read Me files that came with it) and double-click the file icon to launch it.
2. Choose Speak All from the Sound menu or press Command+J. Within just a few seconds, the iMac's little hidden voice will begin talking to you.

Don't expect miracles from your computer's talk-back feature. The speech software doesn't always get context right, and some words will be pronounced incorrectly. For example, "America Online" will be heard as "America Onlin."

3. To stop your computer from speaking, press the universal command to halt an operation, Command+. (period). It will shut up fast!

▲

Read Me files are usually set up so that they can't be altered; thus, you cannot select them. You can turn the speech either on or off. If you'd like to try having your computer read a section of a document to you, try writing one of your own.

Here's how it's done:

▼ To Do

1. Go to the Applications folder and locate your copy of SimpleText.
2. Double-click the program to launch it.
3. Choose New from the File menu (or press Command+N) to make a new document.
4. Type text in your document.
5. Select the portion of the text you want read back.
6. Choose Speak Selection from the Sound menu (it replaces Speak All on a regular document). Or press Command+J. All of the selected text will be read.
7. To stop your computer from speaking, press the universal command to halt an operation, Command+. (period).

▲

Giving Your iMac a New Voice

As shipped from the factory, your iMac's standard voice is one among many provided for your listening pleasure. The lady's name is "Victoria," and if you're not satisfied with that choice (or wish to make her sound a bit different), you do have other options.

Here's how to give your computer a new sound:

▼ To Do

1. Go to the Apple menu, choose Control Panels, and select Speech from the sub-menu. This will open the screen shown in Figure 14.1.
2. To change the speech and pitch of the voice, move the Rate slider switch back and forth with your mouse. Victoria will get a bass voice or become a high-strung soprano, depending on the choices you make.
3. To pick a different voice, click the pop-up menu (see Figure 14.2). Choose another voice from the options offered. Go ahead and try different voices and different pitches to see which one you like best.

The voices on your computer use a small amount of random access memory (RAM) when active. The choices labeled High Quality in the pop-up menu use extra RAM, which means less memory will be available for use with your computer's software.

▼

14

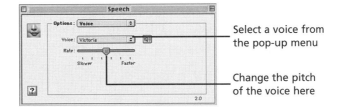

FIGURE 14.1

Had enough of "Victoria"? No problem. You can give your computer a different sound here.

Select a voice from the pop-up menu

Change the pitch of the voice here

FIGURE 14.2

This menu gives you some more voices to select from.

Choose your iMac's personal voice

4. When you're finished making your selection, click the Close box of the Speech Control Panel to send it away.

> Another speech feature of the Mac operating system is the Talking Alert, where a warning message is read back to you after a short delay. If you want to turn off this feature, open the Speech Control Panel, choose Talking Alerts from the pop-up menu, and turn it off. You can also use this feature to change the alert word if you prefer another (and there's practically no limit to what you can add).

> If you'd like to have the iMac sing text back to you (well, sort of), try the Good News voice. It won't make Celine Dion or Madonna jealous, but it will be good for a change of pace.

A Guide to Better Speech

In standard form, your computer is somewhat imprecise with some words, and this might make it difficult to understand some of the text being read back to you.

But there is a way to set up a text document strictly for the spoken word so that it becomes easier to understand. You might have to sidestep a few of the rules of grammar, but if the text is designed to be spoken rather than read, it won't make a difference.

Here are some things to consider:

- **Use extra commas**: Your English teacher wouldn't approve, but if you add an extra comma at an appropriate point, it will insert a brief pause in the speech. This is a technique that radio announcers sometimes use to give a phrase emphasis.
- **Remove emphasis**: The iMac's voice doesn't know when to emphasize a word and when not to do so. This can make it difficult to separate the most important parts of the document from the rest. You can keep a word from being emphasized by inserting the command [[emph-]] before it.

With a few strategic adjustments as described above, you'll be able to improve the quality of your computer's speech capabilities. Nope, it won't win your computer any elocution awards or next year's Oscar, but it will improve matters greatly.

Changing the iMac's Alert Sounds

Your computer comes complete with a set of standard alert sounds. These are the tones you hear whenever the Mac operating system needs to let you know of an important event.

To change the alert sound from those available, here's what to do:

1. Go to the Apple menu, choose Control Panels, and select **Sounds** from the submenu, which opens the screen shown in Figure 14.3.

> If your iMac came with a system software version earlier than Mac OS 9, the functions of the Sound Control Panel were part of a program called Monitors & Sounds. But the steps I'm describing in this hour using your computer's speech feature are pretty much the same.

2. Click the Alert Sounds label (at the left), which opens the screen shown in Figure 14.4.

14

▼

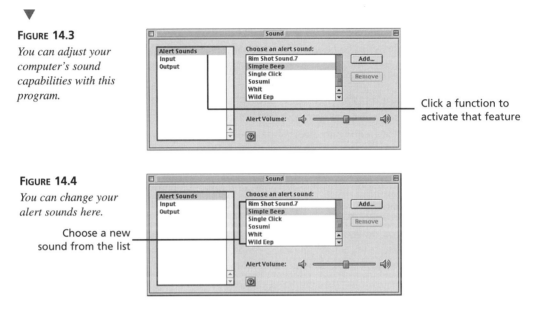

FIGURE 14.3
You can adjust your computer's sound capabilities with this program.

Click a function to activate that feature

FIGURE 14.4
You can change your alert sounds here.

Choose a new sound from the list

3. Select a new sound from the scrolling list.

4. Choose Quit from the File menu to close the Sound Control Panel (or press Command+Q) or just click the Close box. And that's all there is to it.

▲

From here on the new alert sound you've selected will be heard, rather than the standard Simple Beep that was there before.

Installing New Alert Sounds

When you become accustomed to looking for software on the Internet or AOL, no doubt you'll come across sounds that you might like to use for an alert sound. First, you want to look for sounds in the proper format. By default, the iMac works with files labeled as System 7 sounds.

To use such sounds, follow these steps:

1. Click the sound file to select it.

2. Drag the file to the closed System Folder icon.

3. Click OK to store the message in the System file.

In seconds, the sound will be moved inside your computer's System file, and when you open the Alerts icon in the Sound Control Panel, it will be added to the scrolling list.

But not all sounds out there are in the right format. More often than not, you'll find files in WAV format, which is a Windows-based sound format.

Fortunately, you can use those sound files, too, with a little help from Apple's QuickTime Player application (described in Hour 13, "Multimedia Is More Than a CD-ROM Game").

Here's how to change those WAV files to work as alerts:

To Do

1. Double-click the QuickTime Player application to launch it.

2. Choose Open from the File menu (or press Command+O) and navigate to the sound file you want to convert.

3. Select the file and click the Open button in the dialog box, which will bring the file to the screen.

4. After the file is opened, choose Export from the File menu and select Sound to System 7 Sound from the pop-up menu of options.

5. Save the file with whatever name is convenient to identify it.

6. Take the converted sound file and install it in your System Folder (as described previously).

Recording Custom Alert Sounds

Now maybe you're not happy with the sound files that are available, and you'd like to stretch your creative muscles and make one of your own. You'll be pleased to know that your computer can work as a recording machine and that you can record sounds from several sources. These include

- **A home stereo or other external source**: Record snippets from such sources as a broadcast or a video.

- **CD audio**: You can play audio CDs on your computer's built-in player and record the sounds as alerts.

- **A built-in mike**: The iMac's built-in microphone (that little slot above the screen on your iMac) or a separate external mike can be used to record your own voice or live music.

If you want to use a better-quality mike, check your Apple dealer for one that's compatible with the PlainTalk technology.

14

After you've picked the sound source, you'll need to tell your computer where the sound is coming from. Here's how to do it:

1. Open the Sound Control Panel (as described previously).

2. Click the Input label. This opens the screen shown in Figure 14.5.

FIGURE 14.5

*I chose Built-In Mic
for my iMac.*

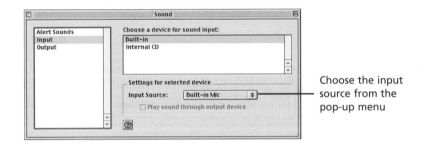

Choose the input
source from the
pop-up menu

3. Click the pop-up menu and select your sound input source.

Let's record your alert sound. First, get your sound source ready. If you are going to use your voice, you might want to rehearse your part a few times to make sure it's right. But don't worry, you can record the sounds over and over again until you get them right. There's no limit to the number of "takes" you can record (as long as you realize that the new sound always replaces the previous one).

Sound bites are limited to five seconds. As a result, phrases or musical *stingers* are about all your computer's recording machine can handle before the process comes to a grinding halt. You'll also want to limit your creation to no more than a couple of seconds, because longer alerts might tend to become distracting or downright annoying when you hear them over and over again.

Now, let's get ready to record:

1. If it is not already onscreen, open the Sound Control Panel as described previously.

2. Click the Alert Sounds option.

3. On the Alerts screen, click the Add button, which will open your computer's little recording center (see Figure 14.6).

FIGURE 14.6

These are the controls for your computer's built-in recording machine.

Click a button to activate that feature

If you're recording from an external sound source or your computer's CD player, you'll want to adjust it (queue it) so that it starts playing just a second or two before the sound passage begins. That'll give you enough time to click the Record button at the right moment.

4. Start your sound source or get ready to speak, and then click the Record button. You'll see animation in the Speaker icon to indicate sounds are being received (see Figure 14.7).

FIGURE 14.7

As you can see from the progress bar, a recording is being made.

5. When you're finished recording, click Stop.

6. Click Play to hear the results of your recording.

7. If you need to do the sound over, follow steps four through six as needed.

8. When you're satisfied with your recording, click the Save button and name your file (see Figure 14.8).

FIGURE 14.8

Select a name for your new sound file.

Click OK to store the sound

Your completed sound will be stored in the System file, together with all of your other System sounds.

14

> If you want to remove a sound from your computer, open the System Folder, double-click the System file, and locate the sound file in the directory. Then drag it out of the System file, which will remove it from the list of Alert sounds. You can now trash the file or store it elsewhere. If you only want a copy, hold down the Option button before dragging the sound from the System file.

Congratulations, you're done! The sound you made will now become part of the list of alerts available on your computer.

Introducing Apple's Speech Recognition Technology

Within some very severe limits, your computer can actually respond to spoken commands. Using Apple's Speech Recognition software, you can activate a number of functions using your own voice. I've not devoted much space to this feature in this book, because the technology is pretty much in its infancy, despite being available for several years.

But if you want to experiment with it, you would need to use your computer's system CD to install the English Speech Recognition software.

I'll cover the subject of system installation in detail in Hour 22, "Giving Your iMac New Software, More RAM, and Other Things." In short, all you have to do is double-click the Install Mac OS icon, and after you select your computer's drive for the installation, you'll see an Add/Remove option. Use that to do a custom installation, which will present you with a list of installation options that includes English Speech Recognition.

> When you add English Speech Recognition, it's a separate installation that's included with your Mac OS system disk. You don't have to reinstall your system software to add this feature.

After Apple's Speech Recognition software is installed, open your Speech Control Panel and click the Help icon to open online instructions on how to use the feature. If you don't expect miracles from it, you might find it an interesting way to experience what might be the future of personal computing.

Is The future Almost Here?

As this book went to press, Dragon Systems was developing a new Mac version of its Naturally Speaking software, and IBM had demonstrated ViaVoice for the Mac. Both programs may be available by the time this book is in the stores. Either program will let you actually dictate, rather than type, your documents. They are especially valuable if a wrist injury or other condition prevents you from using the keyboard and mouse efficiently.

Summary

This lesson focused on Apple's speech technology. You learned how to have your computer read text to you and how to record your own custom alert sounds. True, these capabilities are somewhat limited compared to the awesome features you see in those science fiction movies. But the capabilities are still works in progress and in time, you might well be able to have some sort of conversation with your computer. But when it begins to disagree with you, as Hal did in *2001*, watch out!

When you have completed the first 14 lessons of this book (and congratulations by the way!), you're on the road to understanding a lot about your computer and the Mac OS in general. Beginning in the next lesson, I'll cover the harder stuff, beginning with the Mac OS System Folder.

Q&A

Q I tried to use the Speech feature, but it's not available in my copy of SimpleText. What happened to it?

A In order for your computer to work with speech, you need to have the proper software installed. Please check Hour 15, "What's a System Folder and Why Do I Need One?" and Hour 22 for information on what's inside the System Folder and how to install new software.

Q I know the right software is installed (I checked it). But I still don't hear any sounds. What's wrong? Is my computer's speaker bad?

A It might just be that the volume control is turned down. To check, go to the Apple menu, choose Control Panels, and select Sound from the submenu. Click Output and make sure that the Computer System Volume level control is turned up and that the Mute checkbox isn't checked.

If everything looks right, and you're using a separate speaker system hooked up to your computer, make sure that the speakers are turned on. If they are and you still don't hear anything, make sure that they're connected properly to your computer.

14

Q I tried to install Apple's English Speech Recognition software on my iMac and it wouldn't work. What am I doing wrong?

A The older versions of English Speech Recognition didn't work with the iMac. Fortunately, that was fixed with the version that comes with Mac OS 8.6 and later. If you haven't upgraded your system software, you can find Apple's latest speech software at its support Web site (`http://www.apple.com/support`).

Q I recorded a sound alright, but when I play it back, I hear nothing. What's wrong?

A When you are recording something on your computer's little tape recorder window, you should see animation on the Speaker icon to show sounds are being received. If there's no sign of activity, it might mean that there's something wrong. Try this:

- Check the **Input** in the Sounds Control Panel. Make sure that the right sound source was selected from the pop-up menu.

- If you're using the iMac's internal mike, move closer to it and speak louder. It's not supersensitive, and when you're real close to it, that will help obscure the sounds made by your iMac's built-in cooling fan and other room noises. But if you're too close, you'll hear yourself breathing when you speak.

Q Trivia question: Who is the computer's voice in *Star Trek*?

A Not a trivial answer. It's none other than Majel Barrett Roddenberry, the widow of *Star Trek*'s creator, Gene Roddenberry. And this gifted actress also did a great turn as Counselor Troi's eccentric mom in *The Next Generation* and *Deep Space Nine* series (she also played Nurse Chapel in the original series).

PART III

Learning the Hard Stuff

Hour

HOUR 15

What's a System Folder and Why Do I Need One?

As you use your iMac, you will run some programs and quit others.

But there is one set of software that will run every single waking moment that your iMac is on—your system software.

This is the operating system that gives your computer its special interface and offers the tools that allow your other programs to work. Without a working System Folder, your computer's incredibly fast G3 microprocessor will sit there and do absolutely nothing.

In this lesson, you'll learn

- What is inside the System Folder.
- What most of those files do.
- The real definition of a clean system install.

Welcome to the System Folder

As you've learned more about your computer, no doubt you've given a look at the contents of the System Folder (see Figure 15.1). It's largely a "look but don't touch" area in terms of moving things around. Just about every one of the hundreds of files that lie there provides some essential function that your computer needs. From printing to sharing files to connecting to the Internet, or just your basic screen display, desktop appearance, and file management functions, the System Folder is the heart and soul of all Mac OS computers.

FIGURE **15.1**

*What are all those
folders used for?*

Scroll through the
list to see more

Over the next few pages, I'll dissect the contents of the System Folder, so you can see what most of those files are used for. You'll also have an idea what files you might safely remove without doing any harm to your computer's ability to work.

You will no doubt find files in your computer's System Folder above and beyond the ones described here. I'm limiting this lesson to the files that are standard issue. As you add more and more programs, additional files and folders will be placed there.

Peering Inside the Appearance Folder

15

This folder contains components used by the Appearance application to customize the look of your computer. The settings run the gamut from selecting a new desktop backdrop to choosing fonts and scrollbar enhancements. I'll tell you how to make these settings and others in Hour 16, "Using Control Panels to Customize Your iMac."

Peering Inside the Apple Menu Items Folder

This folder (see Figure 15.2) contains the files that are displayed in the Apple menu. Any file you drop in here will show up in that menu.

FIGURE 15.2
The contents of the Apple menu.

Scroll through the list to see more

Peering Inside the Application Support Folder

This folder contains special files needed by some programs to run or provide custom features.

ATM Font Database

This file is used by Adobe Acrobat and Adobe Type Manager (see the section on Control Panels on the following page and in Hour 16) to simulate fonts that are not installed on your computer.

Many of the files you install in your System Folder are automatically put in the right place. Just drag them to the closed System Folder icon, and the Finder will figure out where they belong.

Peering Inside the Claris Folder

This folder contains files used by AppleWorks and programs by FileMaker and the former Claris division of Apple. Some of the files you'll find here include dictionaries, help files, and settings files.

Clipboard

Although the file isn't directly accessed, it carries the data you put into the Clipboard via the Copy and Paste functions.

Peering Inside the ColorSync Profiles Folder

The contents of this folder are used to provide color information that is used by Apple's ColorSync software to calibrate color.

Peering Inside the Contextual Menu Items Folder

These files support those clever little pop-up menus you see when you click an icon with the Control key held down.

Peering Inside the Control Panels Folder

A Control Panel (see Figure 15.3) is a program that is used to make settings, somewhat in the fashion of your stereo or TV's remote control. I'll cover the settings you can make with these programs in Hour 16. But in passing, I'll mention that some of these files actually work as extensions as well.

Peering Inside the Control Strip Modules Folder

The Control Strip is that cool little palette that appears at the bottom of your computer's screen (or wherever you decide to put it). Each little icon activates a different control function. You'll learn more about it in Hour 16.

15

FIGURE **15.3**

The Control Panels folder contains applications that you can use to make different adjustments to your iMac.

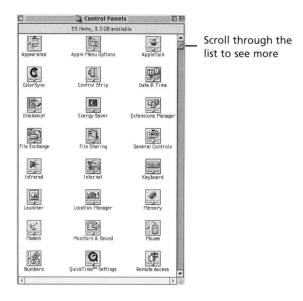

Scroll through the list to see more

Peering Inside the Extensions Folder

A System Extension is used to add functions to your computer (hence the word *extension*). But the folder is really a catch-all place for files that do other things, such as drivers, shared libraries, and support files needed by some programs to work.

NEW TERM — A *driver* is a file that communicates with one of your computer's components (or something attached to it) and makes that component run. A printer driver, of which there are many that came with your computer, makes it possible for your printer to work.

NEW TERM — A *shared library* is a file containing software that can be used by several different programs. Software publishers use these files to avoid having to duplicate efforts and features.

Let's now look over the contents of a typical computer's Extensions folder (mine), as shown in Figure 15.4, and see what the files are there for. If several programs are named similarly and offer similar functions, they're grouped together.

The System Folder contents I'm describing in this lesson are based on the ones that Apple provides with Mac OS 9. If you're using a different system version, you'll find some files aren't there or some different ones are present. But the ones listed in the following list provides most of the important functions.

FIGURE **15.4**

The Extensions folder enhances the functions of your computer.

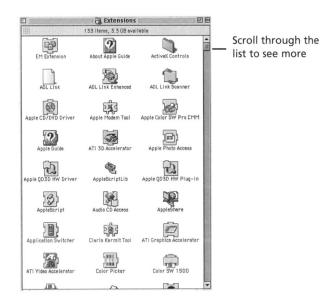

Scroll through the list to see more

- **EM Extension**: This extension is used for Extensions Manager, a program used to manage the add-ons installed in your System Folder.
- **About Apple Guide**: This file is used by your Apple Guide help software.
- **ActiveX Controls**: This is used by Microsoft's Internet software to provide certain graphic display features.
- **AOL Link (etc.)**: These extensions are used by AOL to provide Internet connections.
- **Apple CD/DVD Driver**: Exactly what it says.
- **Apple Color SW Pro CMM**: A driver used for Apple's Color StyleWriter Pro.
- **Apple Enet**: This driver is used to provide ethernet support on your computer.
- **Apple Guide**: Used to provide Apple Guide help screens.
- **Apple Modem Tool**: Used to communicate with your built-in modem.
- **Apple Photo Access**: Enables you to use photo CDs with your computer's CD drive.
- **Apple QD3D (etc.)**: Used to provide QuickDraw 3D capabilities.
- **AppleScript (etc.)**: Used for AppleScript. I'll cover this subject more completely in Hour 19, "AppleScript: Putting Your iMac on Automatic Pilot."
- **AppleShare**: Used for networking your computer with another Apple computer.
- **Application Switcher**: Used to move from one program to another.

15

- **ATI 3D Accelerator (etc)**: These drivers are needed for your computer's built-in graphic acceleration hardware.
- **Audio CD Access**: Used to allow you to play audio CDs on your computer's CD drive.
- **CarbonLib**: This file is used to support applications that will be designed to support the "client" version of Apple's Mac OS X. This is the new generation operating system that Apple is introducing for the year 2000.
- **Claris Kermit Tool**: Used for the communications module of AppleWorks.
- **Color Picker**: This extension enables you to access Apple's color wheel for selection of colors in your programs.
- **Color SW 1500 (etc.)**: Used for different models of Apple's Color StyleWriter printer line.
- **Color Sync Extension**: Provides color calibration capability, which is important if you prepare color documents for printing on a color device, such as one of those cool color inkjet printers.
- **Contextual Menu Extension**: Used to provide those neat pop-up menus showing different software features.
- **Control Strip Extension**: This extension places the Control Strip palette on your computer's desktop.
- **Default Calibrator**: Used with ColorSync for calibrating your screen, printer, and so on.
- **Desktop Printer (etc.)**: These extensions offer desktop printing features.
- **DNSPlugin**: Used with your computer's Internet connection software.
- **DrawSprocketLib**: Used for certain display functions required by your programs (primarily games).
- **FaxMonitor (etc.)**: Used for your FAXStf fax modem software.
- **FBC Indexing Scheduler**: Used by Sherlock 2 to offer scheduled file content scans on your computer.
- **File Sharing Extension (etc.)**: Used for the computer's file-sharing feature.
- **Find (etc.)**: Used to activate Sherlock 2's Find capabilities.
- **Folder Actions**: A support file for AppleScript.
- **Foreign File Access**: Needed by your computer's CD drive to read certain types of CDs.
- **Global Guide Files**: Contains Apple Guide information files.
- **HID Library**: Used with Apple's USB support software.

- **High Sierra File Access**: Another support file for your CD drive, required for some CDs.
- **iMac ATI Driver**: Used with your iMac's built-in graphic acceleration hardware.
- **iMac Modem Extension**: Activates your iMac's built-in modem.
- **Indeo Video**: Used by your Web browser to read Windows-based video files.
- **Intel Raw Video**: Another file for Windows-based video files.
- **InputSprocket (etc.)**: These extensions are used to supply gaming support for various input devices (such as keyboards, mouse-like devices, and similar products).
- **Internet Access (etc)**: These files are used to provide Internet connection features on your computer.
- **Iomega Driver:** This driver is needed if you have an Iomega drive connected to your computer, such as a zip drive.
- **ISO 9660 File Access**: Still another CD drive support file.
- **LaserWriter 300/LS (etc.)**: Drivers to support networked laser printers.
- **Location Manager (etc.)**: Used with Apple's Location Manager software to create custom network and Internet connection settings when your iMac is installed in different locales.
- **Mac OS Tutorial Launcher**: This file is used with Apple's built-in tutorial guide for your computer.
- **MacinTalk 3 (etc.)**: One of several files used by your computer to support speech capabilities.
- **Macintosh Guide**: An Apple Guide support file, offering help information about using the Mac operating system.
- **MacLinkPlus for ClarisWorks 68K**: This file is used to provide file translation capabilities with AppleWorks (despite the label).
- **Microsoft Component Library**: This file is used with certain Microsoft programs to enable you to access certain functions. It's also required by AOL because its built-in Web browser is designed by Microsoft.
- **Modem Scripts**: This folder contains connection scripts used by modems for Internet connections.
- **MRJ Libraries**: This folder contains files used for Apple's Java software.

NEW TERM   The *Java* in your System Folder has no resemblance to the Java you drink. Java is a programming language that works across several computing platforms. Some Web sites, for example, offer special animated features that require Java to be installed.

15

- **MS Font Embed Library(PPC) (etc.)**: One of several Microsoft-related files you'll find in your System Folder that are needed for its Web browser and other programs.

- **Multiprocessing**: Although some programs expect this folder to be there, it was really designed for Macs with more than one microprocessor installed (but leave it be anyway).

- **Multi-User Startup**: This extension is used with Apple's Multiple Users Control Panel to provide secured access to your computer.

- **NetSprocketLib**: Another program needed for Internet connections.

- **Network Setup Extension**: This file is needed to help run your computer's networking features.

- **OpenGLEngine (etc.)**: This set of files is used to provide OpenGL 3D support, which is useful for 3D games and other programs.

- **Open Transport (etc.)**: Open Transport is the name of Apple's networking software. These files are needed for networking, Internet connections, and modem dialing.

- **Printer Descriptions**: This folder contains special PostScript Printer Description (PPD) files that are needed by some printers to work properly with your laser printer software.

- **Printer Share**: This is used with some models of Apple's StyleWriter series for networking capability.

- **Printing Plug-ins (etc.)**: These files are needed for your computer's printing capability.

- **QuickDraw 3D (etc.)**: These files are needed for your computer's QuickDraw 3D feature.

- **QuickTime (etc)**: These files are required for your computer's QuickTime capabilities.

- **Remote Only**: Used by Apple Remote Access for connection.

- **Serial Tool**: Needed by some programs for modem connections.

- **Shared Library Manager (etc.)**: You need both of these files, which are required by some programs to access their shared libraries. Without these files, these programs won't run.

- **SimpleText Guide**: Another Apple Guide support file.

- **SLPPlugin**: Used with your computer's networking software.

- **SOMobjects for the Mac OS**: A support file needed to make some programs work.

- **Sound Manager**: What the name implies.
- **Speech Manager**: Works with the MacinTalk files to support Apple's speech feature.
- **STF Toolbox (etc.)**: Another set of files needed with FAXStf software.
- **SystemAV**: This file is needed by your Monitors Control Panel for it to run.
- **TCPack for AOL**: Needed by AOL's software for Internet connections.
- **Text Encoding Converter**: Offers multilingual text support and is required for some Mac programs to run.
- **Text Tool**: This file adds text capabilities to some communications software.
- **Type 1 Scaler**: This file is used by the Mac OS for handling PostScript fonts.
- **UDF Volume Access**: This is the new universal disk format that is part of the DVD standard.
- **USB Device Extension (etc.)**: These files are used to provide support for attached USB products.
- **Voices**: This file contains voices used by your computer's speech software.
- **VT102 Tool**: Another file used for communications capabilities.
- **Web Sharing Extension**: This file is used by the computer to share Web pages across a local computer network.
- **XMODEM Tool**: This is another communications file, used to support the XModem file transfer protocol.
- **AppleVision**: Used to provide screen display adjustments on an iMac's built-in monitor.

Peering Inside the Favorites Folder

Any file placed in this folder will show up in the submenu of the Favorites folder available from the Apple menu.

Finder

This is an application that runs all the time, offering your basic Mac OS desktop and disk management features. Whenever you open a directory, copy a file, or access a disk, the Finder is at work doing its thing.

15

Peering Inside the Fonts Folder

The fonts you install on your computer reside here.

> As you add software to your computer, you'll be tempted to add fonts, too. Just remember that only 128 font suitcase files can be placed here. If you want to add more fonts than that, you might want to remove some unused ones (you have to close all your open applications first, though). Or just drag one font suitcase and drop it on another (to combine them). There are also programs, such as Adobe's ATM Deluxe, DiamondSoft's Font Reserve, Alsoft's MasterJuggler, and Extensis' Suitcase, that can actually increase the number of fonts you can use.

Peering Inside the Help Folder

The Help folder contains the files used by your computer's Mac OS Help software and by other programs that use this Help feature.

Peering Inside the Internet Search Sites Folder

The Sherlock 2 search program uses the contents of this folder to access Internet sites for the information you want. As you begin to explore the Internet, you'll find more Sherlock 2 files that you can install here.

Peering Inside the Launcher Items Folder

The Launcher is a program that isn't used as much as it could be. It offers a convenient onscreen window with icons representing an application, a file, or a folder. You click just once on the item to launch it. Figure 15.5 shows a Launcher palette already configured with some of my favorite programs. You'll learn more about this feature in Hour 16.

FIGURE 15.5
The Launcher provides convenient, one-click access to applications and documents.

Click once on an icon to launch the program

Mac OS ROM

In older Macs, the software needed to provide basic functions when you start your Mac was placed in a little computer chip called a ROM. For newer Mac computers (such as your iMac), many of the functions are supported in this file, so they can be updated easily to fix problems or improve performance.

NEW TERM A *ROM* (short for *read only memory*) is a chip that offers permanent storage of computer data. The iMac has a very small ROM that doesn't do much more than enable it to start (boot).

MacTCP DNR

This file is used by your Open Transport networking software during your Internet connections.

Peering Inside the MS Preference Panels Folder

This folder contains settings windows needed by some Microsoft programs, such as the Internet Explorer Web browser and the Outlook Express email software.

Peering Inside the Preferences Folder

When you change a setting in a program (or one of those Control Panels I'll discuss in the next lesson), it makes a little file that is stored inside this folder.

Peering Inside the PrintMonitor Documents Folder

PrintMonitor is a program that provides background printing capabilities for your computer (that is, the capability to print while working on another document or program). But because the Desktop Printing software largely supplants this feature, I won't cover it any further.

Scrapbook File

This file is a repository of information you can save for insertion into documents as needed. A program in your Apple menu accesses this feature.

Peering Inside the Scripting Additions and Scripts Folders

These folders contain files you use with your AppleScript software. I'll cover this great feature in more detail in Hour 19.

Peering Inside the Shutdown Items Folder

Some programs perform special functions before you turn off your computer. If these functions are needed, the support files go here.

Peering Inside the Startup Items Folder

If you want a program to launch as soon as your computer has started, you put it here. Some files are already in this folder because some application software requires them.

Peering Inside the STF Folder

Some of the files needed by your fax modem software are placed here. These include your address book and copies of received and sent faxes.

Peering Inside the System File

This is the *heart* of your operating system software. In addition, the file stores keyboard layouts (used when working with foreign language programs) and system sounds (also see Hour 14, "Using the iMac Speech Recording Features").

System Enabler

Sometimes you'll find a System Enabler file in your System Folder. The file might be needed to support special hardware needs. Don't worry if you don't see one; as long as your computer starts properly, it's probably not needed.

System Resources

Wouldn't it be nice if all the System file elements were put in one place? Alas, it is not to be for Mac OS 9. Part of the software required was put in a separate file.

Text Encodings

This folder contains files needed for some foreign language functions.

Summary

The System Folder is not a "no man's" (or woman's) land. It's a place that contains the essential software needed to make your computer operate. If you treat it with care, you'll get trouble-free service and few, if any, system hangs.

The Control Panels on your computer are used to customize various functions, from the speed of your mouse, to the quality of the picture you see on your monitor. I'll explore the subject in Hour 16.

Q&A

Q I've heard about a *clean* system installation. What is it? Do I have to wipe my hard drive clean? Please explain.

A Settle down—you don't have to wipe out all your files. When you reinstall system software on your computer, the normal process is just to update your existing System Folder. When you do it *clean*, a brand new System Folder is created. The original one is renamed Previous System Folder (how original!).

Clean installs are done to help fix recurring performance problems or constant crashes. Sometimes starting with a fresh slate is the way to go, and nothing to fear. Nope, you won't lose your old files.

Q I want to reduce the amount of memory my computer uses. What System Folder files can I remove?

A Most of the files in the System Folder actually don't take memory (or use very little) unless they are being used. Many of these files are drivers, software that communicates with your iMac and something connected to it to provide a specific function. For example, a printer driver is needed to process the information about your documents that goes to your printer. Unless you're printing, it just, well, sits there and does nothing.

15

You should also be careful about what you attempt to remove from the System Folder. As you saw in this lesson, many of those files provide essential functions to make your iMac run properly. Without them, you'll find that CDs don't work, documents don't print, or you are suddenly not able to connect to the Internet.

Q All right, now I'm confused. I looked over my System Folder and found many files that aren't part of your list. What do they do?

A Many programs scatter their own sets of support files around the System Folder. I've covered only the standard files that ship with your iMac (using Mac OS 9 as the starting point). As Apple updates its system software (or you install new programs), your System Folder will swell to support those new elements. If you're not sure what those files do, check the program's documentation or contact the publisher for the information.

Q Will all those extra files slow down my computer?

A Not really. Some of those files might actually speed it up (such as those ATI drivers for your built-in graphic acceleration hardware). It really doesn't matter to your computer whether it has 125 files in the Extensions folder or 225. But you don't just want to add files that have no purpose.

Q Whenever I try to start my computer, I see a little disk icon with a flashing question mark. Is it broken?

A The most common cause of this problem is removing a file from the System Folder that is needed to run. At the very minimum, you need the Finder, Mac OS ROM, System, and System Resources files to start your computer. But you need the rest of the components of your System Folder for it to perform all of its functions properly.

If you encounter this problem, go get your copy of your computer's System (or Software Install) CD, open the CD tray, and place the CD inside. After closing the tray, hold down the C key to allow the iMac to boot from the CD.

After you're up and running, examine the System Folder on your computer's drive for missing items. If you can't find anything missing (or can't find the files to restore them), you should reinstall your system software. See Hour 22, "Giving Your iMac New Software, More RAM, and Other Things," for more information.

HOUR 16

Using Control Panels to Customize Your iMac

Your mouse is too slow, the picture looks a little crooked, and wouldn't it be nice if you could change that desktop pattern so it looks prettier? Fortunately, you can do these things and more by using the various programs in the Control Panels folder.

In this lesson, you'll learn

- What the iMac's standard Control Panels do.
- The ideal settings for different iMac functions.
- Which adjustments you should make and which you should leave alone.

Introducing the Control Panels Folder

I can't tell you how often I visit a fellow Mac user and see that he has never once looked inside the Control Panels folder or attempted to make any new settings. He just leaves things well enough alone.

It's true that your iMac will run just fine as it is, but as you become used to your computer, no doubt you'll find things you'd like to change, the way you might move furniture around in your home or plant new shrubbery in your backyard.

Over the next few pages, I'll cover the Control Panel functions that you are apt to want to change first.

The easiest way to get to the Control Panels folder is to access the Apple menu and select Control Panels. The window containing those Control Panels will open (see Figure 16.1).

FIGURE 16.1

You can use one of these programs to change the look and performance of your computer.

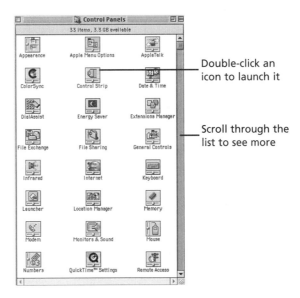

Double-click an icon to launch it

Scroll through the list to see more

Using the Appearance Manager

The Appearance Control Panel is used to redecorate your computer's desktop (see Figure 16.2). Each tab is used to control a different setting.

FIGURE 16.2

Change your iMac's desktop with this program.

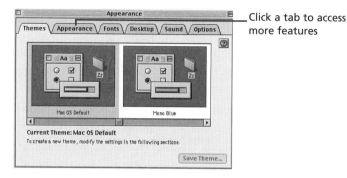

Click a tab to access more features

I'll show you the results of a desktop makeover shortly. But first, here's what the various components of the Appearance Control Panel do:

> The desktop theme you see on your iMac when you install it might be different than the ones I've used in this book. It all depends on the system version you have and, perhaps, whether the technician who prepared your computer for delivery might have changed it.

- **Themes**: These are preconfigured sets of appearance motifs, complete with desktop patterns, display fonts, and more. Just use the horizontal scrollbar to see the various choices.

> When you create a custom desktop environment, you can save it as a theme, using the Save Theme feature, for instant recall later on.

- **Appearance**: This setting controls the look of the menu bar and directory windows and the color used when you highlight (select) an item.
- **Fonts**: Use this setting to pick the fonts used for window and directory display.

> If the text onscreen looks a little jagged to you, you can use the Smooth All Fonts On Screen feature in the Fonts tab to make it look better. The downside of this smoothness, though, is that text might display a little slower on your screen.

- **Desktop**: Use these settings to select new desktop art from Apple's selections. You also might use one of your own pictures.
- **Sound**: If you want, you can have sounds play when activating a function on your computer. This is not recommended for a busy office, where the sounds (which can be a little strange sometimes) might disturb others.
- **Options**: These settings change the look of scrollbars, and they also offer a setting for the "window shade" feature, where you can double-click a title bar to collapse the window.

Making a Customized Desktop Theme

Now that you've seen how to make the settings, let's do a little home redecorating.

Here's what to do:

1. Open the Appearance Control Panel.
2. Click the Appearance tab.
3. Change the Highlight Color and Variation colors from the pop-up menus (pick whatever motif you prefer).
4. Click the Fonts tab.
5. Change the Large System Font option from the pop-up menu. This setting chooses the fonts used for menu bars and title bars. I'll be switching from Techno for this lesson.
6. Choose a Small System Font (if one is available from the pop-up menu). If none is available, it means this option won't work.
7. Click the View Fonts pop-up menu and pick a new font. This adjustment controls the fonts used for directories and icon labels. I selected Courier, which resembles an old-fashioned typewriter font.
8. Click the Desktop tab and select a new desktop pattern from the scrolling list. As you click a choice, you'll see it on the sample window at the left (see Figure 16.3).
9. When you've selected the one you want, click the Set Desktop button to activate it.

> If you have pictures you've created on your computer, you can use them by clicking the Place Picture button in the Desktop window and selecting your choice from the list. If the picture is not in a compatible format, it won't appear on the list.

FIGURE 16.3

You can use one of Apple's standard desktop patterns or additional choices available on your system CD.

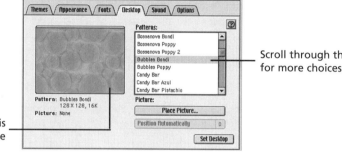

Scroll through the list for more choices

Your selection is previewed here

10. Click the Sounds tab and pick a Sound option from the pop-up menu if you'd like to have relief from the silence that covers most things you do on your computer.

11. From the Options tab, click the Smart Scrolling check box. This changes the look of the scrollbars.

12. To save the theme you've just made, click the Theme tab.

13. Click the Save Theme button and give your selection a name (Custom Theme is the default, which you can change). The result is shown in Figure 16.4.

FIGURE 16.4

I just created a new custom theme. Notice how the look of the desktop, title bar, and icon labels has now changed.

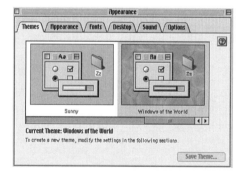

I'll use my new Windows of the World theme for the rest of this lesson, so you can see it in practice.

Setting the Apple Menu Options Control Panel

This Control Panel activates the handy submenus you see in the Apple menu. The other settings control the number of items shown in the Recent Applications, Recent Documents, and Recent Servers (networked Macs) folders available in the Apple menu.

Setting the AppleTalk Control Panel

This Control Panel is used to adjust the network scheme you're using. The default is Ethernet, and unless you're using the iMac's Infrared feature or the Apple's new AirPort card for networking, you can leave it alone.

> The infrared port was removed from the iMac product line beginning with the so-called "Revision C" version (the first ones to "come in colors").

Setting the ColorSync Control Panel

Apple's ColorSync is used to match up your computer's screen with scanners and printing devices. You can use the Monitors Control Panel to calibrate your screen for the most accurate color appearance. Then you can select from your color profiles here.

Setting the Control Strip Control Panel

That little palette of icons at the bottom of your computer's screen is used to activate some Control Panel functions. This Control Panel can be used to hide or show the Control Strip. In addition, you can adjust your Control Strip with these techniques:

- Hold down the Option key and drag the curved end of the Control Strip to move it around.
- Click once on either end of the Control Strip to collapse it (or once collapsed, to expand it again).
- If the left end has a pointed arrow, it indicates that all of the Control Strip modules are not fully displayed. Just click and drag the curved end of the Control Strip to expand it.

Setting the Date & Time Control Panel

You can control the look of your menu bar clock with the Date & Time Control Panel (see Figure 16.5). Here are some of the settings you can make:

- **Date Formats**: Customize the date display to conform to your taste or the standards of a specific country.
- **Time Formats**: Use these settings to change the way time is displayed. You might prefer a 24-hour clock or the scheme used in another country.
- **Time Zone**: This is a setting you make when you set up your iMac with the Mac OS Setup Assistant. If you move to another time zone, you will want to change this setting (and indicate whether daylight savings time is used in that area).

- **Server Options**: These settings allow your computer to adjust its clock when logged on to the Internet or at predetermined intervals.
- **Clock Options**: Choose whether your menu bar clock will include the day and seconds. You can also customize the font used for the clock display.

FIGURE 16.5

Click one of these buttons to change the way the time is displayed.

16

Setting the DialAssist Control Panel

If you need to dial a special number for outside access, or if you're using a phone calling card for long-distance access to an Internet provider, you can make your settings here.

Setting the Energy Saver Control Panel

Your iMac is designed to go into an idle (sleep) mode or shut itself off completely at preset intervals. You can make those changes here (see Figure 16.6).

FIGURE 16.6

You can set your computer to enter sleep mode after a period of inactivity.

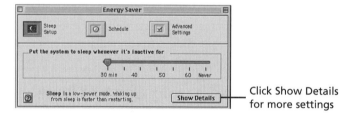

Click Show Details for more settings

Setting the Extensions Manager Control Panel

Apple's Extensions Manager offers a convenient way to manage your Extensions and Control Panels (see Figure 16.7). Click the check box to turn something off (after which you must restart).

The Extensions Manager is also useful for troubleshooting. By systematically activating and deactivating extensions, you can use the program to help you find a possible software conflict. But make any changes with care, because turning off the wrong things (as I explained in Hour 15, "What's a System Folder and Why Do I Need One?") can disable some important functions of your computer. I'll cover this subject in more detail in Hour 23, "Crashin' Away: What to Do?".

FIGURE 16.7

The Extensions Manager controls the programs that are activated when you boot your iMac

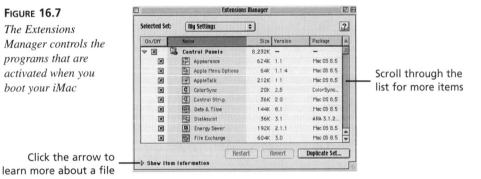

Scroll through the list for more items

Click the arrow to learn more about a file

If you need to run your iMac with a special extension set, you can make that set by using the New Set command in the File menu.

Setting the File Exchange Control Panel

This program gives your computer the capability to read disks made in the Windows environment and also to open documents from that platform with a compatible Mac program.

Setting the File Sharing Control Panel

You can turn file sharing off and on with this Control Panel. You can also rename your computer and change your network password (those settings were first made with the Mac OS Setup Assistant when you first set up your iMac). You can also set Users & Groups access settings by clicking the appropriate tab on the File Sharing Control Panel.

Setting the File Synchronization Control Panel

In Hour 21, I discuss backup methods. Apple's File Synchronization utility can be used for simple backups. It allows you to match up the version of a file you have on your iMac with the version of a file that's on another disk or networked computer.

File Synchronization comes already installed on a "slot loading" iMac. If you have Mac OS 9 on your older iMac, you can run the installer CD to add it, too. Just use the installer's Add/Remove function, pick a Custom installation, and you'll find File Synchronization listed among the Control Panels. When the installation is done, you'll be ready to do simple backups of your important files.

16

Setting the General Control Panel

General Controls are used for a grab bag of functions (see Figure 16.8). Most of the changes you make require a restart to activate. Here's what those settings do:

FIGURE 16.8

Use General Controls to make several adjustments to your iMac.

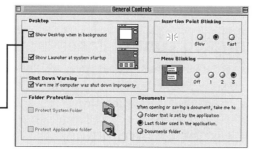

Click a check box to activate a feature

If a check box in General Controls is grayed out, it means the feature isn't available on your computer.

- **Show Desktop When in Background**: If your desktop icons are cluttered and distract you, you can switch off this option to show a blank desktop backdrop when you're working in a program.

- **Show Launcher at System Startup**: This feature activates the neat little Launcher Control Panel, which puts up an icon launching "dock" on your computer's desktop.

- **Shut Down Warning**: If your iMac is not shut down properly (perhaps due to a crash or power failure) or you have to force a restart, you'll see a warning when you start up with this function turned on. In addition, Apple's Disk First Aid software will run automatically to see that your hard drive's directory is healthy. I suggest you leave it on.
- **Insertion Point Blinking**: If the blinking of the insertion point when you're writing text is too distracting, you can change the setting here.
- **Menu Blinking**: This setting adjusts the rate at which the menu bar blinks when you select a command.
- **Documents**: Use this setting to configure the default location where documents are saved.

> The most convenient place to save documents is, naturally, the Documents folder. If you check that option in General Controls, such a folder will be set up the next time you restart. And all of the documents you want to save will point there by default in the Open or Save dialog boxes (but you can still put them elsewhere).

Setting the Infrared Control Panel

This Control Panel is used if you want to try out the iMac's Infrared Networking feature, but you need another iMac or a PowerBook around to use it. This feature was available only in the very early generation iMacs, by the way.

Setting the Internet Control Panel

When you join an Internet service, a number of settings are made to control how your email is addressed, the Web browser you use, and so forth. You can view and change those settings from the Internet Control Panel (see Figure 16.9). Here's a description of what each tab window offers:

> Some of the settings in your Internet Control Panel are put there when you set up an Internet service. They are needed to work with that service. You can change your Personal and Web settings without causing a problem, but other settings might affect your ability to connect to the service.

FIGURE 16.9

These settings control how your computer works with an Internet connection.

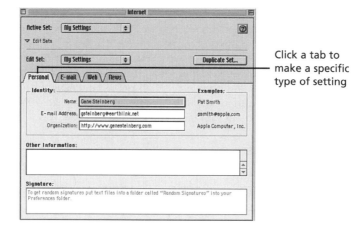

Click a tab to make a specific type of setting

- **Personal**: These settings determine how you're identified when you send email and whether a default signature will be used.
- **E-mail**: This panel contains the settings needed to send and receive email. Don't change them unless you change your Internet service.
- **Web**: You can change your Web browser, the home page, and the page used for Internet searching here.
- **News**: These settings should also be left alone unless you change your Internet service. They enable you to access Usenet Internet message boards for discussions.

> **NEW TERM** *Usenet*, short for "user net," is the common name for Internet-based message or discussion boards. These are the online equivalent of the bulletin boards in your supermarket or civic club. You can use them to read messages from others or place your own statements about one subject or another.

Setting the Keyboard Control Panel

Use these settings to choose a foreign language keyboard or the speed at which your keyboard repeats a keystroke.

Setting the Launcher Control Panel

If the Launcher isn't turned on, select this Control Panel to activate it. See Hour 15 for more information about the Launcher.

To add a program to the Launcher, simply drag the program icon (or its alias) to the Launcher window. Within seconds, it will be available from the list of buttons. But you might have to scroll or click the resize bar on the Launcher window to see all the icons you've added. You can remove an icon by holding down the Option key and dragging the icon from the Launcher. The button size can be changed by pressing the Command key and clicking your mouse and then choosing the new size.

Setting the Location Manager Control Panel

When your iMac travels with you from place to place, you might want to set up such things as custom Internet, network, printer, sound, and time zone settings here.

Setting the Memory Control Panel

This Control Panel is used to activate several features (see Figure 16.10) that have a direct connection with your computer's performance under regular usage. The changes require a restart to activate. The following list describes what those features are used for.

FIGURE 16.10

The settings you make in the Memory Control Panel can impact the performance of your computer.

The best way to set the Memory Control Panel is to click the Use Defaults button. That will establish the optimum disk cache and virtual memory settings for your iMac (depending on how much RAM is installed). Change it only if you add more RAM.

- **Disk Cache**: This setting reserves a small amount of RAM to store frequently used data from your hard drive. The default setting offers a decent speed boost for your iMac. Setting it too low to conserve RAM will slow down some functions (such as display of document windows).

- **Virtual Memory**: Virtual memory sets aside a part of your hard drive to simulate RAM. It's useful to extend available memory when you want to run more programs. But because a hard drive is much slower than real RAM, it might also slow things down somewhat, especially if you set it too high. The normal setting establishes virtual memory at 1MB above the amount of built-in memory on your computer. This setting actually can make some programs run faster (and besides, they also use less memory for some highly technical reasons).

- **RAM Disk**: This feature sets aside RAM to use to simulate the functions of a hard drive (such as copying files and so on). But the memory used here is lost to your computer to run programs. *Use this feature only if you have a lot of RAM installed.* I'll tell you more about RAM upgrades in Hour 22, "Giving Your iMac New Software, More Ram, and Other Things."

16

Setting the Modem Control Panel

This Control Panel offers a pop-up menu that is used to select a different modem. Because your iMac already has an internal modem, you'll probably never use this one.

Setting the Monitors Control Panel

This convenient program is used to make several flavors of screen settings on your iMac (see Figure 16.11).

FIGURE 16.11
You can adjust screen settings with this program.

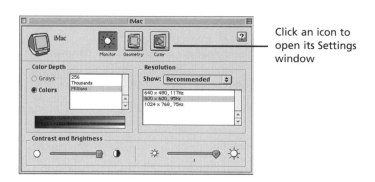

Click an icon to open its Settings window

Here's a brief discussion of the Monitors Control Panel features and what they do. The settings you make here go into effect right away.

- **Monitor**: Use this to change the number of colors on your screen and the resolution (how big or small lettering and icons will appear to be). You can also adjust basic monitor brightness and contrast.

- **Geometry**: If your iMac's screen display seems too small, is off center, or is turned at an angle, you can customize it here. Yes, much like the serviceman who adjusts your TV.

> If your monitor settings get messed up, just click the Factory Settings button in the Geometry panel to restore them to their original settings.

- **Color**: Use this setting to calibrate the color of your iMac's screen, to provide a more accurate color balance.

Setting the Mouse Control Panel

Double-click this Control Panel if you find your mouse is too fast or too slow. You'll be able to make several speed adjustments here.

Setting the Numbers Control Panel

Sorry, this Control Panel won't help you in Las Vegas. It's used to change the way numbers are displayed in the country in which you live.

Setting the QuickTime Settings Control Panel

This program is used to direct the way QuickTime works on your computer. If you upgrade to QuickTime Pro (as described in Hour 13, "Multimedia Is More Than a CD-ROM Game"), you'll need to type the registration number Apple sends you here.

Setting the Remote Access Control Panel

You use this Control Panel to set the phone number and access information needed for your Internet provider. After things are set up, you'll need to use this program only to connect and disconnect.

Setting the Sound Control Panel

OS 9   You were introduced to this handy program in Hour 14, "Using the iMac Speech Recording Features," in the lesson about using sounds and speech with your iMac (see Figure 16.12).

FIGURE 16.12
You can adjust audio settings with this program.

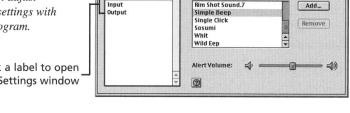

Click a label to open the Settings window

Here's a brief list of Sound Control Panel features and what they do. The settings you make here go into effect right away.

- **Alert Sounds**: Choose the sound for your standard alert tones. If you want to add new alerts or record one of your own, see Hour 14 for the particulars.
- **Input**: Use this to select your computer's sound input sources.
- **Output**: Set your computer's volume level and sound-related options (such as the iMac's 3D Surround Sound effect).

Setting the Speech Control Panel

I described the functions of this Control Panel in Hour 14.

Setting the Startup Disk Control Panel

This isn't necessarily an adjustment you'd need to make unless you zapped the PRAM (which clears the setting) or wanted to use another startup disk (the feature works only with a CD as of the time this book was written).

Setting the TCP/IP Control Panel

The settings used to connect to the Internet, or perhaps a network, are created here. Usually, these adjustments are made by the installation software used by your Internet service, so you should rarely have to open this program unless you want to switch to another setting.

The arcane numbers and words used in the TCP/IP Control Panel are necessary for certain Internet or network hookups. If you change even a single character or number, the connections won't work. It's best not to change any setting without detailed instructions on the information you need to enter.

Summary

In this lesson you discovered ways to customize your computer's settings so that it looks and runs better. As you add new software to your iMac, you'll find additional Control Panels that provide even more interesting functions.

In previous lessons, I described how you can create documents in various programs, such as AppleWorks. In Hour 17, "Now That I Wrote It, How Do I Print It?," you'll learn about installing a new printer and setting it up for the best quality printouts.

Q&A

Q I'm confused. In Hour 15, you described extensions as programs that enhance the functionality of a Mac OS computer. But the Control Panels seem to do the very same thing. What's the difference?

A The biggest difference is that an extension doesn't have a user interface for you to make an adjustment. The Control Panel does. But the waters get muddied after that. Some Control Panels work in concert with an extension to provide some features, such as Extensions Manager and the EM Extension. Some Control Panels (such as the Memory Control Panel) do their stuff without any other programs. As I said, the major difference lies in the word *control*, the ability to set things.

Q Suddenly I see folders labeled Extensions (Disabled), Control Panels (Disabled), and so on. What are they for, and can I remove them?

A Best thing to do is leave them alone, unless you know the contents aren't needed (and more often than not, it's difficult to tell, unless the item is clearly labeled as something you don't need). When you turn off an Extension or Control Panel with Extensions Manager, it goes in one of these folders. When the program is reactivated, it goes back to its regular folder.

Q Some of the programs I want to use say I need to create an "Apple only" extension set to install them. How do I set it up?

A This is easy, because the Extensions Manager Control Panel already has it. Just click the Selected Set pop-up menu to find Mac OS 9 All and Mac OS 9 Base settings (or whatever system version you're using). For normal software installations, choose the latter and restart. After your program is installed, you can open up Extensions Manager, click My Settings from the pop-up menu (or whatever name you've given your set), and restart yet again to set things back the way they were.

Hour 17

Now That I Wrote It, How Do I Print It?

I've focused several lessons on how to create work. You've learned how to use AppleWorks, an integrated program that lets you write, draw pictures, and store financial and other information.

In this lesson, I'll show you how to get a printout of those documents. You'll learn

- What kinds of printers are available for your computer.
- The advantages and disadvantages of inkjet and laser printers.
- How to hook up and configure your new printer.
- How to switch printers on a network.

Buying a New Printer

When you visit your dealer or look over a computer catalog, no doubt you've seen a bewildering array of printers. And a great range of prices. You can buy printers for not much more than one hundred dollars, while others cost thousands.

You want your documents to look their best, but with all the confusing claims about dots-per-inch, four-color, six-color, inkjet versus laser, and photo-realistic, how do you pick the one printer that is perfect for you?

In this part of the lesson, I'll list the kinds of printers that are available, and I'll also define a few of the buzzwords, so you can see which ones matter.

- **Dot-matrix printer**: This sort of printer owes a lot to the traditional typewriter. A printing head puts the image on paper in the form of little dots. Such printers aren't available these days, but older Apple ImageWriters still run and many folks still use them. There is an ImageWriter printer driver on most Mac OS computers these days, although you will need a special adapter plug to allow you to hook it up to an iMac.

- **Inkjet printer**: Here's another printer that owes something to the original type-writer. Instead of keys or a little "ball" with letters, the inkjet printer uses a small bottle of ink (the cartridge) that is run back and forth across the paper on a little sled-like device. Such printers can be quite cheap, and they offer color reproduction and terrific printouts of photos and artwork. But because these printers are still using ink (no matter what the technology), the text isn't quite as sharp and clean as the laser printer.

- **Laser printer**: Laser printers are similar to copying machines. They use fine black powder (toner) to paint the image on paper, and their printing engines use laser devices (like your CD or DVD player). Such printers generally have their own computers, so they cost much more than an inkjet printer, but they offer great out-put quality, especially with text. Color laser printers, though, are especially expensive; they can cost several times what your iMac set you back.

- **Four-color and six-color**: In commercial printing, the various colors in a full-color page are created by using four primary colors (one printing plate for each) and mixing them to various degrees. Six-color printers provide more accurate reproduction of color prints, at least in theory, but you can get great quality from four-color printers, too.

- **Networked printer**: This sort of printer attaches to your computer's ethernet jack and can be shared by other Mac OS computers across a network. Both inkjet and laser printers may come with the proper networking electronics for this sort of connection.

- **Dots-per-inch**: The printed page is made up of little dots, or *pixels*. The more dots per inch, the smaller the dots and the sharper the output. Because laser printers produce sharper dots, though, they will offer better output quality for a specific dots-per-inch specification.

Setting Up a New Printer

Regardless of the kind of printer you buy, the basic hookup steps are similar. The process usually takes just a few minutes from the time you crack open the box until the printer is up and running.

The setup steps for inkjets and laser printers are pretty similar, so I'll describe them together here, with a few notes to show where things may diverge.

1. Unpack your printer and check the device for little bits of tape and cardboard that are needed for shipping.

> I cannot overemphasize the need to remove packing materials before you try to use a printer. Some of those little bits of tape and cardboard can literally lock up the printer (maybe damage it) if you try to use it without removing this material. If in doubt, check the printer's setup manual for information.

2. Plug it in to the power source (AC line or power strip) and install the ink cartridges or toner assembly (whichever applies) as instructed by the manufacturer.

> Inkjet printers are usually set up so that you may have to actually turn them on and push a button to move the inkwells into the proper place to install the cartridge or cartridges. In addition to documentation, such printers may also have a little chart inside to show you how to install cartridges.

3. Use the manufacturer's connection cable to attach the printer to your computer. Depending on the kind of printer or connection setup you have, you will be using either the ethernet port or a USB port (you can use the empty jack on your keyboard for this connection).

If you're using an ethernet printer, you will need to either install a hub (a special connection interface) or use a crossover cable for the hookup to work. Check with your dealer for the requirements.

4. Get out the manufacturer's software CD, insert it into your computer's drive, and install the printing software.

Some printers come with floppy disks rather than CDs for software (these tend to be older models). Unless you bought a SuperDisk drive or other floppy device for your computer, you'll have to contact your dealer or the manufacturer for a software CD (or just install it on another Mac and transfer the files via networking).

If you are setting up a new laser printer, you may be able to save a little time in installing the software. Your computer already has a LaserWriter printer driver that works with most products. Just locate the correct PPD file (which contains custom printer settings) and install it in the Printer Descriptions folder (inside the Extensions folder on your iMac).

5. After software installation is done, restart your computer.

6. The next step is to select the printer driver on your computer. To do that, you need to go to the Apple menu and select the Chooser (see Figure 17.1). The printer's name will appear in the Select a Printer side.

If you're installing a laser printer, you'll see a button labeled Setup at the bottom of the Select a Printer window. Click that button to complete the configuration process.

Not all printers can be identified by the Printer icon in the Chooser (not very convenient!). You may have to check the documentation to see what you have to pick. For example, my Epson Stylus Color 850ne color inkjet printer is identified in the Chooser as SC 850(AT).

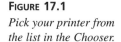

FIGURE 17.1
Pick your printer from the list in the Chooser.

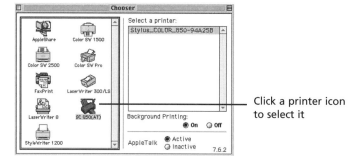

Click a printer icon
to select it

7. Close the Chooser window. You'll see an acknowledgement message that your printer has been selected (see Figure 17.2).

FIGURE 17.2
Your printer has been selected, and you're ready to go.

Click the OK button to
dismiss this message

▲ Congratulations, you're now ready to print your documents.

If you have more than one printer, you'll be revisiting the Chooser every so often to switch from one to the other (unless it's between two laser printers).

Configuring the Page Setup for Your Inkjet Printer

As you see, hooking up a new printer to your computer can be done in a matter of a few minutes at most. And now you're ready to print your documents—well, almost. When you first print your document, you will have to set up a few more things to make sure that your document comes out properly.

That will require a dialog box called Page Setup, which is available from the File menu in most of your programs. See Figure 17.3 for the one that comes with a typical Epson inkjet printer (I'll cover the one for laser printers in a later section).

The Page Setup dialog box will change from printer to printer, and also when you switch from one program to another. I'm covering just the basic features here. Your printer's documentation will offer extra setup instructions.

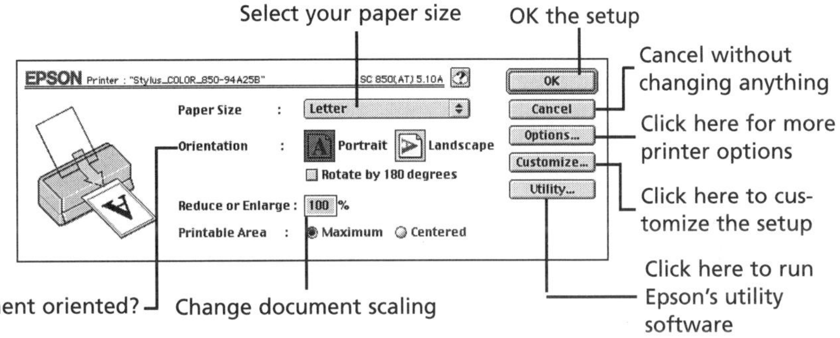

FIGURE 17.3

This is the Page Setup dialog box for an Epson inkjet printer when you're using AppleWorks.

Select your paper size   OK the setup

Cancel without changing anything

Click here for more printer options

Click here to customize the setup

Click here to run Epson's utility software

How is your document oriented?   Change document scaling

By default, the designers of the printing software will guess that you're using a regular, letter-size page and establish the other settings shown in Figure 17.3. If you need to change things, here's what the settings mean:

- **Paper Size**: This pop-up menu is used to pick a different paper size and type, such as legal size, envelopes, and so on.
- **Orientation**: Is your document set up in horizontal or vertical form? Make your change here.
- **Reduce or Enlarge**: If your document is too large for the paper you have, you can scale it down here (or make it larger for a smaller-size document).

Be careful about making a small document larger to fit a paper size. When you enlarge some documents (such as those containing pictures), the quality is reduced in proportion to the amount you increase the size.

- **Options**: Click this button (see Figure 17.4) to make additional printer settings. You can increase printer resolution for sharper printouts or make custom settings for color or for paper type.

FIGURE 17.4

These are the options available when you set up an Epson printer. Other printers will have their own sets of features.

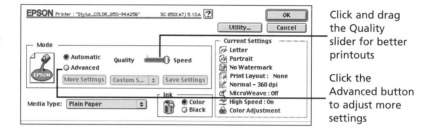

Click and drag the Quality slider for better printouts

Click the Advanced button to adjust more settings

There's no perfect printer setting. You may want to try several and do a sample printout to see which works best with the sort of documents you make. You can save time by using a low-resolution mode when creating a document (because documents print much faster that way) then using the higher-quality mode for final printouts.

- **Customize**: This particular setting lets you create custom profiles for some jobs, so that you can recall them without having to fix up every setting each time you change page size or document style.

- **Utility**: Click this button to access special printer utilities, such as a program that cleans the printer heads when the quality gets a little muddy.

When you save your document, the Page Setup information you set will usually be stored with it. You shouldn't have to reconfigure it every time you want to print the same document.

After your settings are made, click OK to put them in effect.

Printing Your Document on an Inkjet Printer

After you've checked the Page Setup dialog box and set it up, it's time to actually print your document. Unless you intend to change something, here's what you do:

1. Choose Print from the File menu (or press Command+P), which opens a dialog box similar to the one shown in Figure 17.5.

▼

Select the number of copies ⌐   Identify the range of pages to print ⌐   Click Layout to change ⌐print order and scaling

FIGURE 17.5

Activate the printing function from this dialog box.

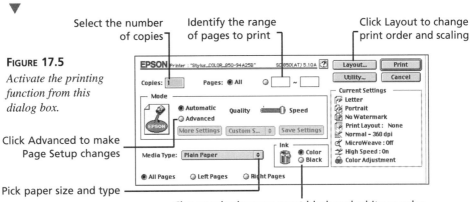

Click Advanced to make Page Setup changes

Pick paper size and type

Choose whether you want black-and-white or color

2. To print your document, click the Print button. This will get you one copy of each
▲   page in your document.

You will see a printer dialog box on your screen showing the progress of your job. Within a few seconds, you should hear some activity from your printer, indicating that the process has begun. You'll regain control of your computer when the last document has been printed. How long that takes depends on how big your document is and the print quality choices you set (higher quality and color take much, much longer, often several minutes per page).

Using Background Printing

If you've grown tired of waiting for the print job to finish before getting back to work, you'll want to try out the background printing feature. If you check Figure 17.1 again, you'll see a check box on the Select a Printer half of the Chooser window that lets you activate this feature.

When you turn on this feature (and it is on automatically when you set up a laser printer), your printer will make a copy of the file in the printer's own language and then feed it to the printer automatically as needed (in the background), letting you get back to work after a few seconds.

Not all printers support background printing. If the choice isn't in your Chooser (or grayed out), you may want to check the printer manual to see if the feature is available and what you need to do to get it to work.

Inkjet printers use your computer for processing the document you're printing. If you want to switch to another printer for a job, wait until printing is done. If you go to the Chooser and pick another printer while the inkjet printer is working, you'll interrupt the printing process, and all you'll get is an error message, rather than your printed document (or just part of the document). If you're using a laser printer, networked, it's okay to switch to another printer before printing is done when using background printing.

Using a Laser Printer's Page Setup Box

A regular, garden-variety, black-and-white laser printer doesn't have nearly as many settings to make as a color printer or an inkjet printer. But the basics of paper type and orientation are the same.

Here's a typical Page Setup box for a popular office laser printer (from HP), as shown in Figure 17.6.

FIGURE 17.6

This is the Page Setup dialog box for a standard laser printer.

Icon illustrates setup choice

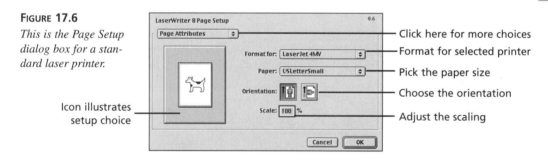

Click here for more choices
Format for selected printer
Pick the paper size
Choose the orientation
Adjust the scaling

I'll briefly describe what the various settings mean.

- **Page Attributes** (pop-up menu): Click this menu for other printer options (such as PostScript options).

NEW TERM   *PostScript* is a printer language from Adobe Systems that is used in the professional publishing and printing industries. The language describes mathematically the content of the printed page. Most laser printers for iMacs support PostScript.

- **Format for**: If you have more than one laser printer installed, you can skip a trip to the Chooser and select a different one here.
- **Paper**: Pick your paper size and type from this pop-up menu.
- **Orientation**: Pick portrait or landscape as you do with the inkjet printer.
- **Scale**: This feature is the same as the Reduce and Enlarge feature of the inkjet's Page Setup box.

When you've made the setups you want, click OK to put them in motion. As with the inkjet printer, when you save your document, the Page Setup changes you make are also included.

Some programs, such as AppleWorks, remember your last printer setting. Some programs don't. So before you print a document the first time after creating it, it's a good idea to double-check the Page Setup dialog box to avoid any surprises.

Printing a Document with Your Laser Printer

There's little difference in printing a document with your laser printer and inkjet printer after you perform the basic setups. But because the dialog boxes are different, I'll describe the laser printer variation here.

To activate the Print feature, choose Print from the File menu. This opens a dialog box similar to the one shown in Figure 17.7.

FIGURE **17.7**
Activate the Print function on your laser printer from this dialog box.

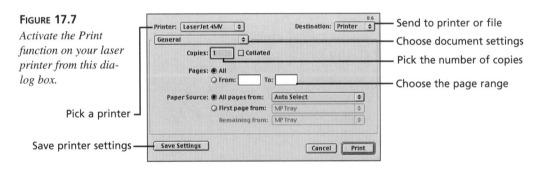

Send to printer or file
Choose document settings
Pick the number of copies
Choose the page range

Pick a printer

Save printer settings

Unlike with inkjet printers, background printing is the default for most laser printers (so you don't have to change anything unless you prefer to switch it off).

You'll notice that a few features are different. Under most circumstances, you'll just click Print and sit back and wait for the document to finish. But if you want to change things, here's what the other functions are used for:

- **Printer**: You can switch between networked laser printers from this dialog box.
- **Destination**: When you use a PostScript laser printer, you can make what is called a printer file of your document, rather than just print the pages. Some printing firms use this file with their own equipment to make final copies for reproduction.
- **General**: Click this pop-up menu to bring up some custom printer and document features.
- **Copies**: Pick how many, if more than just one.
- **Paper Source**: Some laser printers have more than one paper tray, so you may want to set it up to pick from different trays (such as the letterhead in the top tray, the rest in a lower tray).
- **Save Settings**: The laser printer driver lets you save your settings, so you don't have to do them again the next time you want to print a document.

I just want to remind you that the printer dialog boxes you see are going to change a small amount or a lot when you use different printers or different programs to make your documents.

When you set up most laser printers (and only a few inkjet models), you'll see a desktop icon representing the printer. If you drag one or more documents to that icon, the application that made the document will be launched automatically, and you'll see a Print dialog box. When you click the Print command, the print process will begin and the program will quit. Cool!

Summary

There are many great printers from which to choose for your documents. Whether you want to print color art, photos, or your first novel, you'll be able to find the right product and easily hook it up to your computer.

In Hour 18, you'll see how the iMac works in a world where lots of other people are using computers for that "other" platform.

Q&A

Q **I'm using background printing, but whenever my inkjet printer is printing something, everything runs like molasses. I thought my computer's PowerPC microprocessor was supposed to be the fastest thing on the planet. What's wrong?**

A As fast as the iMac works for regular work, it bogs down when it has to perform two or more tasks at once. Part of the reason is the way the Mac multitasks. The method is called *cooperative* multitasking because each program has to share its processing time with another when needed. When you use an inkjet printer, your computer serves as the printer's computer (or *raster image processor*, RIP for short), too. So things can bog down. But you should still be able to do many tasks on your iMac during the printing process, including word processing and even Internet visits. Until Apple addresses the limits of multitasking (which they plan to do with the client version of Mac OS X, a future major upgrade scheduled for the year 2000), you will have to put up with this sort of response.

What you get with a laser printer, by the way, in addition to its superior handling of text and speed, is the fact that it has its own computer. So your computer does not feel as sluggish.

Q **I have an old Apple StyleWriter. When I tried to hook it up to the iMac, I couldn't find any place to plug it in. I need this printer, and I don't want to buy a new one. What can I do to make it work?**

A The newest Mac OS computers uses a different type of expansion port than other Macs, USB, so it has no place to plug in that StyleWriter. But all is not lost. Check with your dealer and ask about a "USB to serial" adapter plug. That will enable you to run your older printer without a problem. Figure on paying $50 to $100, depending on the sort of adapter you need. You can also get adapters that work with older printers that support LocalTalk hookups.

Q **I tried to print a document, but I kept getting error messages. What is wrong?**

A The first thing to do is to see if the message tells you what's wrong. It's not always easy to solve printing problems, because a small error in the Page Setup box (for example, wrong paper size) or a lack of paper may cause the problem.

Here are some things to check:

- **Out of paper/paper jammed:** Make sure that your printer has enough paper, and check to see if a page has jammed inside it. If there's a paper jam, check the manufacturer's directions on how to fix it.

- **Make sure that it is on and connected:** It's very easy to disconnect something (maybe during redecorating or to use the outlet for another item). Double-check your connections and make sure that the printer's on light is running. Also check your printer's documentation on error lights and what they mean.

- **Look at the Page Setup box:** If you choose the wrong paper size or the wrong paper orientation, the printer may just give up the ghost. You'll want to double-check those settings.

- **For laser printers:** Choose the right PPD file. So-called "PostScript" laser printers use special files called PPDs that tell the printer driver about the printer and its special features (such as extra trays, larger paper sizes, and so on). You need to make sure that your PPD file is installed (inside the Printer Descriptions folder, in the Extensions folder). You should also make sure that you did the proper setup routine when you selected the printer in the Chooser. If the PPD file isn't there, check your printer's software disks or contact the dealer or manufacturer to get one.

- **Out of memory:** The software used for background printing consumes memory on your computer. If you get an out-of-memory warning regularly, you might want to consider opening the Chooser, selecting the printer you're using, and turning off the background-printing feature.

17

Q **You mention PostScript printers from time to time. Can I get that feature on an inkjet printer? What is it good for?**

A Yes, there are programs that will let you use PostScript with your inkjet printer. Three products that come to mind are Birmy Script, Epson Stylus RIP (for many Epson printers), and Infowave's StyleScript. Another product coming to market when this book was written was Adobe PressReady, which was designed to offer a similar set of features for many inkjets. You'll want to check with your dealer about which products are compatible with your inkjet printer.

PostScript doesn't help much if you use just text, but if you do complex graphics (such as those made with a PostScript drawing program, such as Adobe Illustrator, CorelDRAW, or Macromedia FreeHand), rotated pictures, and so on, you'll find a PostScript option gives you sharper, more accurate output. If you are doing work for the professional marketplace, PostScript is essential.

HOUR 18

Coping with the Windows World

I won't ignore the obvious. The majority of personal computers out there in the world use Windows, but that doesn't mean you should feel compelled to abandon the Mac operating system in favor of that "other" platform.

But there are times when you will still have to recognize reality and handle documents that have been created in a Windows program or even use software that isn't available in Mac trim.

In this lesson, I'll show you ways to cope with the Windows world and stick with your iMac. You'll learn

- How to use File Exchange to read Windows documents and disks.
- How to locate a compatible Mac program for your Windows files.
- How to share files with other computers, Mac or Windows.
- How to actually set up a real DOS or Windows environment on your computer and instantly switch between it and the Mac OS.

Using PC Exchange for Windows Files

Apple Computer has recognized the reality. There are times when you will receive documents made in a Windows program, such as Office 97 or Office 2000, and there are times you'll have to use a disk made on that other platform.

Fortunately, there are ways around this dilemma, and the best part is that your iMac comes equipped with software that is perfectly capable of reading those files and disks.

It's called File Exchange. You can access it by going to the Apple menu, selecting Control Panels, and choosing File Exchange from the submenu (see Figure 18.1).

By far the most effective way to read a Windows file properly on a Mac is to buy the Mac equivalent of the Windows program (if it's available). For example, if you handle lots of files created in Word or another Microsoft Office program, you'll want to consider the Mac version of Microsoft Office. If all you need is Word, consider the Word 98 Special Edition for the iMac and iBook, which was being offered for less than $100 when this book was written.

FIGURE 18.1

You can use this program to access files created on a PC.

Open PC documents in programs from the file list

Mount PC disks on your computer

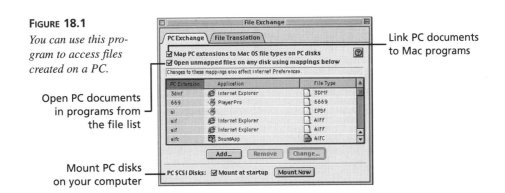

Link PC documents to Mac programs

You cannot mount a PC disk on your iMac without a drive in which to mount it. If you have a CD from the "other" platform, no problem. But if you have a PC floppy or a disk created in another removable format, such as the SuperDisk or zip drive, you need to buy a disk drive that supports one of these formats.

There's no mystery about using File Exchange, and usually there's nothing to learn. You just double-click a file and, so long as you have a Mac program that reads the type of file you have, you're home free. That program will open.

> The first time you open a program for which you don't have the application, File Exchange will put up a dialog box listing applications from which to choose. After you've made that selection, files of the same type will open in the future without further intervention on your part.

There are some considerations, though:

- **Document Formatting**: If you don't have the Mac version of the PC program that made the file, you may lose a bit in the translation. Complex text formats, tables, and so on may not translate accurately. And if the PC document uses fonts that aren't installed on your computer, the fonts will look different. The translation process is very flexible, but there are no miracles.

- **Missing Data**: Sometimes files just don't translate intact; some content is missing. If you need to work on a PC file, ask the folks who created the file to send you a printout so you can compare it for accuracy.

Special PC Exchange Features

Here's some more information about the features available in PC Exchange:

- **Map PC Extensions to Mac OS File Types on PC Disks**: In the PC world, files are identified by a three-letter code, a file extension that explains the sort of program that made it, or the type of file it is. For example, if you get a file with the suffix or extension .doc, it is a file created in Microsoft Word for Windows.

- **Open Unmapped Files on Any Disk by Using Mappings Below**: This is a customized list, where you can tell File Exchange which programs you want to open for certain file types. Usually, the standard settings work fine, so you will probably want to leave this setting alone. What's more, it affects your Internet settings (the programs that run when you download some material from the Internet).

- **PC SCSI Disks**: This selection doesn't really apply to the iMac, because it lacks support for drives using the SCSI protocol. You'd only be interested in this feature if you purchased a USB-to-SCSI adapter interface from your dealer, so you can use SCSI drives.

18

Making File Translation Settings

When you double-click a file and you don't have the program that created it, File Exchange will go into action to translate it automatically. The feature isn't just for PC files; it works for Mac files, too. Because there are thousands of Mac programs out there, it's highly unlikely you'd have even a fraction of them available.

To adjust your file translation settings, open File Exchange from the Control Panels sub-menu; then click the File Translation tab, which opens the screen shown in Figure 18.2 (with default settings).

FIGURE **18.2**

Here's where you tell File Exchange how to handle its translation process.

Choose programs from a network

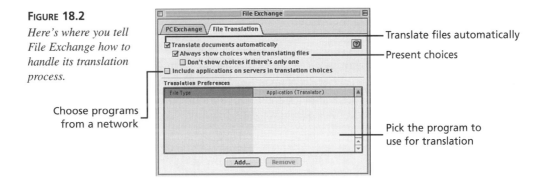

Translate files automatically

Present choices

Pick the program to use for translation

As with the main File Exchange window back in Figure 18.1, the factory settings usually work just fine. But I'll cover the rest here in case you want to give them a whirl:

- **Translate Documents Automatically**: Whenever you open a document (Mac or PC) and you don't have the program that made it, File Exchange will try to convert it for you, so you can read the file.

- **Always Show Choices when Translating Files**: If you have more than one program that works with the file, you'll see a window giving you the choice to pick one. Best thing to do is select a program you use regularly, so it will be a lot easier to handle the translated document.

- **Don't Show Choices if There's Only One**: It's off by default, but you may just want to check it if you prefer having File Exchange always accept your lone choice.

- **Include Applications on Servers in Translation Choices**: This option is needed only if the program you want to launch is on a network server.

- **Translation Preferences**: If you have several programs that might be suitable for file translation (such as more than one word processor), you might want to state a preference here. But this is not an essential setting otherwise.

Exchanging Files with Other Computers

In the old days, when only large companies used computer networks, sharing files was done by a technique known as *sneaker net*. You copied the file to a disk and physically walked the disk over to the other computer. It was a great form of exercise, if you had a big office.

Nowadays, though, you can set up a network in minutes, and your computer can easily communicate with other Macs or Windows-based computers by way of its ethernet networking jack. All you need is an ethernet crossover cable or a hub (a central connection module).

The basic process of sharing files is simple (Nike and Reebok shoes aren't required). Here's how you do it:

▼ To Do

1. Click the folder (Sharing) icon on the Control Strip.

2. Select Turn File Sharing On (it will toggle to Off next time you open it). You'll see the folder icon animate for a moment and, when it stops, you'll be in Sharing mode.

3. When you want to turn off sharing, simply click the Sharing icon in the Control Strip and select Turn File Sharing Off. You'll see a dialog box notifying you that sharing will turn off in 10 minutes (you can change this), to give other users on your network enough time to finish up.

▲

And that's all there is to make your computer's drive available to others on your network. If you want to control access to your computer, open the File Sharing Control Panel and click the Users & Groups tab (see Figure 18.3) and make your settings.

18

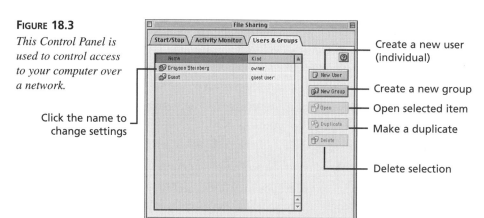

FIGURE 18.3

This Control Panel is used to control access to your computer over a network.

Click the name to change settings

Create a new user (individual)

Create a new group

Open selected item

Make a duplicate

Delete selection

For each user or group, you have the option to allow them to access your computer and whether or not they can access your hard drives.

> If you don't need to give password protection to your computer on your computer network, click Guest, choose Sharing from the pop-up menu, and click the option to allow guests to connect to you. That will let another computer user on your network link up without having to give a username and password (use this feature with caution).

Connecting to Another Mac

Connecting to another Mac on your network is just as simple. All you have to do is

1. Confirm that the computer you want to access has Sharing turned on.

2. Go to the Apple menu and select Network Browser, which opens the screen shown in Figure 18.4.

FIGURE 18.4

This screen shows the computers available on your network.

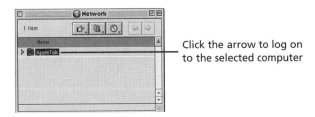

Click the arrow to log on to the selected computer

3. Click AppleTalk (if you've also shared computers via the Internet, you see an option for that, too).

4. After you've selected AppleTalk, you'll see a list of shared computers on your network. To access one of them, simply click the arrow at the left of the computer's name. It will point downward, and you'll see a password prompt (see Figure 18.5).

5. Type the password exactly as it was established on the other computer. That includes upper- and lowercase letters, as needed.

6. Click Connect to bring up the list of available drives in the Network Browser.

7. Double-click the selected drive to open it on your computer's desktop.

8. When you're done sharing files, you may disconnect from that computer simply by dragging its drive icon to the trash (same as you eject a floppy, SuperDisk, or CD).

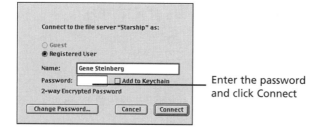

FIGURE 18.5

Enter your password to access that computer's drive.

Enter the password
and click Connect

Sharing Files with Windows Users

It gets a little more complicated if you have Windows users on the network, but there are ways to do it. Here are two possibilities:

- **Printers**: If the network laser printer uses ethernet, you can connect to the printer as easily as to another Mac. You can set it up in the Chooser, simply by picking LaserWriter 8 and selecting the printer's name from the list shown. Such printers usually allow for sharing jobs between Macs and PCs without special setups. If the printer doesn't use ethernet, you'll have to see if an AppleTalk upgrade card is available, and then you'll have to add an AppleTalk-to-ethernet interface to your computer. Ethernet is a lot easier.

One company, Infowave, has a product that you can use work with non-PostScript network printers. It's called PowerPrint for Networks, and it is designed to support more than 1,600 PC printer models and allow Mac OS computers to work with them. To explore the details of this product, pay a visit to the publisher's Web site at http://www.infowave.com.

- **Files**: One of the easiest ways to access a Windows or Windows NT network is a program from Thursby Software Systems called DAVE. With this program, you can connect to the Windows network as easily as you can access another Mac on your network (and that includes networked servers running Windows NT or Windows 2000). It also gives the PC user the capability to communicate with your computer just as simply. You can order a copy of this program at most computer dealers or visit the company's Web site at http://www.thursby.com for more information.

Making a Mac Do Windows

As easy as it is to use PC disks on your computer and access a network with computers from the "other" platform, there will be times that you'll actually need to run a PC program, too.

Fortunately, there's a way to do it without having to get a new computer. That way is with a DOS or Windows emulator.

Two software publishers, Connectix and FWB, offer solutions to this problem. Using these products, you get the best of both worlds. You can continue to use your Mac's programs the same as you currently do and have the added advantage of summoning a Windows setup when necessary.

 Having the ability to quickly jump between the Mac and Windows environments is great for writers like me who have to prepare books covering both platforms. A real time saver!

FWB's answer is its SoftPC line. These programs are specially optimized to run the PC operating system they ship with. Here's what the products do:

- **RealPC**: This program creates a real DOS environment on your iMac's desktop. It's useful for strictly running DOS programs or using DOS games. You can install Windows 95 or Windows 98 at a later time if you prefer.

- **SoftWindows 95**: You can use this program to offer a genuine Windows 95 desktop on your computer. You can access most Windows and DOS programs and copy text and pictures between the PC environment and your iMac.

- **SoftWindows 98**: This program offers Windows 98 instead of Windows 95, but is otherwise virtually identical to SoftWindows 95.

From Connectix you have

- **Virtual PC**: This program actually emulates a genuine Intel Pentium microprocessor on your computer. You can get the basic program and install any PC operating system, including Windows NT, Windows 2000, and various flavors of the industrial-strength UNIX operating systems. Or you can get versions bundled with DOS, Windows 95, or Windows 98.

A Case History: Connectix Virtual PC with Windows 98

An example of how clever these programs are is the version of Virtual PC that comes with Windows 98 already installed. It takes just minutes to install it from a CD, and after it's set up, you'll see a screen much like the one shown in Figure 18.6.

FIGURE 18.6

Is it a Mac or is it...? Yes, it's the author's iMac, running Windows 98.

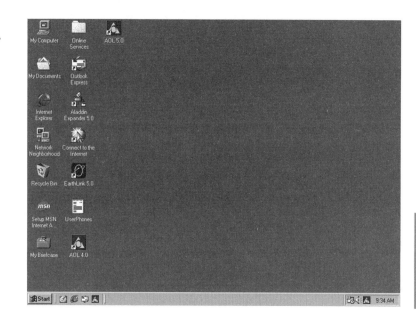

18

In order to do its magic, the Windows emulator has to map (link) some native PC functions to your Mac. But setting it up is quite simple. The Preference box from Virtual PC shows how you can configure it to provide near-seamless PC performance (see Figure 18.7).

FIGURE 18.7

Microsoft Windows runs on your Mac through these settings.

Click an icon to change a setting

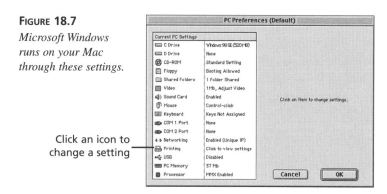

The settings options for Virtual PC are close enough to that in SoftWindows that the following description applies in great part to both programs:

> I've based my descriptions of Virtual PC preferences on version 3.0, which began to ship in the fall of 1999. Earlier versions did not, for example, support USB peripherals or a shared IP address.

- **C Drive**: Virtual PC puts a file on your computer's drive that emulates a genuine Windows drive. You can use the program's tools to make the drive larger if you need to install more programs.
- **D Drive**: This setting lets you create a second drive file on your iMac.
- **CD-ROM**: Use this setting to control access to your computer's CD-ROM drive.
- **Floppy**: This setting enables Windows to start (boot) from a floppy (if you have the appropriate drive installed on your iMac).
- **Shared Folders**: You can set aside a folder on your computer's drive to share files between the Mac and Windows environments.
- **Video**: This setting is used to set aside RAM to emulate a PC graphic card.
- **Sound Card**: Use these adjustments to set up sound emulation on your Windows emulator.

> Unlike Macs, computers from that "other" platform require a special sound card to produce anything more than a beep for sound events or for playing a sound file. Most PCs, though, come with sound cards already installed.

- **Mouse**: This setting lets you link a Macintosh keyboard and mouse combo to emulate the infamous "right mouse button" under Windows.
- **Keyboard**: This setting lets you link Mac keyboard characters to Windows keystrokes. The manual for the program explains what you need to do.
- **COM 1 Port**: This is used to make your internal modem work with a Windows communications port.

- **COM 2 Port**: Use this setting to configure a second port to connect with a modem.
- **Networking**: This setting lets you decide whether Virtual PC can share the same IP (Internet provider) address as your Mac environment. This is useful when you connect to your Internet provider and then fire up Virtual PC to share the connection and use Windows-based programs.
- **Printing**: You will set this up to allow you to use your computer's printer under the PC environment.
- **USB**: This setting allows Virtual PC to share your USB drives.
- **PC Memory**: This indicator shows how much of your computer's RAM is allocated for the PC emulation. The more the better.

> The amount of memory displayed under PC Memory doesn't show all the memory that the program needs to run. Another 8 to 12MB of RAM is needed to cover the emulation functions of these programs. In order to set up 37MB of PC memory (as shown in Figure 18.7), I had to have nearly 50MB of RAM allocated to Virtual PC.

18

- **Processor**: Use this setting to access certain features that are exclusive to the Pentium microprocessor.

Summary

Even though a lot of the world uses Windows, you don't have to feel out of touch with your computer. Besides having a better operating system, you're able to open documents made in compatible software or even emulate the complete Windows environment. So if you must use a program that has no Mac equivalent, you don't have to switch computing platforms.

Hour 19 will show you how to allow your computer to do multiple tasks with a single command. This feature is called *AppleScript*. I'll show you the built-in tools that Apple gives you with your computer and how to write your own special scripts.

Q&A

Q **I've seen ads for expansion cards that can put "Intel inside" a Mac. Can I use that with my iMac?**

A The great thing about the iMac is that it's a totally self-contained computer. You have to attach only a mouse and keyboard. Beyond this, you just need a printer, and you're ready to roll. But there are no expansion slots to add such things as PC processors. The solution for you is emulation software, such as the products described in this lesson.

Q **Tell me the truth. How fast do those PC emulators run?**

A There's really not a pat answer to this one. The basic consideration is that you want to have a lot of RAM installed on your computer and give the emulation program a good chunk of it to run. These programs don't begin to "sing" until they can occupy 48MB to 64MB of RAM all by themselves. Because you need a bunch more for your computer to run, I'd recommend 96MB built-in memory as ideal for using your iMac with SoftWindows 98 or Virtual PC.

Once set up with a good chunk of memory, you can expect an iMac to give you about the performance of a 133 to 166MHz Pentium. The program may feel faster, though, because the clever designers of PC emulation software try to accelerate tasks such as pulling down menus, which have the most impact on perceived speed.

Q **It's time for the final decision. Which program is better: SoftWindows 98 or Virtual PC? And why?**

A I'm not going to duck the question, but I won't be able to give you a straightforward answer, either. SoftWindows 98 is a program especially optimized to work with Windows 98. Virtual PC is a complete software emulator for the DOS and Windows environments. Each publisher can produce benchmarks to show that it is faster. But this really means that one program may perform a calculation or a display function that looks better on their benchmark than the other one does.

In practice, I have used both programs with great success. They both take advantage of your computer's PowerPC microprocessor to gain as much of a performance advantage as they can. But if you intend to move beyond Windows and try another PC operating system (such as Windows 2000 or a UNIX-based program such as Linux), you'll find that Virtual PC is better at that.

And, by the way, there is a version of Linux that will run on PowerPC Mac OS computers, but it would require initializing your drive (wiping out the data) or partitioning the drive (dividing it into multiple volumes, which also requires initializing). That's the only way you could switch from the Mac OS to Linux and back again. If you want to go this route, though, you'd get better performance than any emulator would provide, but bear in mind that Linux is nowhere near as user-friendly as the Mac OS.

Q I thought I could open PC files on my computer without extra stuff. But I've got this file with the extension .exe on it, and it won't run. What do I need?

A That file is an executable file, one that can be launched to bring up a program or an installer for a PC program. It's not a document file. The only way you can run PC programs on your computer is with one of those DOS or Windows emulators.

Q Help! Whenever I try to insert a PC disk into my SuperDisk drive, I get a warning that it wants to initialize the disk. Should I do it?

A No. If you OK that message, the disk will be erased, and if you need files from it, they'll be history. What you should do is Cancel the request, which will result in the disk being ejected. Then go to the Apple menu, select Control Panels, and make absolutely certain that File Exchange is available in the submenu. If it's not, open Extensions Manager and make sure that File Exchange is active (that it has a check mark next to it). If it's not active (but listed), click the check box and restart. That ought to take care of this problem.

18

HOUR 19

AppleScript: Putting Your iMac on Automatic Pilot

As powerful as your computer's PowerPC microprocessor is, you have to use your keyboard and mouse to perform a lot of tasks. When you need to save a document, you have to select a menu bar command (or type the keyboard equivalent), name the document, and then accept a dialog box to save the file.

Just imagine how it would be if you could call upon your computer to think for you when it came to performing such mundane tasks. Fortunately, your iMac comes equipped with software that lets you do just that. It's called AppleScript and, after you get the hang of it, you'll be able to make your computer take over some repetitive tasks for you. There are even folks who make AppleScript do hundreds of operations for them (such as basic editing and saving of photos), and they go off to lunch, confident that the computer will purr away happily at its task until they return.

In this lesson, you'll learn

- How to use your computer's collection of standard scripts.
- The easy way to learn about Apple's Script Editor software.
- How to use Script Editor to record your actions and make a script from them.
- How to use the Folder Actions feature.
- How to use some other tools for desktop automation.

Scripting Without Programming

When you set up your computer, you don't have to do anything special to turn on AppleScript. The program is already active and running, ready for you to create and run scripts.

To get started, you can take a look at the handful of scripts that Apple gives you to activate common functions. You'll find it simply by going to the Apple Menu and choosing Automated Tasks (see Figure 19.1).

FIGURE 19.1

These are some of the canned scripts Apple gives you to try out AppleScript.

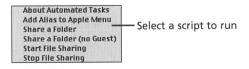

Select a script to run

There are additional scripts for you in the Apple Extras folder. Just open the folder, look for the item AppleScript, and open the More Automated Scripts folder. There are also scripts devoted to Folder Actions (which I'll describe later). Additional choices are available on the Mac OS 9 CD in the AppleScript folder.

Most of these sample scripts work simply by selecting them from the submenu. When you do that, they will perform their functions without further intervention (with one exception that I'll describe later).

Here's what these scripts do:

- **Share a Folder**: This script creates a folder named Shared Folder at the top level of your computer's startup drive (the one used to boot the computer). Then it turns on file sharing and allows guest access to the folder. The folder serves as a sort of drop box for files picked up and retrieved across a network.

- **Share a Folder (No Guest)**: This script works exactly as the one above, with one big exception. Users must log on with a name and password to access it.

- **Start File Sharing**: You can try this as an alternative to turning on file sharing with the command in the Control Strip (or using the File Sharing Control Panel). It's no different, really.

- **Stop File Sharing**: This script simply turns off file sharing.

- **Add Alias to Apple Menu**: This is a fast way to customize the Apple menu with the links to the files you want. Before you call up this script, you must first select the item (or items) for which you want to make an Apple menu alias. After you do that, run the script, and the alias will appear in just a jiffy in the Apple menu, along with an acknowledgement that the job was done (see Figure 19.2).

FIGURE 19.2
Some scripts, such as this one, give you notice when they do their work.

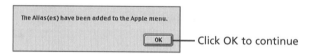

The Alias(es) have been added to the Apple menu.

     OK — Click OK to continue

A Primer on Creating Your Own AppleScripts

When you think of scripts for computers, no doubt you expect some sort of arcane computer-like language that requires lots of training to understand.

Fortunately, AppleScript commands (while not always in plain English) are usually clear enough to learn without needing a translator at your side. And you can even make AppleScripts without knowing a thing about the lingo.

All you need is Apple's Script Editor program, already installed on your computer.

To begin, let's look at a real live script, the one to create an alias and drop it in the Apple menu, and see what it contains.

Here's how to open it:

▼ To Do

1. Go to the Apple Extras folder and open it.
2. Double-click the folder labeled AppleScript.
3. Locate and double-click the Script Editor application icon. This will open the screen shown in Figure 19.3.

19

FIGURE 19.3

This simple interface is used to create an AppleScript from the ground up.

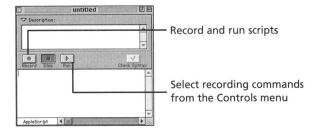

Record and run scripts

Select recording commands
from the Controls menu

4. Choose Open Script from the File menu (or press Command+O) and navigate to the Automated Tasks folder.

5. Open the document labeled Add Alias to Apple Menu (see Figure 19.4).

FIGURE 19.4

Here's a real AppleScript. While not all the syntax is obvious, some of it is in plain English.

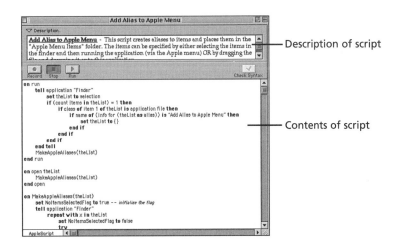

Description of script

Contents of script

After you've studied the script, go ahead and close the document.

Making an AppleScript Without Writing Anything

As I said before, you don't have to understand all of the scripting language to create an AppleScript. Script Editor can go to work and build a script for you, simply by recording the actions you take. In this little exercise, I'll perform some basic Finder functions and then build a genuine AppleScript that repeats the steps.

After you get the hang of it, you'll be able to quickly create your own scripts by using the same technique.

The Script Editor record function can only monitor functions that actually change something in your document. You can move the mouse around, talk on the phone, open and close the CD tray, or attach something new to your computer, but unless what you do makes a real change in the document you're working on or in performing a Finder function, it won't be recorded.

I'm going to take you through a very simple set of Finder routines. Now let's do a take:

1. If it's not already running, launch Script Editor.
2. Click the Record button.
3. Open the Utilities folder.
4. Click Drive Setup and any other item and drag the two icons to the desktop.
5. Close the Utilities window.
6. Return to the Script Editor window and click the Stop button. In the blink of an eye, the result of your scripting efforts will appear in the document window.
7. Click the Description window and write a short description of the script you've just created (see Figure 19.5).

FIGURE 19.5

If I can script, you can script. Here's the one I just made.

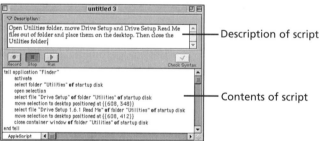

Description of script

Contents of script

19

The ability to record a script works only if the program supports the feature. The fastest way to find out is to check the program's documentation or Help menu—or just try it out and see. AppleWorks, for example, doesn't support the Record feature (at least at the time this book was written).

▲

Now you're ready to check your script just to make sure it performs the actions you want, removing those items from the Utilities folder. To do that

▼ To Do

1. Restore the two items to the Utilities folder.

2. Return to the Script Editor and click the Run button. If everything is working, you should see, quick as a flash, the two icons appear on your desktop, and the Utilities folder will be closed (see Figure 19.6).

FIGURE 19.6

The two icons moved from the Utilities folder are now on my computer's desktop.

3. If the script is what you wanted, it's time to save the document. The easiest way to save it is in run-only form, which is basically a small application that you can double-click to launch (but not edit). So click the File menu and choose Save As Run-Only.

4. Name your script.

5. Choose Application from the pop-up menu and make sure that the two check boxes are unchecked. The result is shown in Figure 19.7.

FIGURE 19.7

Click Save to store your script.

6. After your script is saved, double-click it to launch it. You'll see a dialog box explaining the purpose of the script (see Figure 19.8).

7. Click Run to activate the script, Quit to cancel.

FIGURE 19.8
This screen lets you decide whether to run your script or not.

After you become accustomed to doing scripts by automatic pilot, you'll want to begin to study the syntax. You can, for example, easily change the name of the folder manipulated by writing a new title in your script. Remember, though, that if you make the script read only, it can't be edited.

Introducing Folder Actions

If you are involved in file movement and manipulation in a big way in your business, you'll want to take a gander at another terrific feature of AppleScript. It's called Folder Actions.

After you apply a Folder Action to a folder, whenever you do something with that folder again, such as opening it, closing it, resizing it, or adding and removing items from it, the script is triggered.

Here's a brief idea of what you can do with a Folder Action (and I'm just covering the most basic features here). There are lots of possibilities for such scripts.

- **Open items as labeled**: You can apply a priority label for any item. The feature is available from the Preferences command in the Finder's Edit menu. Any item in a folder with a certain label can be launched when the script folder is opened.

- **Keep a folder open**: If you accidentally close a folder with this script attached to it, it will open again. That way, the contents are always visible to you.

- **Close subfolders**: Great for preventing desktop clutter. This action automatically closes all open windows within the scripted folder.

- **New item alert**: This script is quite useful when you are using a folder for sharing files from a network. Whenever a new item is placed in the scripted folder, you get a warning.

19

- **Reject added items**: This item does what the name implies. It prevents items from being added to the scripted folder.

- **Duplicate to folders**: You can use this script to automatically back up the files. When the item is placed in a scripted folder, a copy is automatically placed in another folder that you select. I'll describe this feature in more detail in Hour 21, "Backup, Backup, Backup…How to Protect Your Files."

- **Retrieve items**: This script is used to move files back in the folder from which they were removed.

The Fast and Dirty Way to Make a Folder Action

Creating a Folder Action doesn't require a visit to Apple's Script Editor. You can do it without having to open any other program. Here's how:

1. Select the folder you want scripted.

2. Hold down the Control key and click the selected item, which opens a Contextual Menu similar to the one shown in Figure 19.9.

FIGURE **19.9**

Pick a command from the Contextual Menu.

3. Select Choose a Folder Action, which opens the Open dialog box.

4. Navigate to the Scripts folder, inside the System Folder.

5. Open the folder labeled Folder Action Scripts, which opens the screen shown in Figure 19.10.

FIGURE **19.10**

These are the standard Folder Actions you can apply.

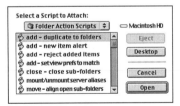

6. Choose Add – New Item Alert and click Open. In a few seconds, the folder's icon will have a little script icon attached to it.

From here on, any time someone adds an item in that scripted folder from across the network, you'll get an onscreen notice about it. No more secrets.

To remove the Folder Action

1. Select the folder from which you want to remove the Folder Action.
2. Hold down the Control key and click the selected item to open the Contextual Menu.
3. Choose Remove a Folder Action from the menu and then select the script you want to remove from the dialog box.

The Script icon will soon disappear from this folder and so will the Folder Action. You can then apply another script to it if you prefer.

> If you ever need to adjust the script for a Folder Action, you can use the Edit a Folder Action command in the Contextual Menu to open the Script Editor and open the script for editing.

A Look at Macro Software for the Mac OS

AppleScript isn't your only road to putting your computer on automatic pilot. You'll find as you get adept at making scripts that not all programs support the feature.

Fortunately, there are other solutions; some came with software you may already have, and some came as separate macro utility software that can script all of your programs, even the ones that don't speak AppleScript.

NEW TERM A *macro* is just another way of identifying a script. It refers to the process of storing a set of repetitive functions and playing them back with a single command.

Here are some of your choices:

- **Macro features**: Such programs as Microsoft Office for the Macintosh have macro features. You can use their built-in script editors to record actions and play them back.

NEW TERM As you've seen, some programs call their automation routines *scripting*, while others call them *macros*. Some programs from Adobe Systems, such as Illustrator and Photoshop, label the routines as *actions*.

19

Although the Mac version of Microsoft Office works extremely well, you are best advised to buy some virus protection software before you fiddle with the macro feature. There are a large number of so-called macro viruses around (they infect Mac and Windows users of Office). I'll tell you more about virus protection options in Hour 24, "An iMac Safety Net."

- **QuicKeys**: This is one of the oldest Macintosh scripting programs. In addition to observing and making scripts from the things you do, it has loads of built-in routines that work with many popular programs (see Figure 19.11). You can also create custom toolbars for fast playback of scripts and program and document launching. If you want to know more, take a visit to the Internet, set your Web browser to `http://www.cesoft.com`, and check out their time-limited demonstration version of the program.

FIGURE 19.11

This is the QuicKeys macro editor, used to add and modify scripts that work in all programs or just a few.

- **OneClick**: Here's another popular scripting program. At the heart of OneClick is a set of floating palettes of repeated functions that can be customized to work in one program or all (see Figure 19.12). You are also able to access the same features via keyboard shortcuts. You can learn more about the program at the publisher's Web site: `http://www.westcodesoft.com`. When you visit the site, you'll find a bunch of OneClick modules that support many programs. Users of the program created them. There's even one for AOL that many members use regularly.

FIGURE 19.12

OneClick creates convenient toolbar palettes that provide easy shortcuts to a program's features.

Summary

After you set up an AppleScript routine, it's really fascinating to see your computer do your work for you while you sit back and watch. Fortunately, the techniques to create scripts aren't so hard that you have to have a degree in computer science to figure them out. You'll be able to get going by using the information in this lesson.

In Hour 20, "Adding More Goodies to Your iMac," I'll tell you something about the many extras you can add to an iMac, using the ethernet and USB ports and the new AirPort. You'll find there are hundreds of products, ranging from digital cameras to printers and extra drives, that can really enhance the capabilities of your computer.

Q&A

Q I tried writing an AppleScript for a program, but it won't work. I checked the language, and it seemed okay. What is wrong?

A The Mac OS Finder and a great number of operating system parts can be scripted. Many of the programs you buy also support AppleScript, but not all of them. If you need to know more, check the documentation that came with your software. You'll be pleased to know that AppleWorks already has some built-in scripts for you to work with. Just check the Scripts icon in the AppleWorks menu bar to access what's available. Unfortunately, this program isn't supporting the script record function with the version available when this book was written.

Q Okay, I'm hooked. This AppleScript stuff sounds great. Where can I learn more about it?

A The first place to start is Apple's own special Web site devoted to the subject. Just aim your Web browser to `http://www.apple.com/applescript`, and you'll find some solid information on the subject. You'll want to check out their technical information document, "Using AppleScript Documentation," which will definitely take you to the next great level of script creation.

19

HOUR 20

Adding More Goodies to Your iMac

In Hour 17, "Now That I Wrote It, How Do I Print It?," I told you how you can add a printer to your computer, so you'll have top quality prints of your work.

NEW TERM But printers aren't the only things you can attach to your iMac. Your computer comes with a flexible connection port called USB (short for *Universal Serial Bus*). It lets you attach up to 127 separate and distinct items that will expand its capabilities. And it's *hot-pluggable*, meaning you can attach and detach the item (with a few cautions) without having to turn off your computer.

In this lesson, you'll discover

- The wide range of USB devices to expand your computer's capabilities.
- The safest ways to install new devices.
- What USB hubs are and why you need them.
- How Apple's new AirPort provides networking freedom.

Making Your iMac Do More

Without a doubt, just adding a printer offers a great enhancement to the capabilities of your computer. You begin to see a printout of all the great things you've visualized on the screen. As sharp as your computer's screen may be, there's nothing like seeing it in print (book authors like me depend on it).

As time goes on, no doubt you'll want to look for other expansion possibilities, to extend your computing prospects still further.

Here's a brief look at the sort of USB devices available for your iMac (and I'm just scratching the surface here):

- **Printers**: Okay, you've added one printer. But there's nothing to prevent you from adding a second printer, either to the ethernet port or the USB port (one black-and-white, one color, two color, and so on).
- **Scanners**: A scanner is a device used to take pictures of artwork or photos and store them in digital form on your computer. Consider it comparable to one half of a copy machine (the part used to pick up the document information). Using a scanner opens up a whole range of possibilities for doing creative work. In addition, you can use a scanner with special software (OCR) that lets you scan manuscripts and then edit the copy on your computer.

   NEW TERM *OCR* is short for optical character recognition. And the description applies to software that can "read" the text in a scanned document and save that text in a form that you can edit on your computer.

- **Cameras**: Yes, you can still make pictures with film, but there's a new generation of digital cameras that record pictures that you can store on your computer without having to take it to the photo finishing store and wait for the prints to return. It will open whole new possibilities for photography. In fact, some of the photos you see in this book were taken with a digital camera. The instant response made it possible for me to reshoot pictures, on the spot, until they were as good as possible.

   You can also purchase miniature video cameras (such as the iREZ Kritter USB and QuickCam), which let you record videos. They won't replace your camcorder, but they are nice for simple images. And you can use them with a special type of software, videoconferencing, which lets you send videos out over the Internet.

- **Storage Devices**: If you need to expand storage beyond your computer's hard drive, you'll find several categories of drives available. I'll cover the most common ones.

- **SuperDisk**: This is a product from such companies as Imation and Winstation that reads regular, high-density floppy disks (from both Macs and PC computers), and also a special high capacity disk, also called SuperDisk, that stores up to 120MB of data.
- **Floppy Drive**: This device lets you read floppy disks on your iMac.
- **Zip Drive**: The zip drive is a popular storage medium from Iomega Corporation that puts either 100MB or 250MB of data on a disk that looks like a floppy with a weight problem. The zip format is supported by millions of users, and it is worth looking into if you exchange files a lot with other folks.

The great thing about USB is that you don't have to stick with just one extra storage device. You can add a number of extra drives to suit your needs. Just bear in mind that things will bog down if you try to use them all at once.

DVD-ROM Drive: This is a product that lets you play a new generation of high-capacity CDs based on the DVD format. It's not necessarily for movies (which would require special decoding hardware not normally available for your computer) but to allow you to back up your files to a near-permanent storage medium. Another type of DVD drive, DVD-RAM, also lets you record on special CDs.

This book is based on the first couple of generations of the iMac. It's quite possible that there will be an iMac with an internal DVD drive (and movie decoding hardware) by the time you read this book or shortly thereafter.

- **Hard Drives**: You can add extra hard drives to your computer for additional storage. The only consideration is that the USB port doesn't really exercise the maximum speed of a large hard drive. It's fine, though, for occasional use or just to back up your precious files. You'll learn more about backup possibilities in Hour 21, "Backup, Backup, Backup...How to Protect Your Files."
- **Input Devices**: You're not limited to your iMac's keyboard and mouse. Not everyone digs the circular mouse (especially if you've used the egg-shaped variety used on older Macs and most other computers). But it's nice to know there are alternatives. In addition, you can purchase joysticks for computer games, keyboards for special needs (or just in the form of those offered on regular Macs), and even trackballs (sort of an upside-down mouse), which some prefer to a regular mouse.

20

- **Cable/DSN/ISDN Modems**: If your iMac's 56K modem seems a little slow, you'll be pleased to know there may be ways to get better performance. One way is the cable modem (which works with the ethernet port), if your cable company offers service in your city. Another is DSL (short for Digital Subscriber Line), an ultra high-speed protocol that uses your regular phone line (this one also uses your iMac's ethernet port). Another alternative is an ISDN modem, which will hook up to the USB port. This sort of modem can virtually double the speed of Internet connections, but before you take this route, check your local phone company for pricing and features.

- **Hubs and Cables**: When you hook up a large chain of USB devices, you may need a hub, which is a central connecting device. Some items work as hubs (such as an iMac's keyboard), and some don't. Before you buy a USB peripheral, you'll want to check the requirements to see if you need anything extra. Bear in mind that, when you run out of jacks to hook up to, you'll need a hub to get more jacks.

The Fast, Safe Way to Install USB Devices

If you've connected peripheral devices to computers from that "other" platform, no doubt you've become used to playing with special interrupt settings. And when you add extra drives to a Mac or a PC, you need to check for ID settings and termination (a device that closes the electric circuit).

With USB, you don't have to worry about dealing with those arcane setups. Instead, you can easily add USB devices as you need them and remove them just as quickly.

Here's a tried-and-true USB installation method (some changes may apply to specific products, and they'll tell you that in the documentation):

1. Unpack the USB device and check for an installation CD.

2. If there's an installation CD, it means that special software (a driver) is needed to make the device work. The SuperDisk and zip drives are examples. Just place the installation CD in your computer's drive.

3. Double-click the Installer icon and follow the instructions to install the new software.

4. After installation, restart your computer.

5. Connect one end of the USB device's cable to the free plug on your iMac's connection panel or the free plug on your keyboard.

If you cannot find a place to plug your USB device, you'll probably need a hub, which extends the number of ports available for USB connections. You can buy a hub at your dealer. Before you purchase a USB device, you'll want to check the available connections so that you don't have to make a return trip to your dealer for another item.

6. Connect the other end of the cable to your USB device.

7. Turn on the device. You'll then want to check your instructions about using the device. Some products, such as scanners, require that you run special software to operate them.

I don't want to mislead you about a USB device being hot pluggable. There are times when you shouldn't unplug the device. For example, if you have a disk in a SuperDisk drive, zip drive, or similar product, eject the disk first before removing the drive. And if you are working in a document that is using the device (such as a hard drive or scanner), make sure that you quit the program before removing the device. Otherwise, you'll risk a crash or possibly a damaged file.

A Look at USB Facts

If you're used to Mac computers that have ADB (Apple Desktop Bus) and serial ports (labeled modem and printer), no doubt you're wondering why the need for a change. Here are some more USB advantages, in addition to the ones I mentioned at the beginning of this lesson:

- **Faster**: The USB port is capable of up to 12 megabits per second transfer speed. That's over 125 times faster than the ADB port and up to 50 times faster than the Mac's regular serial port. It's not nearly as fast as a speedy hard drive, but it does present lots of possibilities for getting speedier performance.

20

In the future, there may be an even faster USB technology. USB version 2.0 has been reported to be on the horizon for the year 2001, with speeds from 30 to 40 times faster than current USB ports. Should this happen, of course, it will require a new generation of Mac OS computers to support it.

- **Easy Hookup**: As you've seen from the seven steps mentioned previously for hooking up a USB device, it's about as easy as it can get. So if you are anxious to try out your new USB peripheral, you'll be glad to know that it will be up and running in minutes.

- **Growing Selection**: From almost the very first day the iMac came out in August 1998, there were products available for it in many categories. And in this cross-platform world, the maker of a USB product for the "other" platform can easily make it work on a Mac, simply by writing a new software driver (and with some mice and keyboards, new software may not even be needed).

Introducing AirPort

In the past, when you wanted to network a computer, you had to run a wire from one to the other or to a hub (a central connecting point). If you've ever tried to do this in a home or office environment, though, you have the problem of wrapping messy wires around walls, furniture, under carpets, and so on. And no doubt you have almost tripped over a stray networking cable.

Apple's AirPort wireless network is designed to get around that limitation. You don't have to fiddle with cables or complex setups. And you can (depending on your surroundings) be up to 150 feet from another AirPort-equipped computer or the AirPort Base Station and still get undiminished performance.

Here's an overview of AirPort products and features:

- **AirPort Interface**: If you have a "slot loading" iMac, which includes AirPort capability , you just need to set up the software to make it run.

  Just launch the AirPort Setup Assistant and choose your wireless networking options. A Control Strip module will let you know if you're in the range of another AirPort access point. You can then connect to any other Mac OS computer that has AirPort installed (up to 10 computers without degrading performance). Or you can connect directly to the next product I'll tell you about, the AirPort Base Station.

- **AirPort Base Station**: This product, which looks like something out of a science fiction movie (see Figure 20.1) forms the hub or central point of an AirPort wireless network. It has a built-in 56K modem and a 10BASE-T ethernet port. You can use it to share an Internet connection across an AirPort network, a regular ethernet network (using cables), cable modems, or DSL modems.

FIGURE 20.1

The AirPort Base Station provides the central hub for a wireless network consisting of iMacs, iBooks, Power Macintosh G4s, and even a regular wired ethernet network.

Once hooked up, your AirPort wireless network can be used to connect computers within your home or office or in a classroom. And because it's wireless, you don't even have to be inside a building to connect. As long as you're in range of another AirPort-equipped computer or the AirPort Base Station, you can connect as efficiently as if you were connected with old-fashioned cables.

FireWire Offers Ultra-Speedy Performance

The iMac DV and iMac DV Special Edition include two FireWire connection ports. FireWire lets you hook up all sorts of high speed devices to your iMac.

Most digital camcorders, for example, have FireWire connections. Of course, they aren't always called FireWire. For Sony camcorders, for example, they're known as iLink. And other products, such as Canon's digital camcorders, use the official term for FireWire, IEEE 1394.

As explained in Hour 13, "Multimedia Is More Than a CD-ROM Game," you use FireWire and Apple's iMovie software to turn your iMac DV into a real video editing station, and you can create high quality productions that'll look near as good as broadcast TV.

In addition to editing videos, you can use your iMac's FireWire capability to hook up FireWire-based hard drives, removable drives, CD drives, tape backup drives and scanners. FireWire features a plug-and-play capability similar to USB. You install the software, then plug in the device and it's recognized, just like that.

20

FireWire and USB are totally separate technologies. You cannot hook up a USB device to a FireWire port, or vice versa (even the plug layouts don't match).

FireWire comes into its own when you need the highest possible performance on your iMac. As this book was written, dozens of FireWire products were available, and more were coming to market. You'll want to check with your dealer to see what's available.

Summary

Depending on your needs, there are a great number of peripherals available for easy hookup to your computer. You'll soon be printing, shooting pictures, scanning artwork, and even, perhaps, using a designer keyboard and mouse. And it will all work just about perfectly on your iMac without having to fiddle with weird connections and software.

If you have a computer that comes with Apple's handy AirPort feature, you'll be able to network without having to attach a messy old cable.

When you begin to create your own files, such as word processing documents with AppleWorks or financial data with Quicken 98, you'll want to make a backup copy, in case something goes wrong with the original copy. In the next lesson, I'll cover one of the most important areas of Mac computing, performing backups.

Q&A

Q **I have an old scanner that works really well. But these new Mac OS computers don't have any place to hook it up. Is there some way I can make it work? Or do I have to buy a new one?**

A Don't give up hope. You'll want to check with your dealer and look for a SCSI-to-USB adapter. These adapters will let you use older scanners, hard drives, and other devices on your computer. The only downside is with hard drives; they'll run slower on a USB port, but scanners should work just fine. Just remember to install your scanning software.

Q **I have a really nice keyboard here, especially designed for folks like me with a wrist injury. Can I use it on the iMac?**

A The answer is a definite yes. You only need to contact your dealer about an ADB-to-USB adapter. That'll let you attach that keyboard and other input devices from the older style Macs to your iMac. One such product is the iMate from Griffin Technology of Nashville, Tennessee. You can learn more about it at the manufacturer's Web site: `http://www.griffintechnology.com`.

I should mention, though, that there are ergonomic USB keyboards as well, so you might find a suitable product if you check with your favorite Apple dealer.

Q **How do I recognize the USB connection cable?**

A USB cables have two types of plugs, so that you can connect the correct end to the correct end. The part that plugs into your computer (or a hub) is small and rectangular. The side that goes into the device itself is square. Some USB devices support a different style of connection, but it will always be obvious which end goes where. But I cannot overemphasize the importance of checking the product's documentation before you hook it up. Scanners, for example, require that you unlock the optical assembly with a switch or pushbutton before they will work.

Q **Can I use a USB device from that "other" platform on my iMac?**

A Maybe yes, maybe no. A keyboard or mouse that doesn't need a special driver program may work, but otherwise, you need software that is designed specifically to work with the Mac OS. Because most new Mac OS computers have USB, Apple has developed improved drivers to work with many devices. If you're unsure whether the product will work for you, contact your dealer or the manufacturer.

Q **I'm having problems getting my new printer or scanner to work. I know it's hooked up properly. I checked the instructions again and again, but it just won't work.**

A The best thing to do is try reinstalling the software and then restarting. See if that helps. If it doesn't work, then contact the manufacturer of your printer or scanner (or check their Web site) for information about a software update that may be needed.

Q **I've read your statistics about how fast USB can be. What if I hook up several devices to my computer? Will that slow things down?**

A Depends. Except for disk drives, it will take several devices working together to begin to affect performance. If you scan a document while printing, it's possible to see some performance degradation, I suppose. But most times you'll hardly notice any difference, even if your USB chain is packed with products.

20

Q I have an iMac. Can I attach an AirPort to it?

A You can network to an AirPort Base Station with an Ethernet crossover cable, which will connect you to AirPort wireless networking. But only the second generation "slot loading" iMacs feature Airport capability. There doesn't seem to be any way to add that feature to older iMacs (though I suppose it could be an opportunity for some company to try).

Q My iMac didn't come with FireWire. Is there anything I can do to add the feature, maybe to the USB jack?

A It would be nice, but the FireWire electronics are part of the iMac DV's logic board. The USB port runs at a much slower speed than FireWire, so in theory this doesn't seem possible (though I never say never).

HOUR **21**

Backup, Backup, Backup...How to Protect Your Files

There's one thing that's certain (other than death and taxes, of course), and that is that your iMac will crash on occasion, just as will any personal computer. When that happens, it's always possible that one or more files on your computer's drive can be affected (especially if you're working on a file when the computer locks up).

In this lesson, I'll show you some easy, safe contingency plans to protect yourself against such problems (even if your computer is stolen).

In this lesson, you'll discover

- How to back up your files, so that you always have a spare copy in case of a problem.
- The difference between full backups and incremental backups and how to decide which method is best for you.
- How AppleScript can help you do near-automatic backups.

- A look at different backup software.
- An overview of Mac OS 9's Multiple User security features and other security software that can prevent access to your files.

The Need for a Backup Strategy

Computers drive our daily lives. Nearly every business has a computer system of some sort, whether a personal computer, such as your iMac, or a large mainframe with huge boxes of electronics and disk drives. The systems aren't perfect, no matter how well you prepare for problems.

I don't want to be an alarmist, but it's very true that nothing is foolproof. If you want to create documents on your computer that you need to keep safe (from a newsletter to your personal financial information), you should consider taking steps to make sure that you'll always be protected in case of trouble.

Consider what the big folks do:

- Large companies, including banks, insurance companies, manufacturers, and even online services such as AOL, make spares (backups) of their data in case something goes wrong with their computer systems.
- Hard drives, such as those in your iMac, are not perfect. They use mechanical components that are working constantly to access and save data. Sometimes things go wrong, and a file can be damaged, or the drive may fail. It doesn't happen often, but it does happen. I'll tell you more about hard drive safety software in Hour 24, "An iMac Safety Net."
- Software isn't perfect. Programs are written by imperfect human beings such as you and me, and program bugs or problems with one program getting along with another can cause a computer lock-up. When that happens, the file you may be saving or working in could get damaged (especially if the Save process is interrupted).
- Computer viruses remain a real threat. Even though the Mac platform doesn't have near the problems as the "other" platform, there are some pretty damaging virus strains out there. If you plan on downloading files from the Internet or sharing disks with other users, arm yourself with virus software. I'll tell you more in Hour 24.
- You may have burglar alarms and great police protection, but thefts do occur anyway. You may have insurance to cover you if your computer is stolen, but what about the files? What about your personal checkbook or other financial information?

The danger of losing information may be small, but the time and expense involved in re-creating your files may be far greater than the cost of protecting it.

A Look at Backup Methods

You can follow different types of backup techniques, depending on the kind of documents you're creating and how many of them there are. Here's a brief look at the sort of things you can do without having to buy extra software:

- **Back up only document files**: You already have copies of your programs on a CD. A complete packet of CDs came with your computer, containing all of the software Apple installed on your computer. In addition, any new software you buy will also come on an installation disk of some sort. So the fastest backup method is just to concentrate on the documents you make with those programs.

- **Back up everything**: Even though you already have a separate copy of the software, it can be very time consuming to have to restore all of your software and redo special program settings and all. If you back up everything, it's easier to restore a program with your settings intact without fuss or bother. In addition, having a complete backup of your computer's drive is extra protection in case something happens to both the computer and software disks.

- **Incremental backups**: This technique requires special software, but it is designed to make a backup strictly of the files that have changed since your last backup. A thorough backup plan may include a full backup at regular intervals, say once a week, and then a daily incremental backup. This method also takes a lot less time to do, and you won't need as much disk space in which to store it all.

Making Backups—The Fast and Dirty Way

When you are ready to make a backup, you need a place to put those files. The best method is to get a separate drive with media (disks) that you can remove. That way, you can store the backups in a separate location for the ultimate in safekeeping. That's the method the big companies use.

Here's what you need:

- **Backup drive**: SuperDisk or zip drives are convenient, and the drives and disks aren't too expensive; there are also tape drives that you can use for backup. If you want to be able to archive your files for a number of years, you'll want to consider a drive that writes CD-ROMs or DVD-ROMs. The disks you make from that kind of drive could, potentially, last for decades.

21

Notice, I'm not saying anything about floppy disks here. Unless you only make a few small files, floppy disks aren't practical. You'd need dozens of them at the minimum, and they just aren't as robust as the larger disk techniques. I cannot begin to tell you how many of my floppies have gone bad over time.

- **Networked disks**: If your computer is on a network, a drive on another Mac (or even a Windows-based PC that's set up to handle Mac files) can be used for your regular backups. Before you set up a networked drive for this purpose, you'll want to set up a strategy with the folks who run the network. Some companies plan on having all files backed up to one drive or several drives, and then they do their own special backup routine on those files.

- **A backup plan**: It's a good idea to set aside a time to do your backup at regular intervals—perhaps at the end of your work day before leaving your office (or shutting down your computer if you're at home).

It's just not a good idea to back up your files to the same drive they were made on (such as your iMac's drive). If something should happen to that drive, or the entire computer, your backup would be gone.

- **Careful labeling**: Make sure that your backup disks are carefully labeled as to date and content. If the label isn't large enough, you may want to prepare a short listing of contents in your word processor and then pack it with the disk. But often something such as "Backup for November 21, 1999" would be sufficient.

- **Reuse older media**: If you need to keep an older version of a file, you'll want to keep the backup in a safe place. But when you no longer need a disk, there's no problem in putting it back into service for newer backups. Otherwise, you'll end up with a huge number of disks.

- **Rotate media**: Although SuperDisks and zip media are pretty solid, you'll want to reduce wear and tear by having several disks around. And, in case one backup file goes bad, having another recent one never hurts.

If you're in the market for some USB drives for backups, you'll also want to read Hour 19, "AppleScript: Putting Your iMac on Automatic Pilot," which offers some information on what's available.

- **Multiple backups**: If your files contain important data (financial or otherwise), make a second backup and store it in a secure location (such as a bank vault). In the unlikely event something happens to your home or office, you'll be protected.

- **Internet backups**: If you have a good Internet connection and you don't want to back up a large number of files, you can use an Internet backup service. Such firms offer secured access, so others won't be able to get to your files. Two companies offering this service when this book went to press were Backjack Internet Backup Service (`http://www.backjack.com`) and iMacbackup.com (`http://www.iMacbackup.com`).

After you've decided where to put those files, here's the fastest way to do your backup:

1. When your regular "backup time" comes around, insert your backup media in the drive.

2. Create special folders for your backups on the backup media, labeled as carefully as possible as to their contents (such as the date of backup, the kind of files, and so on). An example would be "financial backup" or "Thursday's backup").

3. Select and drag the files to be backed up to the backup media.

4. Eject the backup media when you're done and put the disks in a safe place.

>
> If you live or work in a climate with temperature extremes, try to locate a cool, dark place (such as a metal closet) in which to place the backup disks. It's not a good idea to subject backup media to hot sunlight, high humidity, moisture, or extreme cold.

> A popular system enhancement program, Speed Doubler from Connectix, gives you a neat way to do incremental backups. It has a feature called "Smart Replace" that will replace only files that have changed since the last time you copied the contents of a folder or disk.

Doing a Backup with AppleScript

You discovered the great features of AppleScript in Hour 19. It's a clever program that lets you automate repeating functions simply by launching a little application.

The feature you'll want to use is Folder Actions, which is a part of the AppleScript version that came out beginning with Mac OS 8.5 (and continued with Mac OS 9).

21

One of those folder actions is called Duplicate in Folders, which automatically makes a duplicate of any file or folder you drop into the scripted folder. That script can really save you the trouble of having to click and drag files manually.

Here's how it works.

1. Click your computer's desktop and create a new folder labeled For Backup (using the Finder's Command+N).

2. Hold down the Control key and click the folder, which opens the menu shown in Figure 21.1.

FIGURE **21.1**
This contextual menu lets you pick a command that applies to the selected folder.

Choose a function from this list

3. Select Attach a Folder Action, which opens the dialog box shown in Figure 21.2.

FIGURE **21.2**
Here's the list of scripts to link to the selected folder.

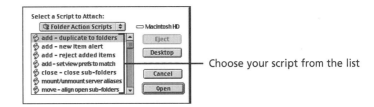

Choose your script from the list

You may have to navigate through the Open dialog boxes to locate the Folder Action Scripts folder. It's located in the System Folder within a folder labeled Scripts.

4. Choose Add – Duplicate To Folders from the list and click the Open button. Within a few seconds, a little script icon will attach itself to the folder you created.

It may take a few moments for folders you put on your desktop to be updated when you add a script to them. Sometimes opening and closing the folder will do the job. But this behavior is normal; there's really nothing wrong when it happens.

5. Open your For Backups folder by double-clicking it.

6. Insert your backup media in your backup drive.

7. Click the backup media's disk icon (this can be done with a disk you're accessing from across a network).

> You can also use a networked drive for step 7, but you may have to answer a password prompt when AppleScript tries to copy a file to it.

8. Choose Make Alias from the Finder's File menu (or press Command+M). This will make an alias file from the backup disk.

9. Click the name of the alias file and add the letters ~! to the beginning of the name. This will tell AppleScript the folder is designed to receive the files you put in the For Backups folder.

10. Drag the alias to your For Backups folder.

And that's it! When you put your files or folders inside that backup folder, the contents will be automatically copied to the drive whose alias is in that folder.

> In order for this clever script to work, you need to open the folder designated for backups. If you leave it closed, the copies aren't made. Don't ask me why. I just work here.

Using Backup Software

Performing a regular backup from a single computer or with a small number of files is easy once you get the hang of it. You can even dig out an alarm clock and have it go off at the appointed time.

But if you have a large number of files, or files need to be backed up from more than one Mac OS computer on a network, you'll do better with some backup software.

Such software can

- **Perform scheduled backups**: You can set the software to perform the backups at a regular time (daily, every other day, weekly, whatever). At the appointed time, you need only have the backup media in place and the computers turned on for the process to go.

21

Although automatic backups are great, a backup can stop dead in its tracks if the media runs out of space isn't ready or the computer was shut down by mistake. If you have a large number of files, check to make sure that your disks have enough space, or be prepared to check the backup process every so often in case of trouble.

- **Perform networked backups**: With the right software, backups can be done from all computers on a network to one or more backup drive.

In order for backups to be done across a network, each computer on the network will need its own licensed copy of the backup software. Many new problems prevent a program from running if there's another copy with the same serial number on a network. Fortunately, networked backup software comes in relatively inexpensive multiuser packs.

- **Back up the entire drive or selected files or folders**: When you set up your backup, you can instruct the software to limit the backup to the items you want. By default, they do the entire drive and then incremental backups for each disk, unless you pick a full backup.

Choosing Backup Software

When you've decided on the backup software route, you'll want to know what to choose. Fortunately, there are several good Mac OS software packages that will give you great automatic backups. They vary in features, and you'll want to pick one based on what you need.

Here's a brief description:

- **Personal Backup**: This simple program, from ASD Software (publisher of the two popular security utilities mentioned in the next section), lets you do simple automatic backups with a number of options (see Figure 21.3). There's also a feature for on-demand backups, where you do them when you want. For added protection, Personal Backup gives you a keystroke recorder feature that makes a text backup of the files you write. In case something goes wrong with the original file, you'll have a way to recover at least the words (but not the artwork or layout).

FIGURE 21.3

You can select most of the settings in Personal Backup from one dialog box.

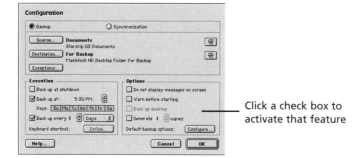

Click a check box to activate that feature

- **Retrospect**: From Dantz, this is a heavy-duty backup program that does just about everything you can imagine in backup planning with little fuss or bother (see Figure 21.4). You can use its EasyScript feature to create a complete backup plan simply by answering some basic questions. Backups are compressed to save space and saved in a special format for efficient retrieval. Unlike other backup programs, Retrospect can work with tape drives, which can store many megabytes of files on little cartridges. Retrospect can also work with Internet-based backup services. For large networks, there's the Retrospect Network Backup Kit and even a Windows version with similar features.

FIGURE 21.4

Though brimming with powerful features, Retrospect is remarkably easy to use.

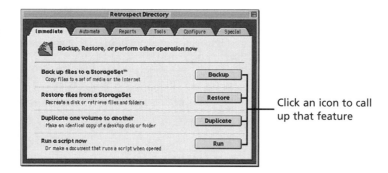

Click an icon to call up that feature

- **Retrospect Express**: This program distills the most important features of Retrospect and puts them in a smaller, less inexpensive package. Express doesn't work with tape drives, and there's no networked version.

- **File Synchronization**: The second generation or "slot loading" iMacs include this control panel. File Synchronization allows you to match up the version of a file on another drive or networked computer with the one on your iMac. You can use it for backup purposes, or simply if you work on more than one Mac and need to make

21

sure the files are in sync. If your iMac has a newer version of the file, it'll be copied to the other drive. The program has a simple drag and drop interface: You drag a file or folder to the control panel's screen, then click the Synchronize button to begin the file copying or matching process.

> If your iMac doesn't have File Synchronization, no problem. The Mac OS 9 installer CD will let you add this control panel as part of the system software installation process.

A Look at Mac OS File Security Methods

If your computer is in an environment where other people may have access to it (such as an office), there are other steps you should consider to keep your files safe—security software, for example. Such software makes it necessary to enter a password to access files folders, or even your computer's hard drive.

Fortunately, Apple has given you tools to secure the files on your computer, beginning with Mac OS 9. Here's a brief overview of those security features.

Keychains

You have a password for your Internet service, and maybe one to get to a special site. Or perhaps you have more than one account, say one for a regular Internet provider, another for AOL. How do you remember all those passwords?

Apple's Keychain Access Control Panel lets you keep track of all those passwords in a safe place. All you need to do is set up one password for access, and then use the Create feature to for your add your passwords, one at a time.

Multiple Users Control Panel

The second weapon in your arsenal against protecting your computer against unwanted access is the Multiple Users Control Panel.

Following is an overview on how this feature works:

1. Open the Apple menu, look for Control Panels, and then pick Multiple Users from the submenu, which will produce the screen shown in Figure 21.5.

2. Click the On button to activate the Multiple Users feature. By default, the name you first entered when you ran the Mac OS Setup Assistant (as shown in Hour 1, "Setting Up Your iMac") is listed as the owner.

FIGURE 21.5

You can use the Multiple Users Control Panel to create a custom environment for each person who uses your computer.

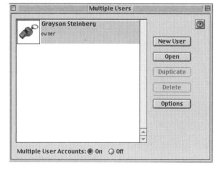

3. Click the Options button to create a set of access features for other users of your computer. Among those features is the ability to log in using Voice Verification, the ability to limit access to certain programs and disks, and even whether another user can create and change his own password.

4. To add extra users, click the New User button, specify that user's name and password, and then select your access choices (see Figure 21.6).

FIGURE 21.6

Create a custom work environment for other users with this setup screen.

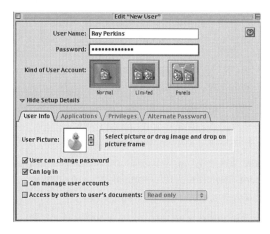

5. After setting up your extra users, click the Close boxes on the various screens to activate the settings.

When you have finished working with your iMac, just choose Logout from the Finder's Special menu. Or you can simply restart or shut down.

21

When another user attempts to use your computer, she'll have to enter the correct name and password at the login prompt (see Figure 21.7). This prompt also appears after you first boot or restart the computer (as long as the Multiple User feature is activated, of course).

FIGURE 21.7

In order for you to use your computer, you must log in first, when Multiple Users is active.

The Multiple Users feature of Mac OS 9 isn't the only security option you have. There are a number of other choices that you might want to consider, such as dedicated security software.

Here are some of the options offered:

- **File access**: You can use security software so that you need to use a password to open an application or document file. Some programs, such as Microsoft Office, give you the ability to protect a document, but the protection scheme usually isn't as robust as a separate security problem.

- **Folder access**: Security software can be set so that you cannot get to a folder without a password. It's common in some offices to keep the System Folder protected, so folks cannot remove or add anything to it.

- **Disk access**: The most potent form of security won't let a user get to a drive without entering the correct password.

- **Special security features**: Some programs offer partial access to files and folders. You can make a file read only, so a user can see the listing for the files and open the files but not change them. Another feature can prevent you from using a removable disk (such as a floppy, SuperDisk, or zip disk) without entering the password. If you don't enter the right password in time, the disk is ejected without further ado.

Here are a few products that might help if you need that extra measure of protection:

- **DiskGuard**: This program, published by ASD Software (publisher of Personal Backup), allows you to control access to disks and folders. If you want, the folder can even be made "invisible" to folks who do not have the password to access it.
- **FileGuard**: Also from ASD Software, this program extends security to floppies, individual documents, and applications. It's designed with networks in mind, and comes in "remote" dress, which allows a single system administrator to control access on all computers in the network.
- **Retrospect**: The regular version of Retrospect also enables you to protect your backups so that unauthorized users can't get access to the contents.

This list isn't meant to be complete. I've just focused on the software that appears at most retail dealers and mail order houses. You may want to contact your dealer directly about these products and others they might suggest.

Summary

Having a regular backup plan is very important, especially if you intend to create documents on your computer that you need to protect. But as you've seen in this lesson, doing backups isn't terribly hard. You just need to follow through on a regular basis to be sure that your most valuable files are safe in case the worst happens.

In the next lesson, I'll show you how to give your iMac a dose of new software and a dose of extra RAM (complete with how-to photos).

Q&A

Q **Tell me the truth: Do you really back up your own files in the same way you tell your readers to back up?**

A Absolutely. I do a regular daily backup. And when I write a book such as this, I usually do three backups of the manuscript every day, on separate disks. That way, I always have a copy of the latest version at hand in case something goes wrong with the original. I've only had to redo a book chapter once over the years (a crash corrupted the original file before the backup was made). And it wasn't fun.

Q **Do you have a personal recommendation for backup software?**

A I've had great luck with Retrospect on my home office computer network. It's absolutely reliable and pretty easy to use. I've used it to restore files every so often, when installing new equipment, and it has never failed me. If you don't have a network, you may do just fine with Retrospect Express.

21

Q **I've got a problem. I tried to restore files from my backup disk, but something was wrong. I can't get those files, and I need them for my work. What do I do?**

A I can't give you a clearcut answer to this one. A program such as Retrospect can sometimes repair a damaged backup disk. But if you have files that you absolutely cannot afford to lose, make an extra backup in case the original backup disk goes bad. You may also want to consider a CD-ROM or DVD-RAM drive with recording capabilities for the safest backups possible.

Q **I'm in bad shape here. I accidentally trashed a file before I backed it up. Is there any way to get it back?**

A Don't get your hopes up high, but in Hour 24 I will discuss software that claims to be able to restore the files you accidentally delete. No promises, but until you read that chapter, best thing to do is not save any files to your computer's drive (if possible), because each file you save makes it more and more difficult for the recovery program to work.

HOUR **22**

Giving Your iMac New Software, More RAM, and Other Things

The great thing about the iMac is that it's almost completely self-contained. You have most everything in one box except for the keyboard and mouse (and the printer or extra drive you may add).

But there may come a time when you need to install something new. Perhaps you've bought some new software or an upgrade to a program you're already using. And maybe you'd like to install more built-in memory to handle more programs at the same time, or run a program that likes lots of RAM (such as a Microsoft Office program or Adobe Photoshop).

In this lesson, you'll learn

- How to install new software.
- How to know if you really need a RAM upgrade.

- An easy, step-by-step process for installing RAM upgrades (complete with photos).
- What to do if something goes wrong with your new installation.

How to Install New Software

After you've used your iMac for a while, no doubt you'll want to add some new software. Or perhaps Apple Computer has come out with a system software upgrade that you'll want to use.

Fortunately, software installation on a Mac OS computer is a relatively simple, uncluttered process. Most software publishers give you basic instructions, but the ones I'm presenting here will cover a great many situations.

For this lesson, you'll be installing a new system software upgrade.

Here's what to do:

1. Go to the Apple menu, choose Control Panels and select Extensions Manager from the submenu.
2. Click the Selected Set pop-up menu, choose Mac OS 9 Base (or the one that represents the system version you're using), and restart.
3. After restart, insert the program's installation CD in your computer's CD drive and wait for a few seconds for the disk's icon to show on your desktop.

If your computer comes equipped with a later operating system, Extensions Manager will have a different version number for the Base set.

4. Most CDs will display a directory of contents. If not, double-click the CD's icon to open its directory.
5. Double-click the icon labeled Install, Mac OS Install, or something with the Install label on it. This will open a screen similar to the one shown in Figure 22.1.
6. You will see one or more intermediate screens, each of which will offer some additional information. One may give you a Read Me, showing basic things you should do before the installation, another may require you to agree to the software license (and you have no choice about this, as not agreeing stops the installation). You may also see a pop-up menu where you can select the drive or folder on which to place the software, but after all these screens, you'll see where you can begin the actual installation (see Figure 22.2).

FIGURE 22.1
This is a typical Mac OS system installer screen.

Click Continue to proceed

Before you add or upgrade any software, be sure to check the onscreen instructions or manual for last-minute information or alerts before you continue with the installation. You want to make sure that there's nothing on your computer that may conflict with the installation of the software or using it later on.

FIGURE 22.2
After you've passed through the introductions, this screen actually starts the installation process.

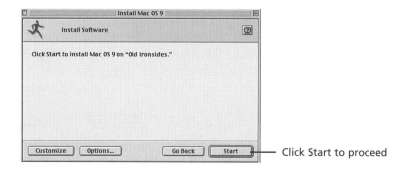

Click Start to proceed

7. You'll see a button usually labeled Install or Start. Click that button to begin.

Before the software installation starts, you can usually opt out by clicking a Cancel button or just quitting the program. If nothing has been installed, there's no harm done in stopping the process if you change your mind.

8. You'll see one or more progress screens showing the installation as it continues. After you've reached the end, you'll see a button labeled Quit or Restart (or both). If it's labeled Restart, choose that option, as it may be required before your software will work.

▼   9. After your computer has restarted, locate the folder that contains the new application and launch it, seeing if it works properly. Hang in there; we're almost done.

> If you have installed a new Mac OS system upgrade, you'll want to make sure that your normal Finder functions (clicking, dragging, opening, and closing items) are normal before you run your regular programs.

10. Return to the Apple menu, choose Control Panels, and relaunch Extensions Manager.

11. Click the Selected Set pop-up menu, choose your regular startup set (usually it's
▲   called My Settings), and then restart.

After restarting, it's time to get back to work.

Updating Apple System Software Automatically

One great feature of Mac OS 9 is the ability to receive software updates from Apple automatically. All you need to set this up is an Internet connection and maybe a minute of your time.

Here's what to do:

1. Click the Apple menu, scroll to Control Panels and choose the Software Updates Control Panel from the submenu. This opens the screen shown in Figure 22.3.

2. If you want to simply check for updates, click the Update Now button. Your Internet service will be dialed up, and Apple's support Web site checked for possible updates.

FIGURE 22.3

Apple lets you download the latest updates for your computer automatically from its Web site.

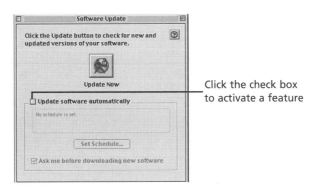

Click the check box to activate a feature

▼

▼   3. If updates are available for your computer, you'll see a screen listing what's available. From there you can click the check boxes for the items you want, and accept the download process.

4. When the downloads are done, the software installers will launch and your computer will be updated with the new software. All you have to do is click the Restart button to finish the process.

5. If you want to have your computer check for Apple software updates automatically, click the Update Software Automatically check box, and then click the Set Schedule button, which opens the screen shown in Figure 22.4.

FIGURE 22.4

Select the date and time of your automatic update scans on this screen.

Click a check box
to select that day

Set Schedule...

Check for new and updated software
at: 12:00 AM ⇅ every:

☑ Monday
☐ Tuesday
☐ Wednesday
☐ Thursday
☐ Friday
☐ Saturday
☐ Sunday

If your computer is not connected to the Internet at a scheduled time, Software Update will check for new and updated software the next time you connect to the Internet.

Cancel   OK

6. When you've set the schedule, click the OK button to activate the feature.

▲   7. Click the close box on the Software Update Control Panel screen to complete the process.

It goes without saying that if your computer isn't on when the scheduled update check is set to take place, it just won't happen. The check will be skipped until the next scheduled run.

Installing New RAM on a First Generation iMac—By the Numbers

You may be perfectly happy with the amount of memory installed on your iMac, but if you want to run several programs at once, you may find the going rough. You'll see onscreen messages that announce that you need to quit one program to use another.

It's also true that there are some programs that simply won't function without lots of installed RAM. Some examples include Microsoft Office and the various graphic arts programs from Adobe Systems, such as InDesign, Illustrator, and Photoshop.

When you find that what you have isn't quite enough, you'll want to consider a RAM upgrade. Fortunately, it's a process you can do yourself.

This section covers RAM installation for the first generation iMacs. If you have one of the newer "slot loading" models, read the next section instead.

When you order a RAM upgrade for your iMac, be sure to tell the dealer what you're using it for. There are many different kinds of RAM available for Apple computers, but only one kind that works in your iMac. Installing the wrong RAM, even if it looks okay, can damage the delicate electronic circuitry. So double-check what you're buying before you install it.

If you've ever put together a toy for your child, or assembled a bookcase or stereo rack, you can probably install a RAM upgrade on your iMac without problem. It's a little more complicated than some other Mac models, but if you follow the steps I'll describe here, carefully, you should do just fine.

I'd like to give my fearless technical editor, Jeff Keller, and his colleague, Robert Jagitsch, hearty thank yous for the photos and some of the descriptive information I'm using here.

Please take extra care in following the instructions on doing a RAM upgrade. You will be taking apart your iMac during this installation, and there is always the danger of damage to some of its delicate components. If you have any qualms about getting involved in this process, you may prefer to have your dealer do it instead.

What You Need

Before you perform your RAM upgrade, I suggest you read through this section at least once, so there are no surprises as you move through the process. Your iMac has two RAM slots. When it leaves the factory, one of these slots (the one located beneath its microprocessor) is already filled. The instructions I'm giving you here will strictly cover installation of RAM into the second slot (the one easiest to reach, by the way).

Now it's time to get ready. Here's what you need:

- A soft cloth or towel on which to place your iMac.
- A desk or other surface large enough to hold all the parts comfortably.
- A Philips head screwdriver.
- And, of course, your RAM upgrade module.

Please don't use a powered screwdriver, as you might damage something. The screwdriver you can get for a couple of bucks at your local hardware store should be fine.

Are you ready? All right, just take a deep breath (I'll wait) and let's dive in:

1. Turn off your iMac, using Shut Down from the Special menu (or by pressing the power key and choosing that command).
2. Unplug all of the computer's cables (power cord and modem cord, too).
3. Grab the handle at the top of the iMac with one hand and hold the front of your computer with your other hand. Lift the iMac up, and turn it over to the front, placing it face down (the monitor side) on the cloth (see Figure 22.5).
4. Take your Phillips head screwdriver and remove the screw from the case cover.
5. Lift the plastic shell up and pull it away from your iMac (see Figure 22.6). Place the cover to the side, or in another safe place.

It may require a hard pull to remove the shell from your iMac, so give it a hard tug. The first time I tried, and I had to tug it a few times (but not too hard) to get it to come loose. If it's still not coming loose, you may want to put it back together and let your dealer do the job.

▼

FIGURE 22.5
The iMac is ready for you to take apart.

Location of iMac's
case screw and handle

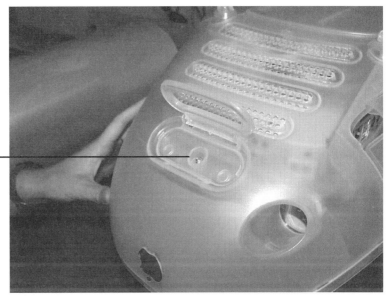

FIGURE 22.6
Grab the shell and lift it off your iMac's case.

Give it a healthy tug
to remove the shell

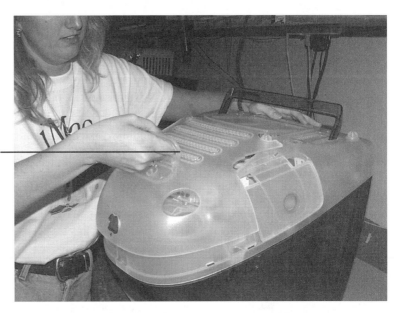

6. It's time to discharge yourself…electrically, that is. Go ahead and place your hand on any exposed metal on the iMac's chassis. This is done to protect it from the nasty effects of an electrostatic discharge.

▼

I cannot overemphasize the dangers of static electricity to the delicate electronic components inside your iMac. While you are doing your RAM installation, don't stroll around your room until you're finished. Otherwise, you may just recharge yourself. Powder room visits are best done before you begin.

7. You will see several connectors attached to the iMac's main logic board. Remove the small plug (a DIN 8 connector, to be precise) at the left first (see Figure 22.7).

FIGURE 22.7
Unplug the DIN 8 connector as shown.

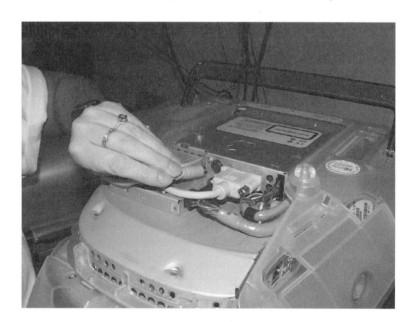

Some iMacs come with a clamp placed over the cables. If the clamp is set down with a screw, remove the screw before undoing the cable connections.

▼ 8. Next remove the connector plug in the middle (DB15) as shown in Figure 22.8.

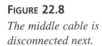

FIGURE 22.8
The middle cable is disconnected next.

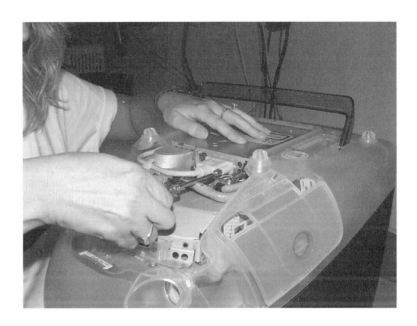

9. Remove the screw from the power cable and then unplug it (see Figure 22.9).

FIGURE 22.9
Detach the power cable from the circuit board.

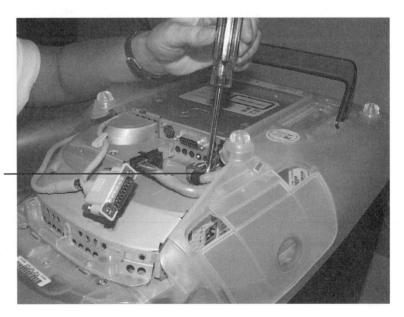

Unscrew the power cable before you try to unplug it

It's always a good idea to put the screws in a small plate or ashtray after unscrewing them. They are very easy to lose.

22

10. You'll want to make room for removing the logic board, so move the cables out of the way (see Figure 22.10).

FIGURE 22.10

Make sure that the cables are moved aside to make room to pull out the logic board.

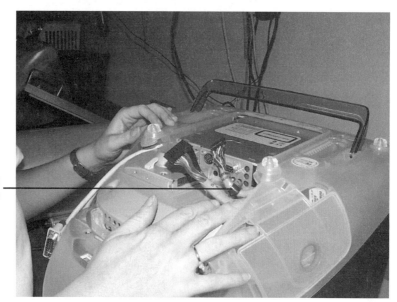

Leave the cables at either end of the case

11. The logic board tray is held down by two screws, located inside a plastic handle. Remove them both (see Figure 22.11).

12. Put your hand on the plastic handle and gently slide the logic board out, moving it straight up and away (see Figure 22.12).

13. Place the logic board on your cloth or in another safe place (make sure that it's not on the edge of the table; this is one item you don't want to drop!).

14. Remove the metal shield by lifting it at both ends. The result is shown in Figure 22.13.

15. Take your RAM module (technically it's called a SODIMM), handling it by its edges (it's inserted at an angle). Align the notch in the module with the small rib in the slot to orient it correctly and insert it into the empty slot as shown in Figure 22.14.

FIGURE 22.11
The logic board is held tight by two screws.

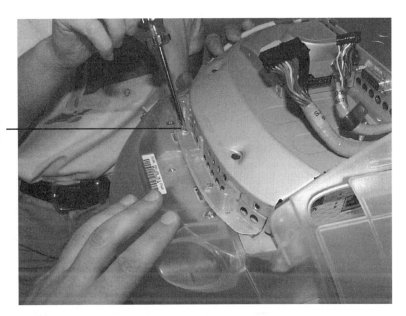

The screws are inside the plastic handle

FIGURE 22.12
Remove the logic board from your iMac.

Make sure it's completely removed

22

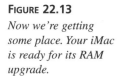

FIGURE 22.13
Now we're getting some place. Your iMac is ready for its RAM upgrade.

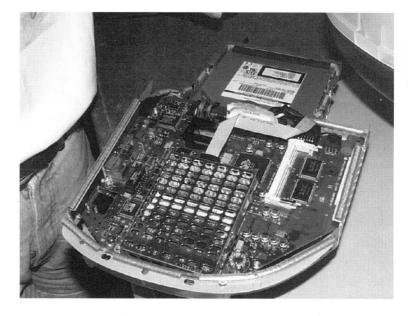

FIGURE 22.14
Insert the RAM module into the slot as shown here.

Line up the RAM module carefully before pushing it down

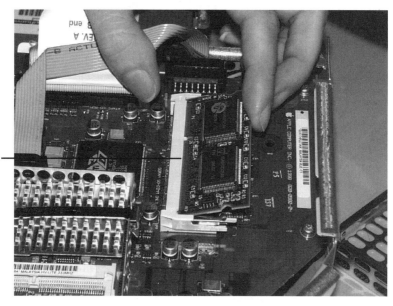

If the RAM slot is filled, it means that a RAM upgrade has already been installed. You'd need to remove that before installing another module (but maybe you want put it all back together and contact your dealer first). And remember, the RAM module is designed to fit in one direction only; don't force it!

16. Press the RAM module firmly into the socket until you hear a faint click.

There's yet another RAM slot, underneath the iMac's G3 microprocessor. But unless you want to stretch the iMac's RAM capacity to the max, you won't need to worry about that one.

17. Before putting things back together again, double-check your RAM installation to make sure that everything looks okay.

18. Place the metal shield covering the RAM slot back into place.

19. Get your iMac's logic board, holding it in one hand. Then lower it carefully into its slot, pushing it straight down until it lies solidly in place. Don't push too hard, but make sure that the silver pin at the edge of the board is under the plastic lip (see Figure 22.15).

FIGURE 22.15
As you see, the silver pin is pressing against the plastic lip, so the logic board can't be inserted fully.

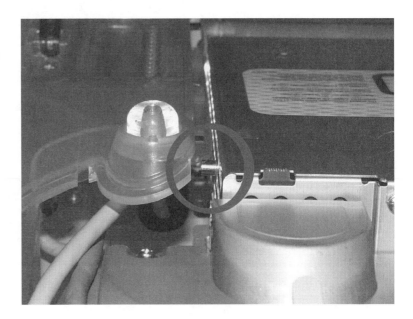

22

▼ 20. Get your Phillips screwdriver and reinstall the two screws that sit at each side of the logic board's handle.

> When tightening the screws, don't go overboard. "Finger" tight is enough. I've seen situations where a screw is tightened just too much and can't be removed without some major surgery. All you need to do is make it secure enough so you need a gentle tug to loosen it again. It's not as if you're going to be doing this sort of thing very often, unless you're upgrading iMacs for a living.

21. Reconnect the cables you set aside in steps 6 through 8 and reconnect them. Make sure that the cables are seated firmly.

22. Use the screwdriver to tighten down the power cord.

> If your iMac came with a clamp over the cables, be sure that the cables are inserted beneath the clamp. If there's a screw slot in the clamp, be sure to reinstall the screw to set it down securely.

23. Take the plastic cover and replace it. Be sure it's snapped back into place on all sides.

> If the cover won't fit securely, remove it and check to make sure that the cables are properly seated; then try again.

24. Before you reattach the case cover, you'll want to make sure your iMac works properly. So lift your iMac up gently, and place it in its normal operating position.

25. Reconnect the keyboard, mouse, and power cord (no need to worry about printers or any other added devices right now).

26. Plug the power cord back into the wall socket (if it's not already plugged in).

27. Start your iMac normally by pressing the power key on the unit or the keyboard and let it go through its full start process.

28. If the iMac starts up in the normal fashion, go right to the Apple menu, choose About This Computer, and check the figure for Built-in Memory. The total should
▼ now add up to the amount of RAM present on both modules inside your iMac.

▼   29. If everything looks normal, go ahead and shut down, and remove the power cord
        and the keyboard and mouse cables.

    30. Turn the iMac over and reinstall the small cover, screwing it down firmly but not
▲   too tight (as I mentioned before).

If everything went according to schedule, your iMac is now ready to roll, with all that
new memory in place. If you run into any problems, check the "Q&A" section at the end
of this chapter for additional help.

To make your iMac run better with the new RAM, be sure to open the
Memory Control Panel (in the Control Panels folder) and click the Use
Defaults button. Then restart your iMac. This will allocate a higher disk
cache, which will make the iMac run a bit faster. Actually this setting ought
to be made automatically, but it never hurts to check.

Installing New RAM on a Slot Loading iMac—By the Numbers

For its second-generation iMac, Apple took to heart requests from customers to do something about the convoluted process of installing RAM. As you see in the previous section, it can take a while and requires a fair amount of attention to a number of details.

As standard issue, Apple gave the "slot loading" iMacs a heavier dose of RAM than the
original models, from 32MB to 64MB (iMac and iMac DV) or 128MB (iMac DV
Special Edition). This is apt to be more than sufficient to get started; however, if you find
you need more memory to run some high-powered programs, you'll want to consider
buying a memory upgrade.

When you order a RAM upgrade for your iMac, be sure to tell the dealer
which iMac you have. The "slot loading" iMacs use PC100 DIMMs. Don't you
worry, any knowledgeable dealer will know just what you're talking about
when you tell them that.

What You Need

Your second-generation iMac has two RAM slots. When it leaves the factory, one of these slots is already filled. Normally you'd add a RAM upgrade module to the second slot. But you could also replace the factory RAM if you want to add a larger capacity upgrade.

Here is what you need to do the job:

- A soft cloth or towel on which to place your iMac.
- A desk or other surface large enough to hold all the parts comfortably.
- A quarter (yes, I'm serious).
- Your RAM upgrade module.

Now it's time to dive in:

1. Turn off your iMac, using Shut Down from the Special menu (or by pressing the power key and choosing that command).
2. Unplug all of the computer's cables (power cord and modem cord too).
3. Grab your iMac's handle (at the top) in one hand and gently and turn it over to the front, placing it face down (the monitor side) on the cloth.
4. At the bottom of the iMac, you'll see the access cover for your iMac's RAM slots (see Figure 22.16).

FIGURE 22.16

This is your doorway to a quick memory upgrade.

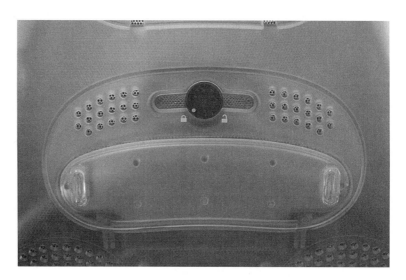

5. Take that quarter and place it in the little circular dial at the top of the access panel (see Figure 22.17).

FIGURE 22.17
Insert the quarter into the slot as shown.

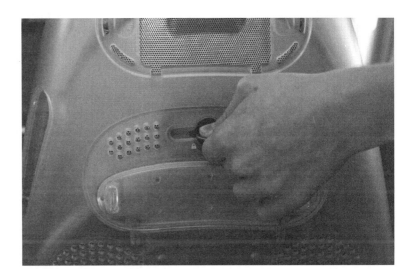

6. Turn the dial clockwise towards the unlock icon.

7. Place your fingers inside the openings at each end of the dial and pull out to open the cover. It may take a tug or two to get it to come loose, so just be patient.

8. When the cover is loosened, open it all the way, so it hangs loose. Now you'll get a clear view of the RAM slots inside (see Figure 22.18).

FIGURE 22.18
As you see, one of your iMac's memory slots is already filled.

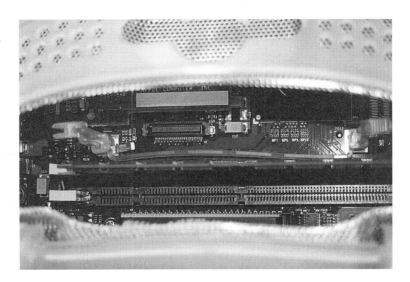

9. Take your fingers and press down the white plastic latches at each side of the empty RAM slot.

10. Get your RAM module, and gently line it up with the latch slots at each end. Make sure that the layout of the pins on the RAM upgrade module matches the layout of the slot (the row with the least number of pins goes at left).

> It is critically important that you make sure the RAM module lines up correctly with the slot. If you insert it incorrectly and try to power up your iMac, you could risk damage to the module or the logic board.

11. Press the RAM module straight down until it snaps into place. You'll feel and hear an audible "clump" when its seated properly (see Figure 22.19).

FIGURE 22.19
When the RAM is properly installed, it'll look just like this.

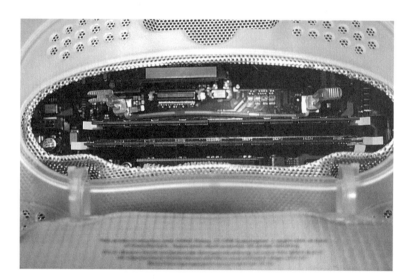

12. Double-check to make sure everything's in place, then grab the top of the access cover and close it.

> The other slot above your RAM slots is designed for installing an AirPort wireless networking module.

▼   13. Take your quarter, insert in the slot and turn it counterclockwise, towards the lock icon.

14. Lift your iMac up gently, and place it in its normal operating position.

15. Go ahead and reconnect the keyboard, mouse, and power cord (no need to worry about printers or any other added devices right now).

16. Plug the power cord back into the wall socket or power strip (if it's not already plugged in).

17. Start your iMac normally by pressing the power key on the unit or the keyboard and let it go through its full start process.

18. If the iMac starts up in the normal fashion, go right to the Apple menu, choose About This Computer, and check the figure for Built-in Memory. The total should
▲   now add up to the amount of RAM present on both modules inside your iMac.

Yes, that's it. In just minutes, you've successfully installed a RAM upgrade on your "slot loading" iMac. Now you're ready to make use of that extra memory, and that, by no strange coincidence, forms the topic of the next section of this chapter.

Making Use of the Extra RAM

After you've installed a RAM upgrade on your computer, you'll be able to run more programs at the same time. But that's only part of the advantage of the upgrade.

You can also allocate more RAM for a program to use, which may make it run faster or more efficiently. Here's how you do it:

1. Make sure that the program you want to give more RAM to is not running (if necessary, quit the program first).

2. Click the program's icon (not the alias!) once to select it.

3. Go to the Finder's File menu and choose Get Info (or press Command+I). This will open the screen shown in Figure 22.20.

4. Click the pop-up menu next to Show and select Memory, which opens the screen shown in Figure 22.21.

5. Click the text field next to Preferred Size and type a higher figure. You should try adding 1000K or 2000K above the original setting to start.

6. Close the Get Info window and launch your application and see how it works. You
▼   may want to increase RAM still further before you're satisfied.

22

FIGURE 22.20
This window gives you
information about the
program that you've
selected.

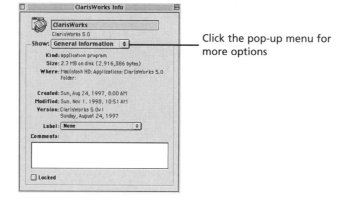

Click the pop-up menu for
more options

FIGURE 22.21
Use this window to
give a program a
healthy dose of extra
RAM.

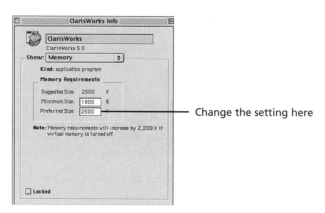

Change the setting here

You should be careful not to give a program too much memory. Your computer needs a certain amount of RAM for the system software. If the total from the system software and your application is higher than the amount you've installed, you'll get a warning message (and you won't be able to run the program). If that happens, just reduce the RAM allocation with the Get Info window.

Summary

As you see from this lesson, you don't have to be a computer expert or engineer to upgrade your iMac. If you just follow the steps shown here, you'll have little trouble adding extra software or even a RAM upgrade. And if you decide to forego the hardware installation yourself, you'll at least know how the process works and what to look for if something goes wrong.

It's inevitable that at some point in time your computer will lock up when you're in the middle of working on something. It's the nature of personal computers to hang from time to time. In the next lesson, I'll tell you why it happens and the things you can do to get your computer up and running smoothly again.

Q&A

Q I tried to install some new software, but I keep seeing a screen message that it won't run on my iMac. What's wrong?

A Possibly, it's the software. Before you purchase software for your computer, make doubly sure that it will run. The iMac will use just about everything designed for a PowerPC Mac (and there are thousands of programs to pick from). Also be sure that your computer has enough built-in memory and available hard drive space to handle the new program (otherwise, you'll want to consider the RAM upgrade described here).

Q My software comes on floppies, but I didn't bother getting one for my computer. What can I do?

A To start with, you may want to contact the software publisher and see if they have a CD version. If you're on a computer network, with some regular floppy-equipped Macs on hand, there's still another possibility. You could install the software on the other computer and then transfer it via a network. Just be sure you copy all the program's elements. A program's installer may put some things in a folder devoted to the application and then in several folders strewn in various parts of the System Folder. You need to cover everything (sometimes the documentation will explain what is installed where). Remember, also, that software is licensed usually for just one computer, so if you want to install a copy on your iMac (when it's already installed on another computer), you will want to contact the publisher about multi-user licensing.

22

Q My dealer tells me that if I try to install RAM on my computer, the warranty will be null and void. Is that true?

A Apple isn't going to stop your warranty protection if you install your own RAM. In fact, they even offer their own technical information documents on how to do it (but not with the sort of photos I have in this lesson). There is a condition, though, and that is if you damage your iMac when installing RAM, Apple won't fix it. But if you carefully follow the steps I described in this lesson, you should do just fine. I've been installing RAM on Macs for years, and I've never lost a patient yet! But if you have any concerns about probing the innards of your computer, go ahead and have your dealer do it (some dealers will install extra RAM for little or no cost if you buy the upgrade when you purchase your computer).

Q How much RAM should I install?

A There's only room for one more, so you should buy the largest size you can comfortably afford. RAM for the iMac comes in 32MB, 64MB, 128MB, and 256MB modules. And you can never have too much RAM.

Q I've seen RAM prices all over the place. One dealer is twice the price of another. Is there any difference?

A For the most part, RAM is a commodity product, so you can probably shop safely on the basis of price. But for added protection (at a somewhat higher price), pick RAM with a lifetime warranty, from such companies as Kingston, Newer, TechWorks, or Viking.

Q Okay, now I'm in trouble. I installed the RAM. I think I followed the instructions, but when I try to boot the iMac, it doesn't work (or I hear weird noises instead of a startup tone)? Is my computer sick?

A Don't panic! Just go back and double-check your installation. When doing a RAM upgrade on the first generation iMac, for example, I suggested that you not finish reassembling the unit until after you've restarted and shut down at least once. That's because the process of RAM installation is so complex. For the second generation iMac, this isn't necessary.

You'll want to open your iMac and make sure that the module is seated firmly (don't force it too hard). If your computer still won't work, remove your RAM upgrade. Then try again. If your computer works this time, then maybe you have a bad RAM module (yes, it happens sometimes). In that case, you'll want to contact your dealer for a replacement or further help.

PART IV

What If Something Goes Wrong?

Hour

Hour **23**

Crashin' Away: What to Do?

In the 1980s, I bought my first Mac computer. I was happily writing a letter to a friend in a word processor program when suddenly a white rectangular screen appeared up with a little bomb icon at one end. It said that a system error had occurred, and there was a little button I could press to restart.

Years and many Mac and system versions later, personal computers still crash. But there's usually something you can do to reduce the number of problems, and, when they do occur, deal with them easily.

In this lesson, you'll learn

- What to do in the event of a system crash.
- How to tell if it involves software or hardware.
- What some of those error messages really mean.
- How to avoid crashes (or at least make them happen less often).

Your First System Crash! What to Do?

It may happen the first day, or the first week, or the first month, but one day the inevitable will occur. You will be working on an important document, and suddenly you won't be able to type anything, or there will be a message that the program has quit.

Personal computers are, well, imperfect, and this is an eventuality you should expect, but it's also something you can prepare for.

Over the next few pages, I'll cover the kinds of system crashes you may see and how to deal with them.

Application Unexpectedly Quits

One of the more common problems you'll face is an application quitting. Suddenly, without warning, the document window disappears from the screen and you'll see a message much like the one shown in Figure 23.1.

FIGURE 23.1

This unfriendly message may sometimes appear when you're working on a document (yes, I actually had to force my iMac to crash to get this picture).

The application "America Online" has unexpectedly quit, because an error of type 3 occurred.

You should save your work in other open applications and restart the computer.

OK ——— Click OK to proceed

Unfortunately, when a program quits while you're working on a document, all of the work you did since the last time it was saved will be gone. That's why I always recommend that you save your documents often, so you won't lose much if something goes wrong.

When you see that message you'll want to do the following:

1. Quit all your open programs.
2. Choose Restart from the Finder's special menu (or press the power button and pick the same option).
3. After you restart, go ahead and get back to work. Don't fret about the problem unless it happens again.

▼ To Do

Even if your computer seems to run satisfactorily after a program quits, don't just sit there and continue working (and definitely don't consider trying to launch the program that quit again). It's the nature of the Mac operating system that it will be unstable after a crash. To avoid an even worse crash (and possibly lose information in your files), you should restart immediately.

23

A Look at Those System Messages

When your computer crashes, you'll often see some sort of message indicating why, only it won't be very helpful. The message will talk of a Type 1 error, a Type 2 error (or the Type 3 error shown in Figure 23.1).

For the most part, the number of the error doesn't matter. It simply means something conflicted with something and made your computer crash. Fixing the problem doesn't depend on knowing the distinct definition of the message, but here are a few definitions that may help a little in finding the cause:

- **Type 1, Type 2, Type 3**: These are general system errors that point to a possible software conflict.

- **Type 25**: This error indicates a program may be out of memory. If you have enough built-in memory on your iMac, you may want to increase the amount allocated to the program by using the Finder's Get Info command (see Hour 22, "Giving Your iMac New Software, More RAM, and Other Things," for more information).

- **Type –39**: Here's a message caused by a corrupted file. The best solution is to reinstall the program. If the corrupted file is a preference file, just delete it and restart.

- **System X won't run on this machine. A newer version is required**: If you attempt to start from a CD containing an older version of the Mac OS, it may not work with your computer. You need to use the system Install disk that came with your iMac or a later version.

Other System Crashes

Not all crashes cause an application to quit. Sometimes you'll see that dreaded bomb message on your screen, or your computer will just lock up completely without a screen prompt of any sort.

If you just experience a lockup in a program, you might try the following:

1. Force quit the program. Holding down the Command+Option+Esc keys and accepting the message to quit the program does this.

2. If the program really doesn't quit, go ahead and restart your computer immediately.

3. If force quitting won't work, or your Mac won't restart normally, follow the steps described in the next section.

Forcing a Restart

If your computer refuses to restart in the normal fashion, you'll have to force the process by using the reset function.

The following instructions apply to the original versions of the iMac:

1. Open the cover at the right side of the iMac to access the connection jacks.

2. Look at the right of the panel for a small triangular-shaped icon. Below that icon will be a small hole (a very small hole). See Figure 23.2 (and look carefully).

3. Take a paper clip, straighten it, insert the clip into the hole, push gently on the button, and then release.

FIGURE 23.2
*The recessed reset but-
ton is used to force the
iMac to restart.*

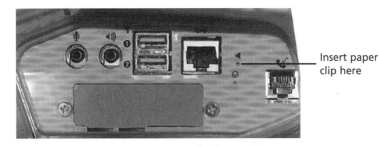

Insert paper
clip here

Don't push the button too hard. Just insert the clip far enough until you feel the resistance of the button and then push it in gently; then release it.

If this paper clip routine seems a bit much, you may want to try something better, the iMacButton. It's just what the name implies, a little switch that fits right into that little slot and lets you dispense with the paper clip restarts forever. You'll find out more about the product at the manufacturer's Web site: http://www.macbutton.com. As of the time this book was written, the price was just $9.95 plus shipping and worth every penny.

As soon as you press and release the reset button, your iMac should restart normally. On a rare occasion, it may not restart. In that event, you'll have to do something a bit more drastic (and remember this is only done as a last resort):

> The reset switch on the second generation "slot loading" iMacs is more sensibly designed. The switch is easy to push without needing a paper clip or any special buttons.

23

To Do

1. Unplug your iMac.
2. Wait at least 30 seconds.
3. Reconnect the power plug and turn on your iMac.

Why Did It Crash!

If a program quits or locks up over and over again, it may just be that you need a newer version. Software is updated regularly (sometimes a couple of times a year) to fix bugs, boost performance, or just give you a different look.

Updates to fix a bug are usually free, but if the program has some new features, the publisher will no doubt charge for the upgrade.

If the program just won't work properly for you, check the manuals or Help menu for the publisher's email address or phone number and ask them for assistance.

> *New Mac OS 9 Warning!*
>
> Beginning with Mac OS 9, Apple added a new error message for some incompatible programs. The message explains that you need a newer version of the software. If you see that sort of message (or a Type 119 error), you'll need to consider whether you wish to stop using the program or contact the publisher for an update.

What's Causing Those Crashes?

A rare system crash, maybe once every few days or so, is normal behavior for a Mac OS computer or even one of those computers from the "dark" side. It's just the nature of the beast. But if you encounter crashes several times a day, then something is definitely wrong. You may be seeing a conflict with some new software or hardware you've installed.

Fortunately, there are ways to check for the cause of such problems. Consider the following:

- **Recent software installations**: What did you do just before your computer began to crash? If you just installed some new software that puts files in the System Folder, maybe one of those files is causing a conflict. You'll want to check the program's documentation (or Read Me, if there is one) to see if the publisher is aware of any problems. As a test, you can go open Extensions Manager (from the Control Panels folder) and disable any system programs that are used with the new software, by running a Mac OS 9 Base set (or the set that applies to the system you have). This restricts it to the bare bones stuff you need to boot your computer. Then restart and see if the problems continue. Of course, you may be disabling something that is needed to make the program run, but at least you'll be able to see what may have caused your problem. If the problem goes away, go back to Extensions Manager and restore the other extensions a few at a time. After a few restarts, you're apt to come to a probable solution.

- **Recent hardware upgrades**: If you just installed a RAM upgrade on your computer and your computer is now crashing away, maybe the RAM module you installed is defective. It's always possible and not easy to test for. You may want to consider removing the RAM upgrade, strictly as a test (following the steps described in Hour 22). Then work with your iMac to see if the crashes go away. If they do, contact the dealer for a replacement module. If you've installed an extra drive, scanner, or other device, disconnect the device (and turn off the software if needed) and see if the problem disappears.

- **Hardware defects**: As with any electronic product, there's always the very slight chance one or more of the components in your computer may fail. In the vast majority of cases, constant crashes are caused by a software conflict (or defective RAM). But if you've tested everything and your iMac won't work reliably, don't hesitate to contact Apple Computer or your dealer and arrange for service. The new product warranty with your iMac includes on-site service (or you can just take it over to your dealer if they feel it needs repair).

Some dealers will offer to sell you an extended warranty with your computer. Such warranties lengthen the standard one-year warranty up to five years. If the cost is real cheap, you may want to get such a warranty as added insurance. But most times, if a computer hasn't failed within a few months after purchase, the chances that it will break later on are slight. So consider that fact if you are presented with the extended warranty option (and also the fact that some dealers make a fairly big profit when they sell them). In all the years I've owned Macs, I've never had the need for one.

A Fast and Dirty Conflict Test

If removing that new software isn't fixing the problem, it may just be that one program isn't getting along with another, and that's why you are experiencing crashes. Most Mac programs are designed to work safely with other programs running. But there are so many possible combinations of operating system versions, program lineups, and Mac hardware that it's impossible for everything to get along all the time.

If you continue to see crashes, here's a way to help you diagnose the problem:

▼ To Do

1. When you restart your computer, as soon as you see the Happy Mac icon, hold down the Shift key. This will disable most system programs, and you'll see an Extensions Disabled message.

2. When you see that message, release the Shift key.

3. If you can restart normally in this mode, go to the next step. If not, go on to the next section on reinstalling system software.

4. When you start your computer, you will see little icons at the bottom of the screen that belong to the Extensions and Control Panels you've installed. If your computer freezes before one of those icons appears, go ahead and force a restart (using the steps mentioned earlier) and when restarting, hold down the Spacebar, which will bring up Extensions Manager.

> If you press the Spacebar too early in the startup process, Extensions Manager won't open. You should wait until you see the Happy Mac icon on your screen before holding down the Spacebar. That should work.

5. Locate the program that appears to be failing in the Extensions Manager directory and uncheck it (to disable it); then let Extensions Manager Resume the startup process.

6. If the problem goes away, you may want to try making the program load in a different order, to see if that helps. You can do that by selecting the program icon (check Extensions Manager to see in which folder it's placed) and clicking its name. Insert an Option+space before the name, to make it load earlier. Or insert a tilde (~) to make it load later.

7. After renaming the offending program, restart and see if it fixes the problem.

8. If the startup crash doesn't stop, hold down the Spacebar at startup to open Extensions Manager.

▼

9. After Extension Manager appears, click the Selected Set pop-up menu and choose Mac OS 9 Base (or whatever operating system version is shown there) and then resume the startup process.

10. If the startup crashes halt, restart and hold down the Spacebar to bring up Extensions Manager.

11. Click the Selected Set pop-up menu to bring back your regular startup lineup.

12. Disable all the non-Apple stuff and resume the startup process.

> It's often hard to know which startup program belongs to Apple because the name may not give a clue. One way to check is to open Extension Manager, select the program from the list, and click the Show Item Information label at the bottom of the screen. You'll see a screen describing what the program does (assuming it's from Apple). Another way is to select Show Balloons from the Finder's Help menu and pointing the mouse cursor above the actual program file.

13. If the problem goes away, reopen Extensions Manager, check on a few more items, and restart. A few restarts of this sort should help you find the cause.

> One really great way to check for startup program conflicts is a commercial program, Conflict Catcher. You'll want to read the "Q&A" section for more information about this terrific product.

Reinstalling System Software

If you've turned off all the non-Apple startup programs (or your computer freezes even when you start with the Shift key held down), you may need to reinstall your Mac system software.

Here's how to get started:

1. Get out your system Install CD, press the CD button, and insert the CD, closing the drive tray.

2. Restart your iMac. If need be, force a restart as described previously.

3. On the first generation iMac, as soon as you hear the computer's startup sound, hold down the C key. This will allow your computer to start from your system CD.

▼ If you have a "slot loading" iMac, hold down the Option key at startup, click on the CD icon, then click on the right arrow to boot from the CD.

4. After you've restarted, double-click the Mac OS Install (or Install) icon and continue through the system installation process as described in the section on installing software in Hour 22.

5. After your system installation is done, go ahead and restart and check that everything is working properly.

▲ 6. If your system installation doesn't work, check the "Q&A" section at the end of this chapter for a discussion about doing a clean installation.

Desktop Icon Problems

The information about all those fancy icons that identify items on your computer's desktop is kept in a set of files called "desktop files." These are files you cannot see, but they're updated every time you add or remove software.

If those icons suddenly become white, rather than multicolored, and you have problems double-clicking an icon to launch a program or document, something may be wrong with those desktop files.

Fortunately, there's a way to fix the damage, or at least update the files so that the icons come back.

Here's what to do:

1. Restart your iMac.

2. Watch your screen and as soon as the last startup icon appears, go ahead and hold down the Command and Option keys.

3. Keep the two keys pressed until you see a message asking if you want to rebuild the desktop (see Figure 23.3).

FIGURE 23.3

Do you really, truly want to rebuild that desktop file? Of course you do!

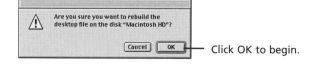

Are you sure you want to rebuild the desktop file on the disk "Macintosh HD"?

Cancel   OK — Click OK to begin.

▼ 4. Release the keys and OK the message to begin the rebuilding process. You'll see a progress bar showing the rebuilding process (see Figure 23.4).

It's a bad idea to cancel a desktop rebuild when it's in progress. The end result will be that the desktop file won't update properly, and that "generic" icon problem will only get worse.

FIGURE 23.4
Your desktop rebuilding process is about halfway done here.

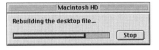

5. When the desktop rebuilding process is finished, go ahead and check to make sure that all of the item icons are back to their normal state.

6. If the icons are still generic, follow steps 1 through 5 again.

7. If the problem isn't resolved, check Hour 24, "An iMac Safety Net," in the section devoted to a discussion about a program, TechTool Pro, which can give you a more robust desktop rebuild.

Summary

As you see from this lesson, system crashes and application quits can be downright annoying, but you are not helpless to do something about them. You can usually restart without much trouble, and diagnosing the cause of a crash can be done without a lot of wasted time.

In addition to dealing with software incompatibilities, you'll want to set up a regular regimen of preventive maintenance. If you download lots of files or share files and disks with other computers, you'll also want to arm yourself with virus protection software. I'll cover these topics and more in Hour 24.

Q&A

Q **Why are programs so buggy? They have all these great programmers. Why can't they make software that won't crash my computer?**

A Your iMac works by a continuing process of communication. Data is being sent back and forth, millions of instructions every second. Every time you type a keystroke, browse the Internet, or draw a rectangle, huge chunks of information have to be handled by your computer to accomplish even the simplest task.

Programs are written by imperfect human beings such as you and me, and one incorrect chunk of computer code, somewhere, can bring the whole thing crashing down.

I remember one instance where a publisher of a popular utility program couldn't figure out why my Mac would lock up whenever I ran their program. Finally, they sent their head software engineer over to my home office (he traveled halfway across the country to get to me), and he hung out one afternoon watching over my shoulder as I duplicated the problem over and over again. Finally, he unpacked his portable computer (an Apple PowerBook) and poured through the code for that program. He chanced upon one small set of instructions, hardly more than a few words really, that seemed to serve no purpose. He said it shouldn't do anything, but under rare circumstances, that set of instructions could be called by mistake, and the program would lock up my Mac. Finally, he just deleted the line of code, rebuilt the program (they call it "compiling"), and the new version worked just great.

Basically, a large computer program may have hundreds of thousands or millions of lines of code. There's just no way to get rid of all the bugs, no way at all.

Q **In your lesson on AppleScript, you discussed ways to let your computer do the work for you. Is there any way to automatically test for a software conflict?**

A Indeed there is. There is one terrific program out there that will not only manage your computer's Control Panels and Extensions, but also actually test for the causes of repeated crashes. It's called Conflict Catcher, and it's published by Casady & Greene. The author of the program, Jeffrey Robbin, used to work for Apple Computer, and he knows the ins and outs of the operating system and what makes software run badly. In addition to testing for conflicts, the program can also automate the process of doing a clean system installation (which installs a brand new System Folder without deleting the old one).

I recommend this program to any Mac user. It earns rave reviews from the computer magazines, and it gets my personal rave review, too. It's well worth the price of admission, and just about every dealer who handles Mac software has this product available. You can find a time-limited demonstration copy of the program for download from the publisher's Web site, at `http://www.casadyg.com`.

Q **I hear the words "clean install" from time to time. I want to install my system software again. Do I need a clean install? And does that mean that I must erase my hard drive, or at the very least reinstall all my software?**

A If your iMac still crashes a lot after you've turned off all of the non-Apple system programs and reinstalled your system software, you're a candidate for a clean install. It's a way to start with a clean slate—and no, you don't have to reinstall all of your programs or erase your hard drive.

When you install your Mac OS software, you'll find an option button on the very first screen of the installer. Click that button, and you'll find the choice of doing a clean installation. When you accept this option, your existing System Folder will be renamed Previous System Folder and a new one will be installed, from scratch.

After you've done a clean system installation and restarted, you'll just need to check that everything is working okay. Then you'll begin the process of locating all of your non-Apple files in the Previous System Folder and moving them to the new System Folder. And that's why I recommend Conflict Catcher; it helps you automate this process, and it will help you figure out what goes where.

Q **Is there no solution for even occasional system crashes?**

A Not with the present iterations of the Mac operating system. But as this book was written, Apple was busily working on an industrial-strength operating system, Mac OS X. This new operating system is designed to make programs run more reliably. And it has a special feature, called "protected memory," which will let programs updated for the new operating system work in their own piece of memory, independent of other programs. So if that program crashes, it won't take down the system with it.

You may expect to see this great new Mac system version some time in the year 2000 (perhaps even by the time you read this book).

Q How do I know if I have a Revision A or Revision B iMac or "slot loading" or something else? And what do you mean by "slot loading" anyway?

A Just check the model number. The original version of the iMac is numbered M6709LL/A. Revision B is M6709LL/B.

The job is easier with later revisions, because of the fruit-color schemes and the higher CPU performance ratings. If you're not sure how fast the CPU is, just click the Apple menu, choose Apple System Profiler, and let it run its own scan of your configuration.

Apple identifies the second generation iMacs as "slot loading," because of the new-style CD/DVD slot, which automatically grabs and pulls in a disc when you insert it. The initial models in this line are clearly identified as just iMac, iMac DV or iMac DV Special Edition. But as the model line is updated, there will no doubt be speed enhancements and other changes that will make clear identification difficult once again.

Q Trivia question: In some of your illustrations, I notice that your hard drive is named Old Ironsides and not Macintosh HD as mine is. How did you do this, and what's the significance of that name? Are you a history buff?

A Changing the name of your drive is easy. First make sure you don't have file sharing on. Then click the disk icon's name, and in a second it'll be highlighted. Now just enter the new name, whatever it is, and press Return or Enter. That'll take care of it. Just remember, though, that changing a disk's name can, on occasion, mess up an alias to a file, and you might have to use the Fix Alias feature of Mac OS 9 when you click the alias.

Now about that second question: The name *Old Ironsides* actually identifies a small space ship that's featured in some of the *Attack of the Rockoids* science fiction novels that my son, Grayson, and I have written. If you want to learn more about it, check our Web site at http://www.rockoids.com.

23

HOUR 24

An iMac Safety Net

I first encountered a computer virus not two days after I bought my first Mac. I installed a new program (I forget which), and then I launched a publishing program that was designed to alert the user whenever it's infected or damaged.

In seconds, I got the warning. I had a virus. It took me the better part of a day and a night to fix the problem. I literally had to wipe all of the files from my Mac's hard drive and start over. I learned a lesson, and the next day I bought a virus protection program.

In this lesson, you'll discover

- What a computer virus is and what it can do.
- How to protect yourself against computer viruses (tell your friends).
- What hard drive directory damage can do to your computer.
- How to fix hard drive problems before your files are damaged.

Computer Viruses Aren't Just for Movie Plots!

Perhaps you've seen that great action movie with Sandra Bullock, *The Net*. An evil industrialist steals her identity with a little computer hocus pocus, and she's on the run, pursued by the villain's personal assassin and the police alike. Finally, she fights back by infecting the industrialist's software with a computer virus.

In the movie universe, the computer virus is sometimes the hero, defeating the bad guy just in the nick of time. The sci-fi flick *Independence Day* also featured a computer virus, this time somehow infecting the alien computers across empty space (with no direct connection) and helping humankind to beat back the space invasion.

Now that's fine and dandy for movies, but when it comes to the real world, computer viruses aren't nice. They are evil, destructive things that can cause your computer to crash and destroy your files.

What Are Computer Viruses?

Without getting overly technical, a computer virus is simply a chunk of code that attaches itself to a document or program. Once the program is run, the virus begins to do its thing. At the very least, it will put a silly message on your screen or play some sort of practical joke. In one instance, the virus would prevent you from typing vowels.

But not all viruses are just funny. Some are downright destructive and will destroy your files and possibly damage your hard drive. The virus I encountered shortly after getting my first Mac is known as nVIR and it can damage files in your System Folder among other things.

Another type of virus is the Trojan Horse, something that appears as a beneficial file, but ends up wreaking havoc. An example of this sort of virus was one that masqueraded as an extension that offered video acceleration, but all it accelerated was the spread of a virus infection that caused crashes and other problems.

Cross-Platform Viruses

Fortunately, most of the computer viruses out there infect computers from that "other" platform, but that doesn't make the Mac-borne viruses any less harmful. In addition, there is a set of viruses that are targeted against Microsoft Office programs (Mac and Windows) called "macro" viruses. Dozens of new strains of these viruses seem to show up every month, and they vary in their effects from silly screen messages to document damage.

If you're using one of the Windows emulators described in Hour 18, "Coping with the Windows World," you'll find that the PC environment is almost as vulnerable to a PC virus as the real thing. You should arm yourself with PC virus protection software if you intend to share files and disks from the "other" side. Fortunately, the publishers of the programs mentioned in this hour also have PC versions.

Protecting Your Computer

I remember the movie promo "Be afraid, be very afraid!" The line sticks in my mind whenever I think of the threat of computer viruses, even though I've long since forgotten the name of the movie it advertised.

Fortunately, there are things you can do to protect yourself against computer viruses and allow you to continue to work in safety.

Here's how to practice, to quote one of the original authors of virus software on the Mac, "safe hex":

- **Don't accept unsolicited files from strangers!** Sometimes you see them on an online service. You get a message saying "Here's that file I promised to send" or something similar. But you never heard of the person and never expected to receive a file. Fortunately, most of those files are PC-based (with .SHS, .EXE and .ZIP attached to the filenames). And even if there's potential damage from a file, if you don't download and try to run that file, you're safe.

America Online will put up a warning message whenever you attempt to download a file of the type mentioned above. Again the danger is primarily to the users of the "other" platform, but there's no telling when some vicious prankster will develop equivalent Mac viruses.

- **Download software *only* from major online services and known commercial sites!** The folks who run the software repositories on AOL, CompuServe, EarthLink, and other services and regular software publishers will check their files for problems before they make them available. That helps ensure the safety of those files (although there's always the slight possibility of a problem with an undiscovered virus).

- **Don't use QuickTime's AutoPlay feature!** One of the most virulent Mac viruses is called "AutoStart." It's triggered when you open an infected CD and run something on it. But you can protect yourself most times simply by opening the QuickTime Control Panel (in the Control Panels folder) and unchecking the options listed under the AutoPlay pop-up menu (as I've done in Figure 24.1).

FIGURE 24.1

Turn off the two options shown in order to protect yourself against a well-known computer virus.

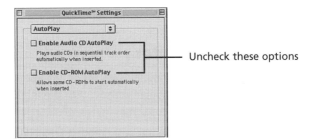

— Uncheck these options

- **Get virus protection software!** This is the best way to ensure that your computer will be kept safe from virus infections. I'll cover this subject in more detail in the next part of this lesson.

If you happen to receive a virus-infected disk from a friend or colleague, don't be shy about telling him. It's no insult to inform folks of such a problem; in fact, it may save their valuable files before it's too late.

A Look at Virus Protection Software

Virus protection software isn't expensive. Each of the two popular products I'm describing here can be had for less than 75 bucks at most computer dealers. When you compare that to the potential loss as a result of getting a virus infection, it's a cheap price for safety and peace of mind.

A free virus program, Disinfectant can be used to protect you against many Mac viruses. But the software is no longer being supported, and it won't detect any recent virus infection. Even the author of this program suggests you buy one of the commercial programs instead.

As with any software product, a specific set of features may be more appealing to you, but either of the programs I'm describing will do the job.

- **Norton AntiVirus**: This program, published by Symantec (see Figure 24.2) is designed to check for viruses every time you insert a disk into a drive, mount a networked disk on your computer's desktop, or download a file from the Internet. So-called "suspicious" activities are also monitored. You can perform scheduled scans, where the program will launch automatically at a predetermined hour and scan your drives. One intriguing feature is called Live Update, where the program will log on to the publisher's site every month and check for updates to protect against newly discovered viruses.

FIGURE 24.2

Norton AntiVirus can be set to update itself automatically with new detection modules.

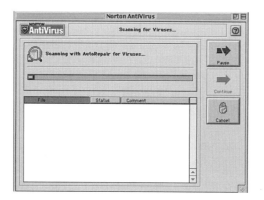

The older version of Norton AntiVirus was known as SAM (short for "Symantec AntiVirus Utilities for Macintosh). If you happen to have this older version, you should upgrade to be protected against the latest virus types.

- **Virex**: This is published by Network Associates (see Figure 24.3). Many of the features offered by Norton AntiVirus are also available with Virex. The program will scan files from a networked drive or the ones you download, and it will do scheduled scans. A special technology, heuristics, is designed to check for virus-like activity, to help protect you against unknown viruses. When you install Virex, there's a drag-and-drop module on your desktop that you can use for on-demand scanning. Updates to the program are usually offered on a monthly basis, and are available via its "Auto Update" feature.

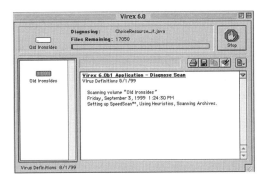

Figure 24.3
Virex offers drag-and-drop detection and regular updates.

The Right Way to Use Virus Software

Buying and installing virus software isn't necessarily a guarantee that you'll be protected. Here are some further issues you should be aware of:

- **New viruses are discovered all the time!** The publishers of virus software share information, so everyone can be protected in case a new virus strain crops up. You'll want to check a publisher's Web site at least once a month for virus detection updates. The information on how to keep updated is usually included with the publisher's documentation. Using a program's ability to do automatic scheduled updates is a real plus.

- **Be careful before you turn the virus software off!** As with any complex program, sometimes virus software may conflict with another program you're using. In addition, it's usually a good idea to disable the virus program before installing new software (Norton AntiVirus monitors installer activity and will offer to turn itself off). But once the software is installed, don't forget to turn the program on again.

- **Virus software may slow things down!** Every time you insert a floppy disk into a drive, the virus program will spend a few moments checking it out. You can defeat this protection and save a few seconds, but I wouldn't recommend it.

Keeping Your Hard Drive Healthy and Happy

In a very general sense, your hard drive is similar to your tape deck. The magnetic particles on the drive are changed when you write files to it. But unlike the tape deck, the files aren't just put down one after another. Working behind the scenes, the Mac file system puts files down wherever space is available. The contents of a file may be spread across the drive, a little bit here, a little bit there…here, there, and everywhere.

To keep track of all this information, a catalog file is kept showing what the files are and where all the pieces are located. Compare it to the catalog card file at your neighborhood library, although it's a lot more complex than just a set of little index cards.

If anything happens to that catalog, there's always the danger that it will lose track of all or part of your file, and you won't be able to retrieve it.

Disk Drive Catalogs Are Easily Damaged!

Day in and day out, thousands upon thousands of files are written, read, and replaced. It's truly amazing that hundreds and thousands of megabytes of data can be tracked, usually without missing a beat.

If you recall my descriptions of a computer's shutdown process throughout this book, you'll see that a little housekeeping is done before you restart or turn off your computer. One of those housekeeping chores is to update the file catalog so that all of the information about the location of your files is accurate.

But the file can be damaged due to the following causes:

- **System crash**: If your computer freezes and you must force a restart, the catalog won't always be updated properly, and there's the danger the catalog may get damaged.
- **Power failure**: You pull the plug by mistake (it gets caught around the vacuum cleaner, for example) or that big storm causes a power failure. Whatever the reason, if your computer shuts down before doing its update chore, there's a possibility of a problem.
- **Virus infections**: A virus infection can damage a file or the hard drive's catalog.

If left unfixed, these hard drive problems can only become worse, and eventually you'll find files come up damaged. Eventually, the iMac won't start up properly because the System Folder or the drive itself cannot be accessed.

Fixing Hard Drive Problems

Your computer comes with a handy tool that can check for and repair a hard drive problem. The program is called Disk First Aid, and you'll find a copy in your Utilities folder (or on your computer's system installer disk if you removed the copy on your hard drive by error).

You can run Disk First Aid at any time, simply by double-clicking the program's icon, and selecting the drive or drives you want to repair (see Figure 24.4).

FIGURE 24.4

Disk First Aid can check your drive for basic directory problems and fix them.

Choose Repair to check and fix your drive

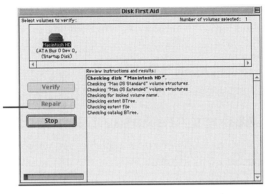

The nice thing about Disk First Aid is that it's free, but it's not a 100, percent solution. There are three popular commercial programs that offer to go beyond Disk First Aid in checking your drive and repairing catalog damage.

If your computer isn't restarted or shut down properly, Disk First Aid will automatically run at the next startup to make sure that your drive is working properly.

Here's a brief description of the better-known hard drive diagnostic programs and what they do:

- **DiskWarrior**: This single-purpose program is from Alsoft, a publisher of several Mac utility products. Its stock in trade is the ability to rebuild, rather than repair, a corrupted hard drive directory file. The original catalog is checked to locate the files on your drive, and then that information is used to make a new directory to replace the damaged one.

- **Norton Utilities**: From Symantec, this is the oldest available hard drive maintenance and repair package. The centerpiece is Disk Doctor (see Figure 24.5), which will check your hard drive and fix problems. There are additional components of the package that can optimize your drive to speed up file retrieval and to recover your drive in the event a crash makes it inaccessible. The program can also help you recover the files you trash by mistake.

FIGURE 24.5
Norton Disk Doctor seeks out and repairs hard drive problems.

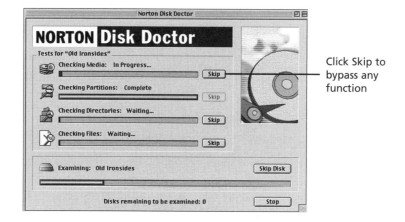

Click Skip to bypass any function

Older versions of Norton Utilities cannot work with the file system on your computer, which is known as HFS+ (or Mac OS Extended). At the very least, they might even make catalog damage worse, and the end result is that your computer's drive's contents will become unavailable. Any version of Norton Utilities from 4.0 on will work with your computer (and may even fix damage caused by using the incompatible version). The version shown in this book is 5.0. If you have an older edition, you may want to check with your dealer or the publisher about a special discount if you upgrade.

- **TechTool Pro**: In addition to hard drive repairs, TechTool Pro (see Figure 24.6) can optimize the drive and even run a wide range of diagnostic checks on all of your computer's hardware and attached devices. One great feature is the ability to perform an extended test of your computer's RAM. This may be helpful if you suddenly face lots of crashes after doing a RAM upgrade.

FIGURE 24.6
TechTool Pro checks all your computer's hardware for potential problems.

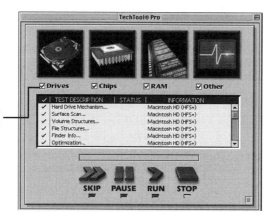

Uncheck a box to bypass that function

There is a free version of TechTool that will do a few simple functions, such as automatic desktop rebuilding. But the free utility cannot run any of the disk repair or diagnostic routines offered by the commercial version.

Using Disk Repair Software

The best way to benefit from a repair program is to install it. Either Norton Utilities or TechTool Pro will work best if you install the package as instructed in the program's documentation.

While the application can be run directly from the CD without installing anything on your computer's drive, the regular installation will provide the following:

- **A catalog directory record**: Both Norton Utilities and TechTool Pro create special ("invisible") files on your hard drive to track information about the drive's catalog. This information is used in case your hard drive crashes so that the files can be recovered.

- **Deleted file record**: The system extensions from Norton Utilities and TechTool Pro track the files you trash. Although there are no guarantees, this information can be used to help recover a file if you dump it by mistake.

- **Automatic scanning**: Both Norton Utilities and TechTool Pro can automatically scan your drive at regular intervals (and before each restart and shut down) to check for problems. If your computer is forced to restart because of a crash, these programs will run a directory scan of your hard drive automatically after startup. These features, by the way, can be switched off if you don't want them.

A Fast Look at Speeding Up Your Hard Drive

As I explained earlier in this lesson, the files you copy or save to your computer's drive aren't all put there in one piece. They are scattered over the drive, based on the available space. Over time, as files are saved, replaced, and removed, little gaps of free space open up between all these files. And the complex electronics in your drive have to work harder to find all parts of a file.

The theory goes that as file elements become scattered about the drive, a condition known as *fragmentation,* the performance of your hard drive may slow down. Both Norton Utilities and TechTool Pro can optimize the drive, which puts all the elements of a file next to each other. That's supposed to make the drive work less to assemble a file, speeding up performance slightly.

Alsoft also has a disk optimization utility, PlusOptimizer, which accomplishes the same purpose.

> The jury is still out about the benefits of optimizing a drive except in cases where so-called fragmentation is really bad. In normal use, you probably won't notice that great of a performance difference otherwise.

Before you optimize a drive, though, you should take a little extra care:

- **Check the hard drive catalog**: During optimization, most or all of the files on the drive will be rewritten, piece by piece, to put all the parts together. The directory catalog should be examined before the hard drive is optimized. Otherwise, directory damage could cause problems. The optimizing component of Norton Utilities (Speed Disk) will run this check automatically, and TechTool Pro's optimization component will also warn you to do such a test.

- **Keep a backup**: It's never happened to me, but there's always the very slight possibility that something will go wrong during the optimization process, and you'll have to restore files. So keep those backups handy.

- **Check the drive in case of a crash or power failure**: If anything happens to stop the optimization process, run your disk diagnostic program right away to make sure that nothing has gone wrong. These programs are designed to check the files (verify them) as they are being rewritten for safety, but a little extra checking is never a bad idea.

- **Don't overdo it!** Unless you are replacing and deleting huge numbers of files on a regular basis, you shouldn't need to optimize very often. Once every month or two is more than sufficient. Some users go for months without optimizing and experience no problems at all.

Summary

I don't want to mince words. Computer viruses are clear and present dangers to anyone who owns a personal computer, whether you have a Macintosh, or a model from the "other" platform. But if you arm yourself with the safety net described in this lesson, up-to-date virus software, you can compute away in safety.

In addition, you should consider getting one of the drive diagnostic programs I've mentioned in this lesson. You may work for months or years and never need what they have to offer. But even one instance of hard drive trouble is enough to cover the cost of any of these products.

24

And that's it: You passed the test, and you've became an expert in using your computer in just 24 hours. Congratulations. If you have any more questions or some information to offer, don't be shy about pointing your Web browser to my Macintosh support site: `http://www.starshiplair.com`.

Q&A

Q **Help! I just received an email message warning me about the "Good Times" virus and to pass on this warning to others. It says I can get a virus just by opening the message. Is this true?**

A There actually was a situation where a bug in some email software made it possible for weird things to happen if a bad file was attached to the message, but in general you cannot get a virus from just reading someone's email. Basically, you can really only get a virus if you try to open an infected file.

   Those warnings you receive from time to time are known as "urban legends." They're not true, although they are spread far and wide anyway. If there's any virus involved, it is the message itself, causing fear and anxiety among many folks who are taken in by these terrible pranks. If you see any messages of this sort, best thing to do is ignore them.

Q **You mentioned those suspicious files that are sometimes sent to you by strangers? What do they do?**

A Such files are sometimes sent to members of AOL or an Internet service. They are Trojan horse files, since they are presented as something you really want.

   If you run those programs (and as I said earlier in this lesson, they are largely PC-based), they will check your hard drive for personal information, such as your online service's password or credit card information. Next time you connect to the service, this information will automatically be emailed to the perpetrator. They can then log on to your Internet service, using your account, to do their mischief. Or use your credit card.

   So, as I said, be wary of unsolicited files.

Q **What's wrong? I thought you said that Disk First Aid would run automatically at startup after I force a restart. Why isn't the program working?**

A Sometimes the program just won't do an automatic scan, and you should run it yourself after your computer has started. If your computer has an extra drive, it's a good idea to run the program anyway because the startup scan only checks your startup drive.

This automatic scanning feature, by the way, is set in the General Control Panel. You'll also want to make sure that the Shut Down Warning option wasn't unchecked by mistake.

Q I scanned my drive with Disk First Aid, and it says there's damage that cannot be fixed. But everything seems to be working satisfactorily. Should I ignore the message?

A Absolutely not! I cannot overemphasize how dangerous unfixed hard drive directory problems are. Over time, you may experience crashes, you may find files can't be found, and one day the drive will go south. You won't be able to use it.

If Disk First Aid doesn't work for you, run, don't walk, to your nearest software dealer and get a copy of one of the disk repair utilities I've mentioned here. They promise to be more robust in ferreting out disk damage and fixing the problems, and they can sometimes repair problems Disk First Aid won't touch.

Q I've used a commercial disk diagnostic program, and it still doesn't work. The damage can't be fixed! What do I do?

A Check the program for instructions about what to do next. It may just be that you have to run the software after booting from the program's CD.

There are two ways to boot from the CD on an iMac, depending on which version you have. If your iMac is a first-generation model (Revision A through Revision D), just hold down the C key at startup with the disk in the CD drive and release the key when the Happy Mac icon appears. If you have one of the "slot-loading" models, including the iMac DV series, pop the CD in the drive, then hold down the option key when your iMac boots. You'll see a screen in which you select the startup disk. Click on the CD icon, then the right arrow, and your iMac will boot right from the CD.

After you start from the CD, try running the program again. If it still won't fix the problem, your next step is to consider backing up all your files and erasing the drive.

That's why I always recommend performing regular backups of your files. This sort of thing doesn't happen very often, but the potential is always there, and you should be ready for it. You'll want to read Hour 21, "Backup, Backup, Backup…How to Protect Your Files," for suggestions on setting up a regular backup program.

24

Q I want the maximum amount of protection. What if I install more than one virus or disk repair program? Wouldn't that be better?

A On the contrary. The virus and disk maintenance programs I am describing here do some of their stuff with a system extension, a program that loads when you start your computer. For example, if two system extensions are performing the same function, it's very possible they will interfere with each other in some fashion and cause crashes. And that can make a hard drive's directory damage worse.

The best approach is simply to pick the program that has the features you want and use that one on a regular basis. Of course, there's nothing wrong with having a second program on hand in case of emergencies, just so long as you run that program directly from the CD, and you don't install any component from it that goes into the System Folder.

Q Help. I tried to start from a drive mounted on my computer's USB port by selecting it in the Startup Disk Control Panel. When I restarted, my computer used the regular hard drive. What did I do wrong?

A Absolutely nothing. The USB feature of the first-generation iMac did not support such an option. So things are working quite normally. However, the second generation "slot loading" iMacs do allow you to boot from a USB drive, so long as it contains a real System Folder.

INDEX

Get **FREE** books and more...when you register this book online for our Personal Bookshelf Program

http://register.samspublishing.com/

SAMS

 Register online and you can sign up for our ***FREE Personal Bookshelf Program***...unlimited access to the electronic version of more than 200 complete computer books—immediately! That means you'll have 100,000 pages of valuable information onscreen, at your fingertips!

 Plus, you can access product support, including complimentary downloads, technical support files, book-focused links, companion Web sites, author sites, and more!

 And you'll be automatically registered to receive a ***FREE subscription to a weekly email newsletter*** to help you stay current with news, announcements, sample book chapters, and special events, including sweepstakes, contests, and various product giveaways!

We value your comments! Best of all, the entire registration process takes only a few minutes to complete, so go online and get the greatest value going—absolutely FREE!

Don't Miss Out On This Great Opportunity!

Sams is a brand of Macmillan Computer Publishing USA.

For more information, please visit *www.mcp.com*

The IT site you asked for...

It's Here!

D1555699

InformIT is a complete online library delivering information, technology, reference, training, news and opinion to IT professionals, students and corporate users.

Find IT Solutions Here!

www.informit.com